Apart or A Part?

Open University Press
Children With Special Needs Series

Editors
PHILLIP WILLIAMS
Emeritus Professor of Education
University College of North Wales, Bangor.
PETER YOUNG
Formerly Tutor in the education of children with
learning difficulties, Cambridge Institute of Education;
educational writer, researcher and consultant.

This is a series of short and authoritative introductions for parents, teachers, professionals and anyone concerned with children with special needs. The series will cover the range of physical, sensory, mental, emotional and behavioural difficulties, and the changing needs from infancy to adult life in the family, at school and in society. The authors have been selected for their wide experience and close professional involvement in their particular fields. All have written penetrating and practical books readily accessible to non-specialists.

TITLES IN THE SERIES

Apart or A Part?

Integration and the Growth of British Special Education

Ted Cole

Open University Press
Milton Keynes • Philadelphia

Open University Press
12 Cofferidge Close
Stony Stratford
Milton Keynes MK11 1BY

and
1900 Frost Road, Suite 101,
Bristol, PA 19007 USA

First Published 1989

British Library Cataloguing in Publication Data

Cole, Ted
  Apart or a part?: integration and the growth of
  British special education.- (Children with special
  needs)
  1. Great Britain. Handicapped children. Education,
  History, Education history
  I. Title II. Series
  371.9′0941

  ISBN 0-335-09226-8
  ISBN 0-335-09225-x (paper)

Library of Congress catalog number is available

Typeset by Burns & Smith, Derby
Printed in Great Britain by Biddles Limited
Guildford and Kings Lynn

Contents

Series Editors' Introduction

In an age when Professor Stephen Hawking, one of the world's leading cosmologists, is grappling with fundamental problems about the origin and nature of the universe while fighting the handicapping conditions which limit his mobility and abilities to communicate, it seems a heresy to ask whether we should segregate or integrate people with special needs. Can we afford to try managing without them? Can we deny ourselves the results of their achievements and their examples of guts? Are we so inhumane as to banish them from the richness of the stimuli of everyday life? Are we so busy 'getting and spending' and so mean-minded in our preoccupation with market forces and cost-effectiveness, that we have neither the time nor the room for the halt and lame?

To get behind the rhetoric of these questions to the reality of meeting the needs of handicapped children and adults we need a broader perspective than that afforded by the false dichotomy of the integration–segregation controversy. This deeply quarried historical study of the growth of special education by Ted Cole is a timely corrective. It demonstrates clearly that the concept of integration informed the minds of many of the pioneers of special education throughout the past century. Some saw integration as the best means of education, some saw it as the goal to be attained by education. For the first time we are able to see, against the background of history, how they addressed the problem of achieving their aims by confronting the reality of limited resources, poverty and indifference.

Fine words and simplistic notions mend no bones. Integration of the physically handicapped is not achieved by building new art galleries which are inaccessible to them, any more than it is realized for the mentally handicapped by putting the patients of our psychiatric hospitals out on the streets. It may sound progressive to say that all our handicapped pupils attend neighbourhood schools but, if the curricula of those schools are inappropriate to 40 per cent of the pupils, the result is disastrous. Ted Cole's study, by revealing the practical examples of early attempts at integration and the thinking behind the vision of pioneers such as Barnhill in nineteenth-century Glasgow, not only warns us against easy solutions, but inspires us to think more deeply and plan more wisely.

In the words of George Santayana, 'Those who cannot remember the past are condemned to repeat it.' In so much of what passes for education planning we can see the tragedy of past historical mistakes being repeated as farce. Who would have thought an over-supply of teachers could, in the space of a few years, become a shortage of teachers – and, of course, a shortage of specialist teachers – while, at the same time, we have a shortage of skilled workers and a shortage of people with management skills at a time of mass unemployment. Who could have imagined that in affluent Britain the priority recommendations of the Warnock Report would be almost completely ignored because of the costs involved and the main outcome would in fact be legislation which has resulted in greater bureaucracy.

Ted Cole exposes the seam of concern for integration throughout the past century and, although his focus is upon England, Scotland and Wales, he directs our attention to the same concerns in Europe and the United States whenever it is appropriate. The summaries of Political, Educational and Special Educational events which precede each chapter provide us with the broader strata. But, because he makes such excellent use of primary sources of material and so often quotes the words of the pioneers, whether it be Bell, Newman or Eicholz, we share their concern and their conviction. We are sure, too, that many readers will feel as we did as we read, the presence of the spectres of generations of pupils, their needs barely perceived by the majority of people.

This book challenges us to do more than address our present problems of meeting the needs of the handicapped. Because of its sound historical base it provides us with a foundation upon which to look ahead and to look more perceptively. For instance, if pioneers discerned so long ago the prime role parents may play in helping their children and in educating them, should we not be thinking about how we can compensate those pupils who have been rejected or abused by their parents? If poverty is such an exacerbating added handicap, how can we develop adequate learning situations for those pupils with special needs who are trapped in poverty? How can we remove the blight of poverty and homelessness? What if parent power seeks to banish the handicapped from nursery education and demands segregation? How much longer can we tolerate having so much research and basic provision of special education dependent upon what Beveridge termed 'voluntary action' – in other words, upon charity? What will be the effects in Britain of assessment at 7, 11 and 14 years on schools' willingness to integrate pupils with severe special needs? How can we be more discriminating and successful in meeting the diverse and changing needs of multiple-handicapped pupils? What will be the effects of advances in medicine and genetics upon the incidence of handicap and upon future provision?

Perhaps, too, we need more radical ways of thinking about these problems. The Warnock Report presented a comfortable consensus when it talked about meeting needs. It never looked at the other half of the equation: how can we release from these pupils according to their abilities. We are adept at itemizing what children cannot do. It is still a matter for surprise when handicapped children demonstrate their abilities in art, music, mathematics, literature or athletics. We parade them through the media as once they were exposed in freak shows and the salons of the wealthy. And shouldn't accountability be extended so that pupils and their parents can have recourse to the courts when speech and other therapies or proper educational programmes are not provided to meet ascertained needs?

Whatever Ted Cole's book may do to inform us of the past it will also, we are sure, make us impatient to do more now and in the future. Segregation and integration are not slogans but mere tools among what should be a whole armoury at our disposal. We accept that for the health of our society we need intensive care and accident units, out- and in-patient treatment, therapies and prostheses, a wide spectrum of specialists and their departments, shock treatment and tender loving care. For the education, survival and development of the full potential of our pupils with special needs we need a similar galaxy of provisions and specialist skills. We do not need Ministers to tell Warnock and other committees that they can propose anything they wish, providing it does not cost money. In human terms, we cannot afford not to provide the money – cost-effectively, of course. That is the lesson of history.

Phillip Williams
Peter Young

CHAPTER 1

Remaking the Jigsaw

A society which forgets its history, the old adage goes, is a society which has lost its memory. In the case of British special education, society has not totally forgotten the past but it has been selective in what it has remembered. It has filtered historical accounts written by an older generation and produced a picture which has been further distorted in the non-specialist press. On other occasions, history has been viewed almost exclusively in terms of a few major government reports, sometimes ignoring the wealth of evidence in the appendices, and then mixed with popular but misleading modern images of the past.

Take a comment written recently in *The Independent* by Hilary Wilce:

> The 1981 Education Act officially marked the end of the Victorian era for handicapped children. Out of the window went the notion that such children must be shut away from others for their schooling, and with it went the many labels of handicap – maladjusted, educationally subnormal, speech defective, and so on – that had put one in 50 children into special schools.[1]*

Perhaps this book will help a little in dispelling the inaccurate stereotype of the past implied in this quotation as well as warning against possible unrealistic hopes for the future.

Subsequent chapters will show that many Victorians, including Gladstone, were worried about special children being shut away and some were as ardent in their desire for the integration of the handicapped in the 1880s as writers in the 1980s. In very general terms

---

* Superscript numerals refer to numbered notes at the end of each chapter.

the Edwardians only decided on the special school route for a minority
of the handicapped after long practical experience suggested that full or
partial integration for the deaf, blind and other handicaps did not work
very well. Further, although a section of opinion wished to place a few
of the severely handicapped in 'permanent care', the people with power
were only marginally impressed. They had doubts about the morality
and practicality of such a course and tended to be mistrustful of Home
Office residential reformatories and also of special boarding schools
unless these were small and non-institutional in nature and
concentrated on training teenagers in trades to prepare them for an
integrated adult life. Between the two World Wars, determined efforts
were made to cure but then to reintegrate the physically defective, and
calls made to provide for those with less severe disabilities including
most of the backward within the ordinary school system. In fact, in
every age, many special educators have sought to minimize the degree
of segregation of the handicapped. Since the advent of mass,
compulsory education over 100 years ago, most handicapped, often
through neglect or lack of government money but sometimes through
parental choice and the schemes of education authorities, have received
their education in mainstream day schools.

To return to Wilce's words, the 'labels of handicap' officially lasted
from 1945 to 1983. They had replaced other labels and were in their turn
to be replaced by new ones within two or three years, whatever
legislators might have hoped. Finally, even in the mid-1980s, when the
highest percentage ever of English and Welsh children were in special
schools, they constituted far less than the 2 per cent often claimed.

These are my impressions after studying a wide variety of source
material, including David Pritchard's excellent 1963 study upon which
so many authors have relied for brief historical resumés.[2] Pritchard's
detailed knowledge and concentration on periods and topics not within
the scope of this book still make instructive reading. However, it was the
product of its time, and the choice of evidence from the myriad of past
events and personalities was largely governed by a belief that the special
school was the way forward and was the most pragmatic way of meeting
the needs of the handicapped. I have much sympathy for this view and
shall be accused of having a vested interest in furthering it as I am
myself involved in running a special school. However, in my research, I
found there were many happenings which struck me as significant
which merited only a brief mention or no mention in Pritchard's work.
Finally, his work only covered the period to 1960, and concentrated
most on pre-war history. There have also been omissions in various pre-
and post-war historical accounts – only rarely can mention be found
there of Victorian integration – all of which have contributed to the

popular view exemplified in the quotation from *The Independent*. There are also factual mistakes and errors of interpretation in both old and new special education publications which need correcting.

Hence the need for a new history which examines the past with the dominating concern of the 1980s, integration, highlighted as the development of the present British system is described. Much of the work for the book was completed before John Hurt's *Outside the Mainstream*[3] was published, and whose latter sections overlap this book a little. However, history is like a jigsaw with thousands of pieces, repeatedly taken by a child and scattered round a large and overgrown garden. Each historian who goes to retrieve it will tend to find different pieces, while some bits fade and rot away leaving each person who remakes it to surmise what goes in the gaps. Hurt's sources were often not the same as the many I examined and the scope and emphasis of his book is very different. Those with an interest in the eugenic movement are advised to read his account which is able to go into far greater detail than mine. One book complements the other.

Limits on the length of the book have unfortunately meant brief treatment for too many ideas and also a neglect of special education in Northern Ireland and, to a lesser extent, Scotland and Wales, which does bring into question the book's subtitle. However, to have talked of merely English special education would have been more inaccurate given the many influential developments north of the border which are described. Similarly, space has not been found for a discussion of the development of special help for dyslexia and only brief mention is made of speech defects and autism.

In the course of my research I did examine various American and a few continental sources to which I make brief allusion from time to time, as quite clearly the microchip and the communication satellite are not necessary for the international exchange of ideas. British representatives attended conferences abroad before 1900 and foreign special education periodicals were available in Britain. Major government enquiries sometimes included a foreign junket for some lucky Commission members. Hence it is no surprise that happenings in special education in America and in Europe influenced events in Britain. However, limited space allows only brief mention of these international influences.

For the sake of brevity and clarity, I have unashamedly used abbreviations such as ESN and its now widely used replacement, MLD, as well as sometimes using the initials rather than the long-winded names of a few professional bodies and official positions. The most common example of the latter is the use of CMO for the Chief Medical Officer of the Board of Education. I have tried to restrict myself to shorthand labels commonly used in the period under discussion. I am fully aware of the dangers of using such labels, but suspect this book could be read by people who also regularly use the modern labels in their day-to-day work while continuing to see children with special needs as individuals for whom any label is inappropriate.

The word 'integration' is also problematic. Only since the Second World War has it gradually taken on its present meaning firmly. The Victorians generally talked of 'co-education'. More recently, reference is made to 'open education' and 'co-operative plans'. Of course Americans usually use the broad term 'mainstreaming'. However, for simplicity and clarity 'integration' is employed as though it was in use throughout the period of the book.

I like the width of Booth and Potts' description of integration as 'the process of increasing the participation of children and young people in their communities'.[4] Integration implies not merely educating children with special needs alongside the non-handicapped in the ordinary primary and secondary schools. It also involves aspects of the community care approach such as fostering instead of placement in a 52-week isolated boarding establishment, or the wish for a small, homely 'cottage style' boarding school with close links with the local community and a child's parents rather than placement in a large institution which frowns on parental contact. Given the aim of nearly every special day and boarding school – except Mary Dendy's Sandlebridge (see p. 43) – was to prepare their leavers to enter normal adult society, I also talk of *adult* integration and sometimes of *community* integration. I also use the Warnock terminology.[5] *Functional* integration happens when a child is a regular full- or part-time member of a class of non-handicapped children. Schooltime *social* integration happens when the child with special needs in a special class or school mixes out of lessons with the non-handicapped. Finally, *locational* integration happens when the child's special class or unit shares the same site as the ordinary school and allows the occasional mixing of the handicapped and non-handicapped. I also refer to *full* and *partial* integration. From the sources it is often difficult to be more precise and, anyway, attempts to tie the degree of integration/segregation to the many stages of models such as the Deno Cascade[6] are fraught with difficulty. Such visual models are simplistic anyway and can be very misleading. Examples in the text below will show that the assumption that full-time education in a regular class automatically equals the maximum degree of integration, or that placement in a special boarding school the maximum degree of segregation, is patently wrong. Galloway and Goodwin shared this concern in 1979.[7] This was shown in the 1830s when blind children from the Edinburgh boarding institution are said to have attended local schools for the sighted.[8]

This example indicates that before the period covered by the book integration was an old idea. In fact, in Scotland, John Arrowsmith had advocated it for the deaf in 1819 after helping his deaf brother to make good progress in an ordinary dame school.[9] Edward Comer tried to implement Arrowsmith's ideas in Liverpool, but in 1825 decided on a special day school instead which developed into an institution with boarding facilities.[10] Earlier in the same town, an asylum for the indigent blind had been founded in 1790. Far from putting its clients 'away' or shielding them from the ordinary community, young blind people had been taken on as day pupils for training as musicians, basket-makers or weavers for up to four years while they lived at home, with friends or in lodgings. J.C. Lettsom was to write approvingly in 1798: 'It preserves the ties of families, restores them to their families, improved and advantaged in the means of life.'[11] The Liverpool Asylum was a model for other pioneer institutions to copy. A few decades later, in Bavaria, Prussia and France, efforts lasting many years were being made to educate the deaf alongside the hearing, and in 1858 integration briefly won a senior minister's backing in France.[12] However, by 1870, for the deaf and blind, the integration movement was in retreat internationally although a near contemporary source claimed there were about 1400 deaf children in special classes in the common schools of West Prussia[13] and some 'auxiliary' classes in the ordinary schools were being developed for the feeble-minded in parts of Germany. Professor Gordon claimed that the majority of international writers had been in favour of integrating the deaf and that 'the institutions were almost without advocates or defenders'.[14] But in the United States in the 1860s, special boarding institutions were the usual response for the deaf and blind as in England.

Boarding institutions in Britain also included the voluntary industrial schools for 'at risk' waifs and strays. In 1854, these schools had been allowed, following campaigns by philanthropists including Mary Carpenter, by an Act of Parliament which laid down regulations and appointed a government inspector to supervise them. Also rescuing destitute children were the poor law 'district schools', dating back to before 1850. These were large barrack-style boarding schools. The school at Sutton had 1543 beds, while that at Hanwell had 1148.[15] Supporters pointed out that they were preferable to keeping pauper children in workhouses where they would live among adults. The development of these schools was halted by the 1870 Education Act and the creation of board schools. It was also stopped by a growing dislike of huge, regimented establishments which did match twentieth-century perceptions of 'the Victorian institution'. Alternative modes of child care were also emerging.

The well-established practice in Scotland of boarding-out poor city children in the countryside, e.g. children from the slums of Glasgow with crofters on the Isle of Arran, spread to England when in 1869 the Poor Law Board allowed some local Guardians to place pauper children in foster homes out of their catchment areas.[16] This approach was preferred by the Poor Law Inspector, Mrs Nassau Senior, to the placement of children in the district schools. In 1874 she expressed her opinion that 'The massing of girls together in large numbers was bad and must issue in failure.'[17] She complained of their poor physical and moral condition, and noted the poor success of their leavers. She believed that better prospects were offered for community integration by boarding-out or cottage-style care linked to children attending day schools.

Her hopes were echoed by Thomas Stephenson, the founder of the National Children's Home, who in 1869 opened his first London home in Lambeth, followed the next year by Thomas Barnardo's first home for destitute boys in Stepney. Barnardo quickly came to share the views of Mrs Nassau Senior, abandoning the 'barrack-system' girls' home he had established in his remodelled coach-house at Barkingside in 1873 and replacing it with a 'village home' made up of 13 small cottages presided over by 'housemothers'. Uniforms were abolished, and 'anything approaching institutionalism . . . scrupulously avoided'.[18] Both Barnardo's and the National Children's Home were later to play a prominent part in special education provision and their approach influenced teachers and administrators working for school boards and, later, local and central government.

Showing a late Victorian attitude which starkly contrasts with hereditarian views often assumed to dominate this and the Edwardian period, Barnardo said: 'If the children of the slums can be removed from their surroundings early enough, and can be kept sufficiently long under training, heredity counts for little, environment counts for everything.'[19] Far from wanting difficult children out of sight and out of mind, he looked after them in his own home. In their 'rescue' work, both he and Stephenson were driven by strong moral and religious beliefs which were shared by many and gave lasting strength to their philanthropy. It also appeared in the early education of London's deaf when the Reverend William Stainer spent much of his own personal money on financing boarding homes for the children in his charge.[20] I dwell briefly on these matters to counteract a modern tendency to characterize the Victorian age as totally materialistic and to see the motivation for helping the handicapped as the economic self-interest of the non-handicapped. It is true that those in power would be swayed by arguments which stressed the prospect of saving government or the taxpayers' money, but this was not the primary motivation. The moral beliefs and liberal humanitarianism of many contemporaries should not be underestimated in the late Victorian age, or for that matter in any period afterwards. The chapters which follow will further reflect my doubts on some aspects of recent sociological interpretations of special education's history.

In 1931, the Chief Medical Officer of the Board of Education saw the development of segregated special schools as the 'growing recognition of difference in children'.[21] Broad, obvious groups were first seen – the deaf, the blind and the feeble-minded. Gradually, differences were seen within each group and the contrasting provisions needed for the deaf and the partially deaf, for the blind and the partially-sighted, for the backward, the educable and ineducable mental defectives, for the cripple and for the victim of illness. Having tried to meet even severe special needs as much as possible in the mainstream but judging it a failure, informed opinion pressed ever more strongly for teaching groups which were homogeneous in age and intelligence and in the nature of their disabilities. To achieve such a teaching situation when the incidence of most conditions was so low, it was necessary to congregate the children in special centres where professionals could provide an efficient service. Inevitably, given the long distance some children lived from these special centres, boarding was necessary and, if the well-to-do saw boarding as beneficial for their children, might it not also help the growth of independence and maturity of the handicapped? Given shortcomings in the ordinary education system, it also seemed the most pragmatic way of providing the trade training which would enable leavers to have the self-respect of being able to earn their own living. Belief in scientific and efficient classification shaped the special education regulations which followed the 1944 Education Act, and the zenith of belief in this approach was reached in the following quarter of a century. In more recent years, with awareness of the needs of the different groupings established, attention has focused more on meeting individual needs. In 1968, foreseeing the modern British integration movement, the senior HMI, James Lumsden, wondered whether instead of taking the handicapped to the experts, might it be possible to take the experts to the handicapped.[22] As the book will show, this was not a new idea. In every period, there were educators fighting to keep segregation to a minimum. This was certainly true in the Glasgow area around 1870 where the next chapter begins.

Notes

1. H. Wilce, 'Bringing all the children together', *The Independent*, 22 October, 1987, p.19.
2. D. Pritchard, *Education and the Handicapped*, Routledge and Kegan Paul, London, 1963.
3. J.S. Hurt, *Outside the Mainstream*, Batsford, London, 1988.
4. T. Booth and P. Potts (eds), *Integrating Special Education*, Blackwell, Oxford, 1983, p.1.
5. Committee of Enquiry into the Education of Handicapped Children and Young People, *Special Educational Needs* (Warnock Report), Cmnd 7212, HMSO, London, 1978, pp.100–1.
6. E. Deno, 'Special education as developmental capital', *Exceptional Children*, vol. 30, 1970, pp.229–37.
7. D. Galloway and C. Goodwin, *Educating Slow Learning Children: Integration or Segregation*, Longman, London, 1979, p.53.
8. A. Barnhill, *A New Era in the Education of Blind Children; or Teaching the Blind in Ordinary Schools*, Glass, Glasgow, 1875, p.vi; *Report for 1908 of the Chief Medical Officer of the Board of Education*, Section VI, HMSO, London, 1909.
9. J.P. Arrowsmith, *The Art of Instructing the Infant Deaf and Dumb*, Taylor and Hessey, London, 1819.
10. J.C. Gordon, 'Deaf-mutes and the public schools from 1815 to the present day', *American Annals of the Deaf*, vol. XXX, no. 2, April 1885, p.137.
11. J.C. Lettsom, *The Blind: Hints Designed to Promote Beneficence, Temperance and Medical Science*, 1801. Reprinted by Sampson Low, London, 1894.
12. Op. cit., note 10, p.131.
13. Ibid., p.129.
14. Ibid., p.123.
15. J. Heywood, *Children in Care*, 3rd edn, Routledge and Kegan Paul, London, 1978, p.71.
16. Ibid., p.81.
17. Ibid., p.72.
18. Ibid., pp.52–3.
19. Ibid., p.53.
20. Op. cit., note 2, p.78.
21. Chief Medical Officer of Board of Education, *The Health of the School Child*, Annual Report for 1930, HMSO, London, 1931, p.64.
22. J. Lumsden, 'Special education for the handicapped', *Teacher of the Blind*, vol. LVI, no. 4, July 1968, p.133.

CHAPTER 2

The New Era: 1870–93

Political and Educational Summary: 1867–93

Major Events and Ordinary Education

1867 Reform Act gives vote to many workers
1868 Public Schools Act – reforms for major upper-class public schools
1868 *Disraeli* (Conservative) PM
1868 *Gladstone's* (Liberal) 1st Ministry
1869 Endowed Schools Act – revised financing and more scholarships for middle-class grammar schools
1870 Forster's Education Act permits non-denominational elected school boards, helped by government grants related to pupils' results, in areas where church schools do not exist – parents can be asked to pay

1874 *Disraeli's 2nd Ministry*

Special Education

1868 Greenock, Scotland; integration of blind begins; foundation of British and Foreign Society (for blind) which soon pushes for adoption of braille (with limited success until 1890s)

1870 Royal Albert Asylum, Lancaster opens under G.E. Shuttleworth
1871 Association for Oral Instruction of Deaf and Dumb founded
1872 Van Praagh starts day classes for deaf in London
1873 London Home Teaching Soc. teachers go into National Schools
1874 LSB concede they have responsibility for deaf – first class in ordinary school in Bethnal Green

1875 LSB appoints peripatetic teachers of blind; Barnhill's *A New Era in the Education of Blind Children* published (describes integration)

1876 Sandon's Education Act – local school boards to enforce attendance; pupils can still leave at 10 for half-time work. Parents to ensure child gets elementary instruction

1876 COS Report *Training of the Blind* published in London – presses for integration of blind; LSB sees braille as force for segregation

1877 COS Report calls for removal of imbeciles from board schools and their special education in boarding institutions

1880 *Gladstone's 2nd Ministry*
1880 Education Act; stricter attendance laws; education to 13, though exemptions
1883 Over 1 000 000 in Board Schools

1881 Governors of deaf institutions vote for oral method; LSB allow cripples, aged 7+ to remain in ordinary infants schools

1883 Managers and Teachers of Blind (at Doncaster Conference) attack COS support for integration

1884 Virtual universal male suffrage

1884 Birmingham School Board inspect London day classes for deaf but reject idea and opt to use Edgbaston institution; Shuttleworth calls for special classes for feeble-minded; Grosvenor House meeting; Duke of Westminster calls for government enquiry into education of blind

1885 *Salisbury's* (Conservative) Ministry

1885 Royal Commission set up to look into needs of blind and later in 1886 the deaf and others; Lord Egerton takes over the chairmanship

1886 *Gladstone's 3rd Ministry* falls over Irish Home Rule
1886 *Salisbury's 2nd Ministry*

1887 Aubert Park home for feeble-minded girls founded ('permanent care' movement begins)

1888 County Councils Act sets up London CC and 62 elected county councils

1888 Maghull institution for epileptics founded; W. Stainer praises boarding schools for deaf; Invalid Children's Aid Association founded

1889 County councils i/c of technical education

1889 Royal Commission reports; pushes integration for blind but

1890	Creation of six teacher training colleges	
1890	Virtual ending of 'payment by results'	
1891	Salisbury's Education Act – free universal elementary education	
1892–4	*Gladstone's 4th Ministry*	
1892	Keir Hardy elected as first Labour MP	
1893	Minimum age of employment up to 11 years	
1894	Bryce Commission wants reform of the national education system	

degrees of segregation for deaf and feeble-minded

1890 Education of Blind and Deaf-Mute Children (Scotland) Act; Norwood Conference debates integration for blind; London Conference debates integration for deaf

1892 Leicester and LSB's first special classes for feeble-minded

1893 Elementary Education (Blind and Deaf Children) Act; duty of school authorities to provide education for blind and deaf children and some state aid provided

In 1870 the Greenock Society heard of the success of local blind pupils who for two years had received their education in the same classrooms and alongside their sighted peers. The Reverend Andrew McFarlane saw this 'as a New Era in the Education of the Blind'.[1] This new era was not confined to the blind. The governments of Gladstone, Disraeli and Salisbury, conscious of a new mass electorate and under pressure from powerful philanthropic bodies such as the Charity Organization Society (COS), founded in 1869, involved themselves in social issues in a way their *laissez-faire* predecessors would not have contemplated, passing housing, public health and child care Acts and responding to middle- and working-class demands for universal education.

In fact the new era was heralded in by a flurry of educational reforms: reform of the public schools in 1868, the grammar schools in 1869 and, in 1870, Gladstone's government turned its attention to mass education for the lower classes by setting up locally elected school boards to fill the gaps left by the voluntary church schools. Further Education Acts in 1876, 1880 and 1891 completed the provision of free, universal and compulsory elementary education.

As a by-product, thousands of children with special needs became the responsibility of the board school teachers. Classes became overburdened with children with learning difficulties who could not pass the annual examinations and whose failure lowered the pay of their teachers until the virtual ending of 'payment by results' in 1890. This produced pressure for these children to be excluded from the ordinary education system.

On the other hand, the law required, if in vague terms, the education of all children, except the 'permanently disabled', a term interpreted differently in different areas. Nor would the law allow the school boards to build separate special schools or provide ancillary services such as school transport or board and lodging.[2] If a child was to attend one of the voluntary special institutions, by now established in most regions of the country, the state would not contribute to the cost unless the child and family were paupers. There were also professionals such as teachers of the blind in Glasgow or 'charitable people' (e.g. the COS) who believed in integration for the good of the individual handicapped child and who attacked the inadequacies and the life-style of the residential institutions.

Gradually, pressure from philanthropists and the staff of the financially struggling voluntary institutions impinged upon central government until in 1885 a Royal Commission was set up by the Conservative Government of Lord Salisbury to enquire into the needs of the blind. In the following year its terms of reference were expanded to include the deaf 'as well as such other cases as from special circumstances would seem to require exceptional methods of treatment'.[3] It reported in 1889 and laws providing state aid and placing a clear duty on parents and school authorities to educate the blind and deaf were passed in 1890 for Scotland and 1893 for England and Wales. Government action on the feeble-minded, physically handicapped and epileptics was to be delayed until 1899.

Throughout these years the integration–segregation debate featured prominently. An awareness of the issues was shown at the highest level by Prime Minister William Gladstone in a speech to the House of Commons on 1 March 1868, urging state aid for the Irish and proposing help for the special institutions:

> I am not now speaking of Institutions in which the Deaf, Dumb and Blind are to be mewed up for life, but simply of schools in which they may receive that kind of instruction which they are capable of receiving for their own benefit, to prepare them to go out into the world to play their part as Providence permits them – as useful members of society.[4]

The fact that his brother Robert was President of the Old Trafford residential school for the deaf might have contributed to his awareness and his support for institutions which actively worked for the integration of its leavers into open society. There were many who shared this hopeful view.

Others were less sanguine. As the COS fought successfully to prevent Henry Gardner's substantial bequest being spent on the creation of another residential institution for the blind, a writer to *The Times* claimed in 1880:

The institution is a little world of its own, into which external influences penetrate but slowly, and which in the course of a few years, is liable to be fenced around by a petrified coverage of usages ... against which the efforts of the reformer are spent in vain ... . The institution has been the greatest possible obstacle in the way of useful and much-needed progress; and managers generally have seemed to think that the blind or the deaf existed for the glorification of the system, not the system for the afflicted.[5]

Given feelings such as these, expressed in the most influential paper of the period, it was to be expected that alternative ways should be sought for caring for handicapped children and that the integration of the blind in central Scotland, publicized throughout England and Scotland by A. Barnhill in 1875, should interest the Royal Commissioners in the late 1880s.

Children who were Deaf or Blind

In the 1870s the voluntary institutions for the deaf and the blind continued to expand and provided a service for most regions. They were generally situated in major provincial towns such as Newcastle and Derby, but occasionally in smaller communities such as Boston Spa. Census returns showed that the numbers of pupils in the institutions for the deaf increased from 1979 in 1871 to 2646 in 1881.[6] Numbers also increased for the blind. By 1889 there were 35 boarding schools for them. Much effort had to be devoted to fund raising. Lack of finance prevented the employment or training of high-quality staff and led to increasing calls for government aid towards the costs of educating all their pupils.

In the 1870s, institutions for the deaf had yet to embrace the oral/speech reading approach and those for the blind still saw braille as an alien language likely to increase the segregation of their pupils as adults from the seeing world. Oralism and braille came to be adopted more widely in the 1880s and 1890s and almost universally by 1900.

International support for the residential approach was seen at the 1873 Vienna Conference for Teachers of the Blind, which called for blind children to be placed in ordinary schools with the sighted only in the absence of special schools.[7] This was in stark contrast to the approach of the Pennsylvania State Institute which in 1874–5 was pressing the state government to allow it to place blind children under 11 years of age in the ordinary schools. The Vienna message also conflicted with A. Barnhill's evangelical 1875 tract publicizing the feasibility of functional integration of the blind as had been practised in Scotland since 1868. Barnhill, the Superintendent of the Glasgow Mission for the outdoor relief of the blind, claimed that 50 children in Scotland were following his 'plan'.

This involved teaching the blind to read by raised non-braille Roman style type for which the child was given separate lessons by an advanced scholar or pupil-teacher. Parents gave extra coaching at home. Similarly, in other lessons such as geography, parents, using embossed maps, were asked to go over lessons with their children at home to prepare for the schoolday ahead. With this extra support, many children had been able to keep up to the prescribed standards. Barnhill preferred full functional integration for as much of the timetable as possible.

He praised the social and emotional value to the child:

> One who has never seen it would scarcely believe the great change that comes over a blind boy by a year or two's attendance at school and education with sighted companions – in his appearance, his cheerfulness, his intelligence, and his smartness.

It counteracted feelings of isolation or despondency, it allowed blind children 'to enjoy the society and happiness of home' and enabled them to go with their brothers and sisters to the same school: 'By mixing freely with those who have their sight he comes to think and feel as they do.' The fear that integrated children are 'laughed at, mocked, or ill-used, foolishly thought by some parents, has been amply refuted'.[8]

He attacked education in institutions: 'Isolation in a strange house with many other children affected by the same calamity, can scarcely but have a depressing and enervating effect.' Later in the book appeared letters of support, including one from S.S. Forster, Headmaster of the College for Blind Sons of Gentlemen, Worcester, who felt there was:

> a growing opinion among some teachers that the massing together of blind children in large numbers, for purposes of education, is not the best means to that end; that the effect is one of gloom and isolation, and a depressing conviction of common helplessness, which is prejudicial to effort and success.

He also noted the low standards said to prevail in contemporary British institutions. The shortage of good staff had led to the appointment of F.J. Campbell, an American, as Head of the Royal Normal College for the Blind, Upper Norwood, who wrote to Barnhill in November 1874 and spoke of the benefits for children placed in institutions if part of their time 'was spent in ordinary schools for sighted children, as this will oblige them to associate and play with the sighted, and thus, to some extent at least, overcome some of the habits peculiar to blind children'.

Barnhill devotes another chapter to the testimony of Scottish teachers following his plan. The Ayrshire teacher, W. Glasgow, was an example of an initial doubter on its feasibility, but his preconceived notions 'had been the result of ignorance'[9] and he now recommended it, as did many other teachers. To convince other doubters Barnhill devotes a chapter to 'Not Interfering with Teachers' Time and School Exercises'. The success of the approach was illustrated by case histories from various towns in central Scotland and was also praised in the *Leicester Guardian* in 1872.

In 1873, in London, the Home Teaching Society arranged for its staff to teach Moon's embossed print to blind children in the ordinary classes of the voluntary national schools. In February 1876, the COS published their report on *Training of the Blind*. This noted the 'perfect success' of the widespread Scottish system[10] and was happy with integration developing in 20 London board schools. The objections of teachers in ordinary schools sprang from ignorance and inexperience of integration and could be overcome. They should be made aware of special aids such as embossed prints and maps and told that fears of the blind being ill-treated by the sighted were groundless.[11] The COS saw only a limited role for the residential institutions; perhaps, giving the young child a preparatory course for a year before letting him pursue the major part of his education in the elementary day schools. Education until 15 with their sighted peers, followed by industrial training to make them self-reliant, useful adults, should be the general rule. In the appendix, self-help advice was given to parents.

In 1875, the London School Board (LSB) employed two blind teachers from the Home Teaching Society to teach the blind children in the board schools using Moon's Roman type embossed print. In 1879 there were 34 children being helped in this way. However, in the previous year, a Board inspector had criticized the quality of the teaching and in 1879 the Board appointed the sighted American, Miss M. C. Greene, an experienced teacher at Norwood, as Superintendent of a new scheme.[12] Also appointed were two other teachers who had been trained at Norwood. They favoured the use of braille and overturned the recommendation of the London School Board Conference, held in 1876, which had preferred an embossed Roman type system and had seen dot systems as a force for segregation.

A new scheme was set up whereby blind children spent half of their time in segregated special classes and the remainder in the ordinary board classes with the sighted, following a normal timetable in the school nearest their home. The system was developed until in 1888 there were 133 children being taught by five teachers working under Miss Greene in 23 centres attached to day schools.

Meanwhile, for deaf children, partial school and total community integration was still on the minds of some educators and was forced on others by the requirements of Forster's Education Act.

In 1872, the young Dutch teacher William van Praagh started a day school where student teachers learning the oral method could practise their craft. A major aim of this establishment was to further the long-term integration prospects of its pupils by making them mix with hearing people outside school hours. If they could not stay in their family home they would live, not in concentrated numbers as would be the case in a residential institution, but in ones and twos, boarded-out with families near the school where they would have to practise their developing lip-reading and articulation skills. Van Praagh had seen this arrangement work well in Rotterdam and was convinced of its superiority over residential institutional life.[13] The Royal Commission was to hear of a similar scheme operating in Schleswig in northern Germany.[14] Van Praagh was to speak up for the day/fostering approach at various conferences in the years that followed.

A model had been established for the LSB to follow. The Reverend William Stainer, formerly employed by the Old Kent Road Institution, was made Superintendent of their new scheme and, in 1874, a classroom in the board school at Wilmot Road, Bethnal Green was set aside as a special class and five deaf children were admitted. By July 1877, there were 120 children in special classes attached to ordinary board schools and some children were fostered nearby.[15] Stainer was also to open special children's homes for deaf children near the receiving board schools. In the early years, Stainer seemed convinced of the superiority of this approach over concentrating large numbers of deaf children in institutions.

Predictably, at the Third Conference of the Heads of the Institutions for the Deaf, held in 1877 in London, his views were attacked. Richard Elliott, Head of the Margate branch of the Old Kent Road Institution referred to the failure of day schools in France and Prussia, claiming that institutions were now the almost universal practice. Foretelling often-used arguments of the 1890s, he said that small day centres did not allow for the efficient division of children into classes. He commented on the possible poor attendance levels of day scholars, an accusation refuted by Stainer at this time.[16]

These arguments were to re-surface at conferences for deaf educators in the early 1880s. While the institution governors met in London in 1881 primarily to discuss the Milan International Conference's call for the adoption of oral methods of teaching the deaf, discussion also took place on the relative merits of day and residential education. Miss Muller, of the LSB, regretted that 'the parents of course like to have their children with them, but this is often productive of unfavourable results'. At home the adults would use sign language with their children, undoing the work of the teachers.[17]

Miss Muller was one of an increasing number of teachers of the deaf who believed it possible, in a controlled environment, to teach deaf children to lip-read and also to speak intelligibly. The process of achieving this might be long and painful for deaf children and, in the majority British view, might well require them to live away from tender-hearted parents in boarding schools, but it was increasingly believed to be the best way of helping the deaf to integrate as adults in normal hearing society. To allow deaf children to use finger-spelling or any form of sign language was to opt for easy short-term gains in communication but would distract the child from learning to lip-read and to speak. Until well after the Congress of Milan, many British educators of the deaf continued to see a place for signing whether by itself or used in conjunction with lip-reading and speech. The latter was known as the 'Combined Method', a term which was to be superseded by 'Total Communication' nearly a century later. During the intervening years throughout the world, the proponents of the rival methods were to engage in long and often fruitless arguments on the relative merits of the two approaches. Allusion to this debate, which started hundreds of years before the period of this book and continues today, will be made at various points in the pages that follow.

In 1882 the Heads gathered again, this time at Doncaster. They were envious of the financial assistance the US government gave to voluntary American institutions, relieving the latter from the time-consuming and sometimes fruitless task of fund-raising. Blaming their parlous finances, the British Heads were in self-critical mood and complained of poor quality staff and equipment. They were also disappointed that training in a trade given to older pupils – for example, students in Edinburgh learned how to print or to make shoes – was inefficient and, even if well done, of limited usefulness. Business men apparently preferred to train their own new staff and the emerging trades unions wanted the correct apprenticeship procedures followed in their entirety.

Van Praagh once again pushed the merits of his day/fostering system.[18] While his views were contested by Richard Elliott, the latter did appreciate the need for increasing the contact of his pupils with the outside world. Holidays, at this time rarely given, were one means of doing this:

> We are educating our children for society – let us give them from time to time an opportunity of going into that society they will afterwards join permanently. What can be a more unnatural proceeding than to keep a deaf and dumb person wholly within the walls of an Institution, leading its artificial life, and then at the end of five or six years to thrust him forth to make his first real acquaintance with the world and its ways.[19]

That Elliott found it necessary to say this suggests that too many institutions were of the type which 'mewed up' their clients. The

Royal Commission also pushed the need for holidays.

William Stainer was also in self-critical mood, expressing growing doubts on the London day classes. The more Stainer experienced the homes and families of the deaf children for whom his classes catered, the less happy he was to leave them there. He, as much as Barnardo, saw the need to 'rescue' children from their home environments for the good of their health, their education, their soul and to enhance their chances as adults. The 1870 Act did not allow the school boards to pay for children's board and lodging, and therefore prevented their establishing boarding schools. Stainer felt obliged to use his own money and raised funds for boarding-out and for financing his children's homes. In this debate, he lamented that his day classes only looked after the deaf children for a seventh of the hours in a week – 'Where are the other six-sevenths spent? I confess if your Institutions were not so large, I should prefer Institutions to the homes of many of these children.'[20] Increasingly, given the practical difficulties he experienced with finding suitable foster homes and in maintaining his children's homes, he came to see the desirability of small residential special schools for the children living in appalling physical conditions. This was reflected in the LSB's evidence to the Royal Commission.[21]

These doubts may have influenced the Birmingham School Board in 1884. Thinking of setting up day classes, members inspected the Stainer system in London but concluded that placement at the Edgbaston institution would better meet the needs of their deaf children.

However, the continuing day schemes of the Scottish and London board schools offered an alternative model which some provincial towns did follow. The day approach was adopted by Sheffield who set up a special class for the deaf in 1879. A boarding hostel was not deemed necessary as the children would be able to walk each day to the deaf centre from their homes. In 1883, Nottingham School Board opened a day centre for the deaf for 35 children taught by two teachers, although they continued to send their blind children to the Midlands Institute until this closed. Also in this decade, special classes for the deaf were set up in Leeds, Bradford, Bristol, Leicester and Oldham. For the blind, a special class was set up in 1882 in Sunderland and in 1885 in Bradford, although, unlike London, the pupils spent all their lessons apart from the sighted.

Meanwhile, developments were occurring in America which were to arouse interest in Britain. After working with his father as a teacher of the deaf in Edinburgh, the Scot, Alexander Graham Bell, had emigrated to Canada and thence to Boston University as a Professor of vocal physiology in 1871. He proceeded to marry one of his deaf students and to pioneer the development of the telephone and later the gramophone.

In July 1884, in Madison, Wisconsin, he addressed the Annual Meeting of the National Education Association. He put forward an optimistic message which was reminiscent of that of his compatriot, Barnhill, for the blind. His ideas were to be given serious consideration by the members of the 1889 Royal Commission. He noted that there were over 7000 deaf children in 58 American residential institutions, but that as many children again were not receiving any education. Society, he claimed, had no right to demand the compulsory education of a deaf child away from its parents unless proven absolutely necessary: 'The separation of a child from its parents at a tender age cannot but be considered a calamity.' He preferred special classes within the ordinary day public schools: 'Segregation in childhood for the purposes of education tends to segregation in adult life. Institution life, by removing deaf-mutes from their normal environment, tends to make them a distinct class in the community.' Leavers mixed with and married other deaf people and there was 'a serious danger of the formation of a deaf variety of the human race'.[22]

Paul Binner, Principal of the recently established Milwaukee Day School for the Deaf, was to tell the meeting how these ideas could be realized in practice. He conceded that 'co-education of the deaf with hearing children' had been tried and 'shelved by the German schools and it is now looked upon as simply ridiculous. We can educate children in schools where hearing children are, but not *with* them.' He went on to advise special classrooms among classes for the hearing, with the deaf and hearing being encouraged to mix at playtimes and on the journey to and from school. He commented that this system had been 'tried and found efficient' in schools in Germany and the United States.[23]

Shortly after, the Superintendent of the existing Illinois Institution representing the viewpoint of many contemporaries, dismissed Bell's plan saying 'our grand-parents had not thought it worthy of handing down to us'[24] and referred to the German experience, as did Professor Gordon in an 1885 article[25] which claimed that integration in Prussia was now only used as a preparation for attending special institutions. The spread of the integration of the deaf child in France in the middle of the century had been limited. This still persisted in a few schools at Toulouse, Poitiers and Orleans and the integration ideal had been pushed in a French pamphlet by Grosselin in 1882.[26] Gordon also recorded Stainer's growing preference for residential schools and concluded from the available sources 'that the theoretical advantages of an environment of hearing persons have never been realised in practice'; that special institutions were a necessity and 'continue to offer superior results, with the greatest economy of time, money and men'.[27]

However, an article written in 1886 suggests there were gaps in

Gordon's knowledge. F.W. Reuschert said there were 97 institutions for the deaf in Germany of which 50 were day schools and 14 worked the inter/externate system,[28] whereby a child would board for two to three years until sufficiently advanced to make use of spoken language. The child would then be boarded out in private families and attend school as a day-scholar. He also said that in Brandenburg, deaf children were taught in the ordinary schools.

'Street Arabs' and Industrial Schools

In 1871 the professional 'baby farmer' Margaret Waters was hanged for murder after the police found filthy, emaciated babies lying neglected around her house. Four died shortly afterwards in the workhouse. The previous year, 276 dead babies had been found by police 'dropped about the streets' of London.[29] Unwanted or neglected children who survived such an early end tended to become the 'street arabs' portrayed by Dickens in Oliver Twist and accurately described as 'the perishing class' by Mary Carpenter in 1851.[30] For these waifs the church schools run by the British and National Societies did not cater. Those who survived babyhood in their overstressed families in the city slums were the clientele for whom the industrial schools, offering a practical and different curriculum from the other existing schools, were established.

They rescued children whose parents were least able to bring them up satisfactorily and sometimes helped their leavers to pursue an adult life away from their roots – in service, at sea, in Canada or in the armed forces. They aimed to stop children embarking upon a criminal or dissolute life. They were run by voluntary managers but subject to certification and inspection by Home Office staff.

By 1872 there were 100 such schools in what was the most fully developed and fastest growing sector catering for what can fairly be called 'special' children. At the end of 1869, 7345 children were living in them.[31] This number doubled over the ensuing decade. They came to be seen as a useful asset by some school boards, some of whom were to set up their own. By 1889, the London School Board had sent 13 000 children from disturbed homes, petty offenders and persistent truants to them.[32]

In his 1870 report, the government inspector and pioneer Head, Sydney Turner, while sympathetic to their work and praising the general standards found within them, regretted trends which tended to make these schools more remote and isolated from the communities they served. There was a tendency for schools to move out of town to better, new premises in rural or semi-rural sites, e.g. from Exeter and

Perth. Turner noted that this was partly for security reasons – to better contain the increasing number of young offenders being placed in these schools and to reduce the number of runaways who escaped, never to be heard of again. It was also for health reasons. Turner noted fatal diseases 'carrying off staff as well as scholars'.[33] In the fresh air of the countryside this was less likely to happen. This trend and the increasing practice of using ships as training schools made it difficult to use them for members of the 'ragged and neglected class' who were not offenders and who could continue to live at home. This he regretted as:

> The admixture of day scholars not only extends the usefulness of a school, but certainly infuses a more free and natural tone into its discipline, and keeps up more thoroughly the relations of the children to the realities of that practical life going on outside the school in which they will have again to mix.[34]

For these children, he urged the new school boards to provide day industrial *feeding* schools, where pupils, usually from impoverished homes, would receive three meals a day and regular baths in addition to basic education and training in a trade. This plea was to be repeated in later reports by inspectors but with only limited results. By 1890 there were 18 day schools for 2599 pupils in Oxford, Yarmouth, Leeds, Glasgow and other towns. The new inspector, William Inglis, praised these happy, low-cost schools.

Another development in the 1880s was the creation of some pioneer short-stay boarding schools for persistent truants who would start their placement in solitary confinement.[35]

Idiots, Imbeciles and the Feeble-minded

During this period, mentally handicapped children could be placed in the five existing large institutions at Earlswood (Red Hill), Knowle (near Birmingham), Colchester, Starcross (Devon) and Lancaster. In the 1870s, the Metropolitan Asylums Board was to open separate children's establishments at Caterham and Hampstead, the latter with its school for imbeciles, transferring to new premises at Darenth in 1878. Two private institutions also existed.

There remained much confusion about definitions of the degree of handicap, although increasingly the lowest grade, idiots, were distinguished from the more able, imbeciles, who in turn were recognized as different from the feeble-minded. Limited ability was frequently confused with mental illness, as was epilepsy. Similarly, the physically handicapped, for whom there was virtually no appropriate provision at this stage, were often confused with the feeble-minded and were occasionally placed in these institutions. For parents to have their children admitted, they had to agree to their children being certified as idiots – a much hated label. In 1877, the Charity Organization Society's Report[36] was to address these problems of definition and to stress the harmless nature of the feeble-minded, but in its proposals for more 500-bed asylums for the young feeble-minded, was to do nothing to try to keep these children integrated into their local communities.

They perhaps shared the enthusiasm of C. Miller who, in 1874, described his visit to the Royal Albert, Lancaster. He observed the children in class:

> Instead of the weary, depressed, bothered air, so common in ordinary school-rooms, we saw a general effect of brightness and briskness, both in pupils and teachers, as if they liked their work, and went at it heartily with a will.[37]

As he saw round the institution he noticed that 'merriment and joyousness are the order of the day'. The Royal Albert had been deliberately built on the moor outside Lancaster as 'all the best medical authorities agree as to the benefit arising from the effect of bracing air in cases of idiocy'.[38] In an appendix to this pamphlet in which an appeal was made to the reader for contributions – perhaps explaining Miller's praise – the Chairman and Secretary of the management committee hint at the 'rescue' side to their work. In open society the feeble-minded were abused and neglected, 'but in an asylum, where he can be isolated from all that degrade and irritate, surrounded by bright and happy associations, and treated with gentle firmness, the idiot's condition may be greatly ameliorated'.

The seriously handicapped who were not placed in the few large residential institutions continued to receive no education, whereas increasingly the more able feeble-minded children attended the board classes following the tightening up of the attendance laws by the 1880 Education Act. They were clogging up the lower standards. The device of creating a 'sink class' often called Standard 0 was adopted by some school boards, e.g. Bristol.[39] Others, such as London, left the children in Standard 1, leading to the claim made by a Medical Officer in the 1890s that almost every London school had 70 children in their Standard 1 class, of whom 25 were almost entirely ignorant. By using them, the school boards met their statutory duty to provide education for all children but, given the huge class size and the fact that young pupil-teachers often had to cope with them, they were unsatisfactory expedients not worthy of the description 'integration'.

G.E. Shuttleworth, although Superintendent of the Royal Albert Asylum and a doughty fighter for the care of the severely handicapped in residential institutions, was one of the first influential people to advocate the alternative of the Norwegian and German style special class for the feeble-minded. At the 1884 Health Exhibition Conference he called for these to be established in each large town. He saw this approach as better meeting the educational and social needs of the feeble-minded while allowing them to remain with their families in their own communities.[40] Sometimes these could be combined to form separate day auxiliary schools. The Egerton Report adopted these ideas.

The 1889 Royal Commission

Lord Egerton was the Chairman of the enlarged Royal Commission which set to work in earnest in 1887. The resulting 1889 Report contained a wide diversity of international opinion and throws interesting light on the integration–segregation debate.

Appendix 1 of the Report contains a rare extant example of the views of handicapped people themselves. Representatives of the Edinburgh, Glasgow, Aberdeen and Dundee asylums for the blind suggested the limited outreach of the Barnhill 'plan' but strongly endorsed his call for the education of the blind in the ordinary board schools. This they claimed:

> would be as convenient, cheap, and efficient as for any other member of the family, without entailing their removal from home, deprivation of varied and suitable companionship, or the intervention of entire strangers. At present, it may be said that there are only the asylum schools for their reception, and the rule and the strict discipline observed in these schools is an objectionable feature in the training and the upbringing of the juvenile blind.[41]

Institutional life, funded by charity, was a poor preparation for self-supporting integration as adults into the seeing world. Their denunciation of Scottish institutional life is echoed by the Huddersfield and District Blind Association's[42] and the Blackburn School Board's belief in special classes in the ordinary schools and at least playtime integration with sighted children.

The Commissioners themselves observed functional school integration. In London, four blind children at the Lisson Grove Board School, seen in March 1887, were to pass their examinations 'as well as any in their class'.[43] In Glasgow, two blind children at the St George's Road Board School were seen to 'take part with the seeing in dictation and other class lessons with perfect facility'. Opinion supporting this approach is also given by teachers. The Head of the Gorbals Board School talked of the 'immense advantages' of teaching the blind with the sighted and said the arrangement 'is perfectly practicable, and works well'.

In the south, after some years' practical experience, the London Home Teaching Society was unanimously in favour of blind children up to the age of 10 receiving education for some of the time with the sighted. The Commissioners were clearly impressed by this evidence and concluded that:

> the free intercourse with the seeing gives courage and self-reliance to the blind, and a healthy stimulus which enables them to compete more successfully with the seeing in after life than those who have been brought up altogether in blind institutions.[44]

The board school was suitable for blind children in good health and living within reasonable distance of the day school until age 12, but then they should transfer to special institutions for the technical education needed to prepare them for self-supporting adulthood. The Commissioners were convinced by what they had seen that most blind children could follow the normal curriculum and pass the standards with their sighted companions. Help should be given in the provision of guides and any travel costs. The Glasgow Board's satisfaction with its peripatetic teacher of the blind, who in 1888 had to support 28 blind pupils in ordinary schools, was also noted. Visiting teachers were also employed in London and Cardiff.

The physically weak and those from poor homes would, however, be better off in institutions. They were conscious of the dangers of institutionalization noted by Scottish and German witnesses. The curriculum of residential schools, they stressed, should be geared to making leavers self-supporting. Rather than a timetable exclusively reserved for academic subjects, more lessons should be devoted to book-keeping, manual dexterity and, in the modern phrase, 'life-skills' training. They admired the Saxon practice of attaching 'guardians' to supervise and support leavers.

The Commissioners were less sanguine about the prospects for integrating the deaf. Attention was given to the ideas of A.G. Bell and also the arguments of Philip Emery, Principal of the Chicago Day School for the Deaf, who complained of residential institutions weaning the deaf from their neighbourhoods. He preferred the deaf and hearing to 'grow up together, and live and die as old friends of childhood and school-days'.[45] Day schools gave deaf children the chance to practise oral skills in everyday life.

These views were echoed by witnesses from Huddersfield, Blackburn, Leeds and Nottingham. Examples of partial integration were described in Dundee where there was a class for the deaf attached to the board school and two children were boarded out locally. At Smyllum Park Orphanage, Lanark, 'great advantage is found to ensue from the association in playtime of the deaf with the hearing children. It makes the former brighter and more energetic.' The Commissioners were impressed by this mixing out of class of the deaf and hearing children at Donaldson's Hospital School, Edinburgh, where for 50 years poor deaf and hearing pupils had boarded together. At Govan, the teacher of the deaf class attached to the board school expressed the same sentiment and felt that the pupils lost nothing by living in their family homes, although she conceded that the parents would sometimes use sign language against her wishes with their children. This last point was also made by teachers in Greenock and Leicester.[46]

No account is given of a child being fully integrated with his hearing peers and the Commissioners listened carefully to the growing doubts of the LSB who now said that the day school principle was not favourable to the education of most deaf children. Small numbers meant inadequate classification at the 13 board schools where there were classes for the deaf.[47] In contrast to Stainer's 1877 view, attendance was said to be poor, 'accounted for by the distance at which they reside from the centres, bad weather, want of boots and clothing, illness and family circumstances'. This led Stainer to write in 1888:

> Boarding Institutions are therefore indispensable for the effective education of the deaf and dumb children of the poor, while the better classes can fall back on private education at home or in day classes.[48]

The Commissioners agreed, particularly in view of the alleged poor quality of child care in Stainer's special homes. All deaf children should go to separate schools, whether day or boarding, except perhaps the children from richer families who could continue to use day school/boarding out arrangements on the Van Praagh model. Bell's fear of the creation of a deaf race led them to propose a further dimension of segregation, i.e. deaf boys and girls attending day schools should be separated from each other.[49]

The feeble-minded received only brief attention. G.E. Shuttleworth's evidence – repeating his 1884 views – was adopted and it was recommended that they should 'be separated from ordinary scholars in public elementary schools in order that they may receive special instruction'. The more severely handicapped idiots and imbeciles were best placed in special residential institutions, but ought to be both distinguished and separated from lunatics.[50]

Reactions and Legislation: 1889–93

Egerton's call for state aid and compulsory education for the deaf and blind was considered and generally approved by gatherings of leading educators at separate meetings in November 1889. Pressure was rapidly applied on the government for legislation.

Further discussion took place at the Conference of Headmasters of the Institutions for the Deaf in January 1890, where the relative merits of day and boarding were again debated. A. Large, the Head of Donaldson's School, Edinburgh defended the institutions. In open society, he said, deaf children were the 'butt and gibe of their associates' from an early age and they could be overprotected by the 'misdirected sympathy of neighbours'. He only favoured day education as a preparation for institutional life where deaf children 'were rescued from all the evils of street influence and bad associates'.[51] He spoke for many delegates when he said children were better fed, housed, clothed, had their health properly looked after and their education was more efficient largely because homogeneous classification was possible. He asked how it could be thought injurious to the deaf to be sent to boarding school when the well-to-do of the land chose to send their children to public schools – an argument to be repeated frequently over the next century.

Large gave qualified support to the notion that both the deaf and the hearing benefited from mixing in the same school environment – the former in intelligence, the latter in sympathy for the handicapped. However, he had watched the deaf and hearing in his Edinburgh playgrounds for many years and was of the opinion that the deaf could not be forced to integrate freely with the hearing and that efforts to force them could be counter-productive. P. Dodds, in 1890, working in the London day classes, had similarly watched the behaviour patterns of deaf and hearing children in a Paddington playground:

> There are a number of strong, healthy, and lively children in the deaf department, with speech, and in close proximity to a large school of hearing boys and girls, having extensive and commodious playgrounds, yet there is seldom any visible desire on the part of the hearing to associate with the deaf, and there is less eagerness on the part of the deaf to associate with the hearing, although it is encouraged in every way, even to this extent – the boys going to drill with the hearing pupils, and the girls to the cookery class.[52]

Dodds had taught the deaf the playground games of the hearing to encourage integration but this seldom happened. He deduced from this that 'the deaf have a decided preference for their own class and their own ways, and a voluntary aversion to mixing with the hearing'. To force integration, 'be it at play, labour or lessons – would be carrying out, to the letter, the proverbial horse taken to the water'. The deaf gravitated to their own kind because 'there is a kind of sympathy which only they can give to their afflicted brothers'. Only a dramatic and, he hints, impossible change in the deeply held attitudes of the hearing, 'that the strong must ever assist the weak', could end this. His view was not unanimously accepted however.

Dodds clearly shared Large's belief in the 'rescue' and other social work functions of boarding schools. Like other day school teachers he was frustrated by the limited influence he had in these areas,[53] and was later to return to residential work as Head of the Exeter Institution where he remained until his retirement in the 1920s.

J.P. Barrett, Head of the Margate Institution, had earlier spoken on the need for improvements in institutional life, although he thought institutions superior to day alternatives. He wished that institutions could be 'attached in some way to a hearing school'. Unlike Dodds he still had faith that this would lead to the frequent mixing of the deaf with the hearing. He thought that when the deaf lived only with each other, each child got a distorted view of his own capabilities, was overprotected and isolated from mainstream society. He was 'a hot-house plant, metaphorically speaking, every precaution is taken to prevent the wind blowing upon him, and his every want is provided beforehand'. If he came from a good home, his lack of independent living skills did not matter, but 'the worse his home is so much the more necessary is it for him to visit it frequently in order to become accustomed to the struggle he may be required to undergo when he leaves school'.[54] He also attacked the lack of homeliness in the big institutions and wanted the cottage system adopted. These self-criticisms produced a lively response. There were objections to the hot-house plant metaphor and claims were made about the success of boarders and the relative failure of pupils on leaving day school.

At this, as at other conferences, Van Praagh was a rather lonely defender of the day school/fostering system, although some support came from St John Ackers who reminded the conference that some parents would insist that their children went to day classes and continued to live at home.[55] He said that the Royal Commissioners, while seeing day classes as second-best, recognized them as a necessary means of preserving liberty of choice for parents. He believed that until attendance for the deaf was made truly compulsory in Britain, it was not fair to condemn the results of the day classes. There was also some support for the German inter/externate system (see p. 20).

In May 1890, the Marquis of Lothian introduced the Education of Blind and Deaf Children (Scotland) Bill proposing state aid and compulsory education. While this was being discussed by parliament, a separate bill was introduced in July for England and Wales.[56]

In the same month at Norwood, London, over 100 leading educators of the blind gathered from most parts of England and Scotland with representatives from Denmark, Belgium and France. In the light of the

Royal Commission's Report the integration issue was fully discussed.

John MacDonald, speaking for the West of Scotland Mission, fervently supported integration. He spoke of 20 years of 'gratifying results' in Scotland and of the support of 'numerous school teachers' who preferred it to institutional care. He reported that 44 blind children attended board schools, of whom 33 lived at home while 11 lived in the blind asylum but attended day schools. Of the 44, 32 had made 'complete passes in their respective standards'. He stressed that these were not specially selected but taken 'from the rank and file of blind children'. He claimed that the idea that the young blind needed to be educated in special institutions was 'now well-nigh exploded'. It merely served to distort their minds, contract their ideas of ordinary society and increased their isolation and dependency.

He attacked the Royal Commission's suggestion that the physically weak blind needed residential care and education. In contrast to most speakers at the Conference for the Deaf, he claimed their need for tenderness and consideration would be better met in their own homes. If a family was not suitable, foster care in respectable families and day school education were preferable. He also attacked the LSB's policy of congregating blind children in a limited number of special centres, preferring individual functional integration. This had the added advantage of being cheaper. While it cost £9 10s 5d per annum for a child to attend a special class in London, it cost £3 17s 6d per annum for a blind pupil educated under the Glasgow School Board scheme.[57]

Predictably, his views and claims of success were attacked by representatives of the institutions for the blind. One speaker asked why many parents opted to send their children to the Edinburgh Institution when the Glasgow Institution parents tried sending their children out for education to the board schools? He further alleged that HMI allowed integrated blind pupils through the grades 'with a leniency not to be allowed to the sighted children'.[58] A former HMI also praised the superiority of the better special schools for the blind. He talked of the 'mistaken kindness' blind children sometimes experienced at home and, echoing the thoughts of Large, scorned accusations that residential placement cut off home ties. This he considered 'sentimental nonsense'. Just as the sons of the rich were sent to public schools for character building and the development of independence, so should the blind be sent to special institutions.

However, the integrators were in the majority, and the following resolution, proposed by the blind person, J. Keir of Aberdeen, was passed almost unanimously: 'In ordinary circumstances, blind children should be educated in the Board Schools, the Boards providing any special appliances found necessary.'[59]

In August, the Scottish Bill received Royal Assent but the English and Welsh Bill was delayed, first for financial reasons and later by parliamentary timetables and then the 1892 general election. Eventually, a fourth bill was introduced by Arthur Acland and received Royal Assent in September 1893.[60] This Act laid a duty on parents and school authorities to ensure that blind children aged between 5 and 16 and deaf children aged between 7 and 16 received an appropriate education, in schools provided by a school board, or group of school boards joining together for the purpose, or in a voluntary institution or school, inspected and certified by HMI. The feeble-minded deaf were excluded and the pauper handicapped continued to be controlled by the Board of Guardians. School boards could also board-out children to facilitate their education. Per capita grants were to be paid to both school authorities and to certified institutions. The Elementary Education (Blind and Deaf Children) Act came into effect on 1 January 1894.

No legislation was proposed for the feeble-minded and it was to take a further five years of growing pressure on their behalf by the LSB and the COS before this was to take place. However, in 1892 the first special class for these children was opened in Leicester.

Summary

The 'New Era' saw the creation of universal, free, compulsory education in Britain and a growing awareness of special children, but disagreement on how best to meet their needs. Voluntary boarding schools grew in number and size for 'street arabs', deaf and blind children. Many argued vigorously that the residential approach was the best way of protecting and educating children and at the same time preparing them for community integration as adults. However, there was also widespread dissatisfaction with the style of care and training provided in some of the latter, and also the large existing institutions for the low-grade feeble-minded and the poor law schools. Faults in the schools for the deaf and blind were admitted by workers within them who were well aware of arguments favouring alternative modes of educating the handicapped.

These alternatives included the education of individual blind children in the ordinary classes for the sighted in central Scotland, copied in various locations in England although to differing degrees of functional integration. In London, special classes in strategically placed elementary board schools were preferred, with the blind pupils spending half of their class time with the seeing. In the late 1880s, the Royal Commission appointed to advise on the best means of providing for the educational needs of the blind, deaf and feeble-minded, observed the functional integration of the blind working well and recommended the continuance of at least partial integration for this group with special trade training for those over 12. International experience suggested functional integration for the deaf was impractical, but special classes in ordinary schools were advocated in parts of America and were started in the London board schools and a few towns elsewhere in Britain. Sometimes, such day provision was linked to fostering or living in special hostels near day schools. However, after a decade of such arrangements the LSB came to prefer small homely boarding schools, at least for the children from poor homes. The Royal Commission listened to this advice and urged that the deaf of average ability receive instruction by the oral method in separate day classes or boarding schools.

Following the Royal Commission's advice, Acts of Parliament were passed for Scotland in 1890 and for England and Wales in 1893, making the education of the deaf and blind compulsory and providing limited financial assistance to the voluntary boarding schools, as well as allowing school authorities to provide their own schools or special classes.

No legislation was passed for the feeble-minded, for whom the Egerton Commission had recommended separate special classes or 'auxiliary schools', while low-grade cases were to be placed in residential institutions. Provision for the physically defective did not exist other than two industrial schools in London, although, after 1881, the LSB had been allowed to admit them to board school classes. A colony for epileptics had been founded in Lancashire in 1890.

It was therefore a period of patchy development of some special educational provision in a few board school areas, with London taking a lead. Integration was a topical issue and a consciously pursued aim. However, many school boards did not help the deaf and blind at all, or sometimes used the voluntary residential institutions for severe cases and for the children from unsatisfactory home backgrounds.

Notes

1. A. Barnhill, *A New Era in the Education of Blind Children*, Glass, Glasgow, 1875, p. v.
2. W. Stainer, 'The powers of the School Board and the Poor Law Guardians in relation to the care and education of the deaf and dumb', *Quarterly Review of Deaf-Mute Education*, vol. I, no. XII, 1888, p.375.
3. *Report of the Royal Commission on the Blind, Deaf and Dumb and Co* (Egerton Report), HMSO, London, 1889.

4. Quoted in Anon., *A Statement with Reference to the Number, Education and Condition of the Deaf and Dumb and Blind of Ireland*, Alley, Dublin, 1877, p.14.
5. H. Bosanquet, *Social Work in London 1869 to 1912: A History of the Charity Organization Society*, Murray, London, 1914, ch. 9.
6. D. Buxton, *Notes on Progress in the Education of the Deaf*, Allen, London, 1882.
7. D. Pritchard, *Education and the Handicapped*, Routledge and Kegan Paul, London, 1963, p.75; O.H. Burritt, 'Education of the blind with the seeing', *Outlook for the Blind*, vol. 4, Spring 1910.
8. Op. cit., note 1, pp.21–6.
9. Ibid., p.56.
10. COS, *Training of the Blind*, Longmans, London, 1876, pp.12–13.
11. Ibid, p.8.
12. Pritchard, op. cit., note 7, pp.78–80.
13. *American Annals of the Deaf*, vol. XXI, p.56.
14. Op. cit., note 3, p.65.
15. R. Elliott, 'The British Conference on the Education of the Deaf and Dumb', *American Annals of the Deaf*, vol. 22, 1877, p.206.
16. Ibid., p.49.
17. *Proceedings of the Conference of the Governing Bodies of Institutions for the Education of the Deaf and Dumb*, London, 1881, p.25.
18. *Proceedings of the Conference of Headmasters of Institutions for the Education of the Deaf and Dumb*, Doncaster, 1882, p.55.
19. Ibid., p.49.
20. Ibid., p.54.
21. Op. cit., note 2, p.377.
22. A.G. Bell, 'Deaf-mute instruction in relation to the work of the public schools', *Report of the Annual Meeting of the National Education Association*, Madison, Wisconsin, July 1884, National Education Association, Washington, 1885, pp.14–18.
23. Ibid., p.50.
24. E.A. Fay, 'Address by A.G. Bell and Dr. P.G. Gillett to the Chicago Bd of Educ., 20th July 1884', *American Annals of the Deaf*, vol. 29, 1884, p.312.
25. J.C. Gordon, 'Deaf-mutes and the public schools from 1815 to the present day', *American Annals of the Deaf*, vol. XXX, 2 April 1885.
26. E. Grosselin, *De La Possibilité de L'Enseignement du Sourd-Muet Dans L'Ecole Primaire*, Picard, Paris, 1882.
27. Op. cit., note 25, pp.142–3.
28. F.W. Reuschert, 'Statistics of the instruction of the deaf in Germany (Dec. 1886)', *Quarterly Review of Deaf-Mute Education*, vol. VI, April 1887, pp.190–91.
29. J. Heywood, *Children in Care*, 3rd edn, Routledge and Kegan Paul, London, 1978, pp.94–6.
30. M. Carpenter, *Reformatory Schools for the Children of the Perishing and Dangerous Classes, and for Juvenile Offenders*, London, 1851.
31. *13th Report of the Inspector of Reformatory and Industrial Schools of Great Britain*, HMSO, London, 1870, p.21.
32. *33rd Report of the Inspector of Reformatory and Industrial Schools of Great Britain*, HMSO, London, 1890.

33. Op. cit., note 31, p.22.
34. Ibid., p.17.
35. Op. cit., note 32, pp.36–9.
36. COS, *Education and Care of Idiots, Imbeciles and Harmless Lunatics*, Longmans, London, 1877, p.15.
37. C. Miller, *Broken Gleams*, 2nd edn, Isbister, London, 1874, p.16.
38. Ibid., p.9
39. *Report of the Departmental Committee on Defective and Epileptic Children* (Sharpe Report), HMSO, London, 1898, vol. 2, p.39.
40. Op. cit., note 3, p.370.
41. Ibid., Appendix 1, p.3.
42. Ibid., Appendix 1, pp.6–8.
43. Ibid., Appendix 2, p.15.
44. Ibid., p.xvii
45. Ibid., Appendix 19, p.327.
46. Ibid., Appendix 1, pp.46–8.
47. Ibid., vol. 2, Appendix 26.
48. Op. cit., note 2, p.377.
49. Op. cit., note 3, p.xxxiii.
50. Ibid., p.cvi.
51. A. Large, 'Institutions and day schools', *Proceedings of the Conference of Headmasters of Institutions for the Deaf'*, Allen, London, 1890, pp.8–10.
52. P. Dodds, 'Theory versus practice', pp.113–16, ibid.
53. J.P. Barrett, 'Improvements in institutional life', p.19, ibid.
54. Ibid., pp.14–16.
55. Ibid., p.26.
56. Op. cit., note 7, p.108.
57. *Report of the Conference of the Blind and Their Friends*, held at the Royal Normal College, Norwood, July 1890, London, 1891, pp.14–19.
58. Ibid., p.24.
59. Ibid., p.26.
60. Op. cit., note 7, p.110.

CHAPTER 3

To the End of the Great War: 1893–1918

Political and Educational Summary: 1893–1918

Major Events and Ordinary Education

1894   *Lord Rosebery* (Liberal) made PM by Queen when Gladstone resigns after failure to push Irish Home Rule through Lords

1895   *Salisbury's 3rd (Conservative) Ministry*

1895   Bryce Commission notes poor finances of grammar schools; wants more scholarships to them; urges more co-education (e.g. after Scots and new central government education board

1890s   Growth of higher grade board schools threatening the grammar schools

Special Education

1894   New Education Act for blind and deaf in force

1894   Miss Sewell's London special class for physically defective starts

1895   Ed. Dept Regulations allow boarding-out for pupils at day special schools

1890s   London phases out part-time special education, amalgamates smaller units, uses boarding more; expansion of boarding schools throughout UK

1896   Burnley parents win day school for deaf

1896   Dept Comm. Rep. on Ref. and Industrial Schools

1897   27 schools now cater for London feeble-minded

		1898	Rep. of Dept Comm. on Def. and Epil. wants separate special schools for better classification
1899	Second Boer War	1899	Elementary Education (Defective and Epileptic Children) Act empowers school authorities to make provision for these children
1899	Board of Education created and takes over from Privy Council's Education Dept		
1899	Cockerton Judgement halts growth of post-elementary education in board schools	1899	Passmore Edwards Settlement School for physically defective opens in London
1900	*Salisbury* re-elected in 'Khaki' election following military successes against Boers	1900	Special class for physically defective in Liverpool
		1901	W. Kirby Residential School for convalescent children opens
		1901	LSB decides younger blind to be educated full time in special schools while maintaining part-integration for older children
		1901	Nottingham starts classes for physically defective
1902	Salisbury's nephew *A. Balfour* (Conservative) becomes PM	1902	Dendy's Sandlebridge School, Cheshire, for permanent care of feeble-minded, recognized by Board of Education
1902	Education Act; 318 LEAs to replace 2500 school boards (N.B. elected Scots school boards continue); central and local govt funding for grammar schools; LEAs to maintain voluntary schools	1902	Education Act permits higher education for deaf and blind
		1903	Chailey Residential School for physically defective starts
		1903	LCC starts White Oak Hospital and School for Ophthalmia
1904–5	About 500 grant-aided English secondary schools	1905	Int. Conf. at Edinburgh of teachers of the blind argue against day school classes and for boarding
1905	*Campbell-Bannerman* (Liberal) becomes PM on Balfour's resignation		
1906	53 Labour MPs elected with help of Lib–Lab pact	1906	Education of Defective Children (Scotland) Act (permissive)
1906	Education (Provision of Meals) Act	1907	LCC opens first UK open air school (Bostall Wood)
1907	Grant-aided secondary schools must provide 25% minimum free places	1907	Int. Conf. for teachers of deaf at Edinburgh wants residential segregation of feeble-minded deaf but classes in ordinary day schools for part-hearing

1908	*Asquith* (Liberal) becomes PM; Tory-dominated House of Lords continue to reject Liberal bills passed in Commons	1908	First sight-saving class (in Camberwell)
		1908	College of Teachers of the Blind founded
1909	Crisis when Lords reject Lloyd George's People's Budget which increased income tax, death duties, etc., to fund pensions and increased defence spending	1908	Royal Commission on Feeble-Minded attacks special classes and favours large colonies
1910	Asquith wins two general elections	1910	320 certified special schools in England and Wales
1911	Start of central (post-elementary technical) schools		
1911	The new King's (George V's) threat to create 400 new peers forces Lords to accept Parliament Act which limited their power		
1911	Irish Home Rule thwarted by Protestant revolt in Ulster. Syndicalism and suffragettes		
1913	Survey shows 72% of urban Directors of Education oppose multipurpose local authorities; would prefer locally elected school boards	1913	C. Burt appointed as first LEA psychologist
		1913	Mental Deficiency Act sets up Board of Control
1913–14	Over 1000 grant-aided secondary schools; over 6 million in public elementary schools	1914	Elementary Education (Defective and Epileptic Children) Act says LEAs must provide for educable defectives
1914	Start of Great War prevents civil war in Ireland	1914	Integration debate at Westminster Int. Conf. for workers with blind
1916	*Lloyd George* (Liberal) becomes PM		
1917	Introduction of national school certificate	1917	Report of Dept Comm. on Welfare of Blind
1918	Fisher's Education Act. Great War ends	1918	Act says LEAs must provide for physically defective and epileptics

As the octogenarian Gladstone entered the final months of his fourth term as Premier, the 1893 Act came into effect. At the start of this period Lloyd George had yet to make a national impression, yet by 1918 was in his third year as Prime Minister, and within four years of the demise of the final Liberal-dominated government. This period thus contained the Indian summer of Liberalism, with its increasing collectivist and socialist tendencies. It also saw the emergence of the Labour party as a significant parliamentary force. It was an era of outward assurance, witnessed by the continued expansion of Empire but inner doubts caused by the Boer War, uncertainty over whether France, Russia or Germany was our real enemy, a worsening arms race, stiff economic and agricultural competition from the New World and domestic troubles with militant trades unions, aggressive employers, suffragettes and near civil war in Ireland. In addition, the House of Lords was unwilling to bow to the wishes of a House of Commons until George V threatened to create 400 new peers. Finally, there was the traumatic Great War.

In addition to these problems, governments now had to appeal to a mass electorate dominated by the working-class vote. This factor, along with the humanitarianism of many middle-class and some upper-class voters, helped to focus attention on education and other social issues. In response to this pressure, the 1902 Education Act was passed. This drew together the voluntary and the board schools into a national system run by new Local Education Authorities (LEAs). It also eased the finances of the grammar schools on condition they responded to increasing demands for wider secondary education by admitting some bright working-class children.

By 1914, in the growing field of special education, the differing needs of the mentally defective, the deaf and the blind, the partially deaf, the partially blind, the myopic and the phthisical (the tubercular) had been identified and special schools and classes began to cater for these groups. Efficient classification was increasingly pursued and with it the necessary corollary, a greater degree of segregation from the ordinary schools. This at least was the approach adopted by key figures at the new Board of Education, created in 1899, and those in charge of the London County Council (LCC). But opinion was far from uniform and the torch of integration continued to be carried in different parts of the country and in America.

The formation of the Eugenics Society in 1907 reflected much contemporary interest in the possibilities of improving the human race by selective breeding. Given the widely held belief in the overweening power of inherited genes in determining the characters and abilities of children, in an ideal world, only the bright, the beautiful and the balanced would breed. Extreme believers in the eugenic approach saw, as a necessary corollary, the need to prevent the insane, the handicapped and particularly the feeble-minded from having children. This last group was frequently blamed for perpetuating and increasing the crime, vice and general fecklessness which was believed to be weakening the nation. The size of their families, much larger than those of people of average or superior intelligence, was also a growing concern. The degeneracy of the race would follow unless action was taken. Asexualization (sterilization) was one option which was to be practised to a limited extent in America. Less extreme and more widely favoured was the policy of placing some of the low-grade feeble-minded in large rural colonies where their lives could be controlled until they died and where liaisons of a sexual nature could be prevented. However, although this *permanent care* was much discussed in this period, most notably in the Royal Commission's Report in 1908, it was not implemented to any great extent.

Most of those who favoured the increasingly segregationist approach did so reluctantly. For the vast majority of the handicapped, including the backward child, the motivation was efficiency of education, hopefully leading to societal integration for the school-leaver. It was true that ordinary school teachers found it difficult to cope with 'backward' children and some wanted them out of the ordinary classes, but the sources do not suggest that there was a problem in controlling them. It was rather that teachers felt guilty about having to ignore their needs. As payment by results largely ended in 1890,[1] two years ahead of the first special class for the feeble-minded, their presence in the ordinary classes did not affect teachers' incomes. They might sometimes be a nuisance and slow down the progress of the brighter children but rarely were they a threat. That so many LEAs did not provide for the feeble-minded, until the 1914 Education Act forced them to, supports this view.

For the less handicapped – the partially deaf or blind and most physically defective, the epileptic and the backward – a degree of integration continued to be advocated and often practised.

Providing for the Feeble-minded

The Egerton Report's call for the separation of the feeble-minded into special classes and schools was reinforced by the American, L.R. Klemm's book which highlighted the success of the German *hilfschule* and special classes. His attention focused on the day special school at Elberfeld to which affluent parents had moved house so as to be able to send their children to the school there.[2] Meanwhile, Dr Francis Warner, a London paediatrician, whose sponsors included the Charity Organization Society, was examining 50 000 children to determine the extent and nature of feeble-mindedness. General Moberley, an influential member of the London School Board was well aware of this work and had been impressed by the progress of a feeble-minded girl he helped to place in a private school. He therefore campaigned for a limited number of special schools for the feeble-minded. In 1891, the Education Department, also aware of more general complaints about the feeble-minded clogging up the Standards, agreed to three such schools.[3]

Before the LSB opened their first new unit, Leicester School Board had selected 12 quite severely feeble-minded for a special class in the Milton Street Board School. This started work in the spring of 1892. A few months later, pending the building of a segregated school on the playground of London's largest elementary board school, three special classes opened in the main part of the Hugh Myddleton School, Finsbury. In 1893 two special classes started in Nottingham[4] and in 1894 some in Bradford.

In 1893 the COS incorporated Warner's findings in their report on the feeble-minded.[5] This praised Elberfeld and called for the majority of England's feeble-minded to be educated in auxiliary schools. For better classification, they preferred a larger central school to scattered special classes appended to ordinary board schools. Free transport should be provided to these and the Education Department should provide grant-aid as they did for the education of the blind and deaf. The curriculum must be radically different from the ordinary schools and there was need for a government-funded Pestalozzi/Froebel training college to supply the special teachers needed. Thus segregation was advocated but there was a concern for integration in so far as they were aiming for adult integration rather than placing the feeble-minded indefinitely in large institutions such as Darenth. They pointed out that the central special school 'need not be far from the child's home' and the 'home-tie' would be maintained 'which there is at present very great temptation to neglect'.

They realized that some children would need residential provision but this should be in 'homes with schools' which were of the 'least institution-like and the most home-like type'. Once again they had Darenth and the enormous poor law boarding schools in their sights. They warmly approved of the pioneer small community-based homes which were developing for teenage feeble-minded girls, e.g. Aubert Park in Highbury. They described life at such a home set in Painswick, Gloucestershire. Staff controlled the girls' lives, and hopefully prevented liaisons of a sexual nature – an important consideration given the supposed fecundity of the feeble-minded. However, these teenage girls were far from being 'mewed up'. They entered into the village and home life as much as possible: 'They have tea with the servants at a neighbouring house; they take walks; they attend the church, and take part in any school meeting or little festivity that there may be. They seem very happy.' They also went out on work-experience at a safety-pin factory and received education in the '3Rs' back at the home where cats and dogs were kept and the owner Miss Wemyss made every effort to preserve 'a cottage air'. Others were warmly recommended to follow this example.[6] By 1897 there were 10 similar homes in Knotty Ash, Morpeth and elsewhere. The longer-term aim, although not one readily achieved, was adult integration. In London, a decade later, feeble-minded girls continued to live in special hostels from where they went to ordinary day schools. On occasion, fostering was also preferred to placement in a large institution.[7]

In the mid-1890s the COS and LSB lobbied central government to extend the 1883 Act to other handicaps. Their case was strengthened by the success of the new classes. In 1895, the Nottingham Board heard that:

> The results so far have been most gratifying, several of the scholars having sufficiently developed under the special instruction to permit of their being transferred to the ordinary Board schools. Both parents and scholars, moreover, appear greatly to appreciate the classes.[8]

By 1897 there were 27 special schools for 1070 pupils in London.[9] In the previous year the COS had sponsored the formation of the National Association for Promoting the Welfare of the Feeble-Minded (NAPWFM).

Responding to this pressure the Committee on Defective and Epileptic Children was appointed with the Reverend T.W. Sharpe, Senior Chief Inspector of the Education Department, as Chairman in December 1896. The Committee was dominated by medical men, including Shuttleworth. This was to be expected as the pioneer psychological work of Galton and Sully was not to lead to the creation of educational psychology as a profession until after the Great War and the few teachers of handicapped children were not specially trained. Doctors were accepted as the *experts* in child development at a time when *phrenology* – the science of diagnosing mental ability by studying the physical characteristics of the cranium – still held sway.

However, the Sharpe Committee did include Mrs Burgwin, the LSB's Superintendent of Special Classes and Miss Townsend, secretary of the NAPWFM. Its task was to enquire into existing systems for providing for the feeble-minded and other defectives who were not idiots or imbeciles and advise on necessary changes. It was also asked how best to provide for epileptic children. The detailed Report was published in 1898.

The Committee recommended that school boards be required to provide special classes for the educable feeble-minded, certainly in towns with populations of over 20 000. For better classification, they favoured larger separate special schools rather than scattered special classes in the ordinary schools. If the special classes or schools had to be on the same sites as the ordinary schools they advocated separate playgrounds, entrances, cloakrooms and corridors. Children should not mix with ordinary children for any lessons.[10] In the interests of society as well as their own, idiots and imbeciles should be placed in permanent care.[11]

Stated thus the message would seem to be starkly segregationist, but closer examination of the Report and particularly the appendices reveals a more complex picture and a wealth of evidence that many at the end of the nineteenth century were loath to cut off the handicapped from society. Where childhood segregation was necessary it was to be limited and used as a stepping stone to reintegration.

The Committee accepted that the feeble-minded left in the ordinary Standards with 60 to a class were neglected and made little progress. In London, before 1892, the feeble-minded over 11 years old had been mixed with 5-year-olds in Standard 1. Dr James Kerr of the Bradford School Board spoke of teachers being so concerned with getting their average children through the Standards and so conscious of HMI's expectations that they would send the feeble-minded to play in a corner with a slate.[12] The great majority of the 1300 children the Committee had observed in the existing special classes had gained little or nothing other than habits of discipline from their previous placement in the ordinary classes, whereas in the small special classes they were making progress.[13] Reports were heard of children's new found happiness and motivation. They were shielded from teasing, particularly where playtimes were staggered.

Moreover, parents in Bristol, Brighton and Bradford were said to be appreciative, although sometimes after an initial reluctance. Further, where the *hilfschule* was well established in Germany, parents were eager for their feeble-minded to gain entrance to them. In Leicester, five parents had moved house to be near the special class.[14]

However, other parents in both Leicester and Bradford had resisted and still objected, perceiving a stigma attached to their child's placement in a special class, or in the contemporary phrase, 'silly school'.[15] Likewise, a witness said that parents 'will admit anything except that their children are defective in intellect'.[16] References are made to parents putting their children into voluntary schools to avoid their being placed by the local board into special classes.[17] This practice continued until the absorption of voluntary schools into the state system following the 1902 Education Act.

In advocating the LSB's policy of the larger segregated special school, the Committee were making a rational but somewhat reluctant recommendation and most members seemed sympathetic to parental doubts. In the opening pages of the Report they wrote:

> Public feeling would revolt, and rightly, against the permanent care of these educable children in institutions, and therefore it is better that they should not be sent to institutions during their childhood, but should be familiar with the world in which they will have to live. [They should] ... associate with ordinary children as much as is consistent with their receiving the special and individual care and training they require.[18]

If children from poor homes did require residential care boarding-out was preferred. The Education Department had sanctioned the fostering of the blind and deaf for some years and the 1895 regulations had stipulated that only two deaf or blind children could live in any one home. The Committee was anxious to maintain a homely, family-style life for the separated child. In like-vein it commended boarding-out for the feeble-minded to keep them in touch with ordinary children rather than 'secluding the feeble-minded child, during its school life, within four walls of an institution'.[19]

The London teacher, Miss Earley, dissented however. She wanted boarding homes near the special school to protect her pupils who would otherwise 'herd with vagabonds and thieves in lodging-houses having all sorts of vile principles instilled into them'. She claimed that others had parents 'less fitted than pigs to train them'.[20] At age 15 she wanted these young people drafted into country homes to prevent their becoming enemies of society. But this was very much a minority view.

A degree of segregation might be necessary but the aim, which was sometimes achieved, was reintegration. Out of 493 former pupils from the London special classes, 193 had gone back to ordinary schools. In a similar survey of special classes outside London, 65 out of 160 leavers had been reintegrated.[21]

Clear opposition to segregation can be found in the appendices and one wonders how great a slice of public opinion these fragments of evidence represent. W.E. Currey, HMI for West Lambeth, answered when asked about teachers' attitudes to special classes:

> Opinion is divided upon the subject, but there appears to be amongst the teachers with whom I have spoken rather a general agreement that the children, where they are tractable, are as well, if not better, in the ordinary schools under ordinary environments than they would be if drafted into special classes.

It was, however, too early to pass final judgement on the subject. Was it not impossible to provide the special curriculum they needed, he was asked? 'By a little elasticity' this could be done in ordinary classes in ordinary schools if the feeble-minded were given 'hand' work while the other children were doing 'head' work. Currey then used an argument which has often been repeated in recent years. Ordinary children were frequently kind and considerate to the feeble-minded and 'a rather valuable influence upon them'. But Mrs Burgwin was not happy with his replies and reminded him that, following parental pressure, he had referred children to her special classes. Accounts of kindness by ordinary pupils to the handicapped were also given elsewhere in the Report.[22]

Thomas Aldis, the experienced HMI for nearby Tower Hamlets, was similarly dubious. He thought segregating the feeble-minded had been 'disastrous'. It was better to let them stay with their age-group where the brighter children helped the weak. In special classes with 30 on the roll, the higher-grade would be dragged down by the lower-grade children. He reported that many teachers did not think backward pupils were better placed in special classes. However, if in the latter teacher–pupil ratios were reduced to 1:6, he would alter his view.[23]

Another angle was given by an HMI for a country district. He reported that feeble-minded children mixed happily with ordinary children in village schools and were best left there working unpressured at a separate table in the corner of the classroom and joining the main class for singing and drill. They learned social skills and out of schooltime helped their fathers on the land. They were thus best prepared for an adult life. The institutional alternative, even a cottage-style establishment, was likely to cut them off from their community. This is an example showing that the feeble-minded were often not viewed as troublesome pupils of whom the teachers wanted rid. If they were to be placed in special classes it was because teachers primarily felt unable to meet their needs in the ordinary classes. Social control was often not a relevant issue and certainly did not play a major part at this time.[24]

In short, the Sharpe Committee heard many arguments for and against special schools which are still paraded in the last quarter of the twentieth century. In those days, as now, critics and defenders of segregated special education tended to see issues in black and white terms, too often generalizing from their own limited experience or viewpoints.

As the government was fearful of financial implications, the resulting 1899 Elementary Education (Defective and Epileptic Children) Act empowered, rather than required, school authorities to provide education for the new official class of mentally (and physically) defective children in certified special classes in public elementary schools or separate certified special schools. They could also board-out children near such schools or classes. A duty was placed upon parents to ensure that their defective child received suitable education when aged 7 if such provision was within reasonable reach. Defective children were to stay at school until age 16. In a further interesting anti-institutional move they also decreed that any resulting boarding school must be built on cottage-style lines with no more than 15 children in any one building and only four such buildings on one site.[25] However, because of the expense, the number was increased to 30 per building in 1904.[26] Similar legislation was passed for Scotland in 1906.

Within 10 years, 133 out of the 318 English and Welsh local authorities had availed themselves of its powers; a few, such as London, in determined fashion.[27] In 1899, there were already 50 London special schools or classes.[28] In that year Manchester also opened a class, followed by Liverpool a year later.

In 1901, Dr Alfred Eicholz, who had been made an HMI in 1898, attended the Augsburg Congress on the feeble-minded. This was attended by 362 German inspectors, teachers, doctors and foreign guests. Their debates clearly reflected the increasingly popular eugenic fears displayed to the Sharpe Committee by Miss Earley. Assuming intelligence was closely governed by heredity and given the large families of the feeble-minded, it was argued that the degeneration of the advanced European races would ensue. The mentally defective were also blamed for most of society's social ills. The Congress thought that the existing 98 German day schools and 13 special classes in ordinary schools for the feeble-minded were a wasted effort. It left the children exposed outside school hours to unwholesome influences which undid the good work of the schools. At leaving age, Eicholz reported, they were thought to become 'wanderers in semi-darkness, helpless, aimless and unrestrained, to swell the ranks of crime and vice'.[29] Early placement for life in colonies was preferred. This was already happening in parts of America where 500- to 2000-bed farm and industrial colonies were now operating.

Reflecting this opinion, the value of the new special classes and schools which started in the wake of the 1899 Act came to be doubted in some quarters, while a greater section of opinion which more clearly distinguished between the low-grade ineducable and the far greater number of trainable feeble-minded, wanted 'permanent care' colonies to supplement the work of the special schools. In 1897, Mary Dendy had founded the Lancashire and Cheshire Society for the Permanent Care of the Feeble-minded. In 1902, the practical expression of her ideas, Sandlebridge Boarding School and Home at Alderley Edge, was recognized by the Board of Education. Despite the integrationist tendencies of many of its members, the COS campaigned in 1901 and 1902 for permanent care. Also active was Ellen Pinsent who was disappointed at the way leavers from Birmingham's special classes fared in their 'after life'. In April 1903 a petition signed by 140 influential people was presented to the Home Secretary calling for a Royal Commission to look into the problems of the feeble-minded.[30] The government responded to this pressure. With respect still shown for the phrenology practised by doctors such as Francis Warner, the resulting Commission, chaired by Lord Radnor, was dominated by medical men.

In 1905, the Commissioners heard that provision of special schools and classes under the 1899 Act was centred on the larger towns. It was most complete in London. None of the new county LEAs and only Darlington of the borough LEAs had yet made any provision other than board-out a few children in bigger towns near day schools run by other authorities. In Scotland, only in Glasgow and Govan did classes exist, although Edinburgh was now planning to follow suit. Provision was almost entirely in day schools. Rare exceptions were a Roman Catholic residential institution in Hillingdon and Mary Dendy's Sandlebridge.[31]

Mary Dendy's views were absorbed by many Commissioners with near reverence. She claimed to have examined 40 000 Manchester schoolchildren and, as a result of her pleading that the feeble-minded among them were hopelessly out of place in the ordinary Standards, special classes had been formed in 1899. By that date, however, she had begun work on Sandlebridge, a permanent home for boys and girls, with sexes strictly segregated and the possibility of their remaining there as adults. She feared that despite their day class segregation, all the 220 children in the Manchester special classes would be 'a definite risk to society. Before they are twenty they will probably have children, and before they are thirty they will probably have a very big family.' Better, she believed, to place them in permanent care. It would lessen their suffering and stop their breeding, saving society expense in the long run.[32]

The Commissioners heard Sir James Crichton-Browne describe the feeble-minded as 'our social rubbish' who 'should be swept up and garnered and utilized as far as possible' and stopped from having children.[33] Compulsory sterilization, as was practised in America, seemed to be discreetly favoured. The near doubling in the number of insane between 1871 and 1901 was blamed on the feeble-minded. The Commissioners were influenced by Dr A.F. Tredgold's claim that whereas the average family size was four, the 'degenerate's' was 7.3. They also heard the results of his study of 150 families which apparently supported the notion that heredity was a major cause of feeble-mindedness. The mild feeble-minded, he reported, swelled the ranks of the insane, the pauper and the criminal. 'We pay much attention', he went on, 'to the breeding of our horses, our cattle, our dogs and poultry, even our flowers and vegetables; surely it is not too much to ask that a little care should be bestowed upon the breeding and rearing of our race.'[34] Much evidence was heard pointing to the degeneracy of the British race and linking feeble-mindedness to criminality, drunkenness, wantonness, bastardy, child abuse and even train-wrecking, the result of all of which was expense for the taxpayer.

Day special schools and classes, it was claimed, failed to prevent these problems and were often a waste of time and money for the true feeble-minded and were likely to give them a taste for freedom and independence which would ill-prepare them for adult life in colonies.[35] However, such classes *were* acceptable for the many children who were dull or backward for environmental reasons.[36] The Commissioners' views were influenced by reports that only a minority of special school or class leavers earned a living and many were thought not fit to enter open society. Better was the Dendy approach at Sandlebridge:

> Our boys are now arriving at the age of sixteen, and they have never slept a night off the place since they have been admitted. Neither boys nor girls show the least restlessness. They are orderly and good. It is rather sad, in a way; you can manage them with a word.

The same boys were to remain at Sandlebridge in the adult colony which was shortly to be built on the site.[37] Other residential homes were reported to be much in demand.

In England, the more community-based approach of fostering, after a decade of difficulty, was now in disrepute. Various witnesses, including Eicholz and Mrs Burgwin, talked of the problems of finding suitable host families and then of successfully boarding-out the feeble-minded.[38] However, since 1885 in Glasgow, harmless lunatics, nearly a fifth of the total, had been boarded-out to avoid the need to extend institutions. The dissenting witness, Dr Macpherson, praised the 'more home-like life and consequently the happiness of the patients'.[39] In France and Belgium similar schemes had been working for some years. However, the Commissioners were not impressed.

Nor were they impressed by many of the arguments put forward by Eicholz, now HMI for special schools.[40] He was not alone in attacking the favoured notions of the Commissioners. While 35 expert witnesses believed heredity to be the all important determinant of mental defect, Eicholz and nine other dissenters emphasized the importance of environmental factors. He claimed Tredgold's and other 'family histories' were scientifically unsound and ran counter to his own experience with the families of the mental defectives in London. 'Drink, phthisis and depravity of living on the part of the parents' seemed a more likely cause. There was a very high death rate among feeble-minded babies. Malnutrition seemed a major cause. He also stressed that the children of the less intelligent tended to be nearer the norm in ability. Further, if all the known feeble-minded were isolated in residential institutions, other families would still produce feeble-minded children. Slum clearance, good nutrition and school health services would be better cures. In better areas the success rate of leavers from special schools was considerably higher.

From another angle, his awareness of the difficulty of running the residential establishments favoured by the Commissioners has a timeless ring:

> Neither teachers nor matrons are easily found willing to sacrifice their own domestic ties for this most trying work. The teachers find the strain of added school duties more difficult than ordinary school life under the most exigent circumstances, and are not inclined to give up congenial work for duty which is incessant and exhausting.[41]

This insight did not stop his support for some boarding schools or for permanent care for some lowest-grade cases, but his support fell far short of the enthusiasm shown by the Commissioners.

He was not alone in his doubts. Mrs Burgwin also saw the need for permanent care for some imbeciles but was not prepared to accept the criticism of the London day special schools she had spent so much of her life developing.[42] Similarly, Maud Lawrence, the Chief Woman HMI, talked of parents' praise for London's special schools and how many moved house to be near one.[43] Elsewhere in the country other arguments were adduced suggesting the success of day special schools and classes. Of the pupils at the Willow Street Special School in Leicester, 34 per cent were transferred back to normal schools.[44] The medical officer of Liverpool produced reports from the Heads of four special schools recording the educational and social advances of their pupils.[45]

The Scot, T.W.L. Spence, advocated leaving the feeble-minded in their own families or under responsible guardians. Aware of their human rights, he argued that if they were not a source of annoyance to the public 'there would not be the slightest excuse for interference on the part of the state'. A harmless imbecile should not be shut up 'on the theory that he might possibly do something wrong'.[46] One suspects that this attitude, so much more in keeping with the tone of evidence given a few years earlier to the Departmental Committee, was much nearer the feelings of the nation than the opinions of the Commissioners. That five years were allowed to lapse and that the 1913 Mental Deficiency Act and 1914 Education Act should largely reject the recommendations of the Royal Commission supports this view. The new legislation also reflected the beliefs and growing power of George Newman, appointed as the first Chief Medical Officer (CMO) of the Board in 1907, with Eicholz as his assistant. They may have had a vested interest in limiting the powers of a new government department as civil service rivalry did seem to exist.[47] However, Newman had a genuine dislike of permanent care for children: 'It seems a monstrous proposition to apply such treatment to young children whose powers are growing and concerning whose future we know little or nothing.'[48] While the ineducable should be kept out of the special schools and classes to give teachers a better chance of helping higher-grade children, permanent care was a different matter. Further, from a practical angle, there was no point in segregating children if there were so few adult colonies.

The 1913 Act did set up the suggested Board of Control, but it did not transfer the running of special schools from LEAs to it as the Radnor Commission had hoped. Furthermore, the 1914 Education Act increased rather than diminished the importance and number of special schools by making *all* LEAs provide them for mentally defective children. This reflected the Board's continuing faith in them. It is true that some colonies in the guise of subnormality hospitals were developed and boarding schools did grow in popularity. However, in 1911, there were only seven certified residential special schools for taking the more severe cases. Pontville in Ormskirk, founded in 1910, helped but more were needed. These schools were also to give children holidays and sought to prepare leavers for life in open society – a very different approach to the proposals of the Royal Commission.

The first of the Chief Medical Officer's detailed annual reports was written in 1909.[49] In this, criticism by the Royal Commission of day special schools was only reflected in a limited way when the CMO pressed for more precise classification for the feeble-minded and by his calls for more After Care Committees to help special school leavers find and keep work. He wondered how the schools' medical officer for Warrington could examine 968 children and yet find no feeble-minded, whereas almost 20 per cent of 135 Northampton children were said to be mentally defective? There were obviously widely contrasting definitions of the condition and the nature of the clientele of special schools differed greatly, no doubt helping to explain the differing rates of reintegration and employment of leavers seen in the Royal Commission's Report. CMO Newman commended London's practice, pushed vigorously by MO James Kerr, of excluding low-grade mental defectives. As a result, in 1908, 212 out of 279 leavers found employment. Liverpool was similarly weeding out the least able. Improved classification enabled a more suitable curriculum for those remaining and better preparation for employment. He wanted all LEAs to recognize three classes – the dull and backward who should, where possible, be kept in ordinary schools, the educable feeble-minded and the non-educable. In 1911 he recorded that he had repeatedly to admonish LEAs for placing the merely backward among the more severely feeble-minded. He commended the seven newly formed classes attached to ordinary schools at Oxford, Leicester, Brighton, Exeter and Croydon for backward children.[50] Table 1 shows the statistical situation at this time.[51] In short, there was steady if unspectacular growth in provision for the mentally defective. In 1909 nearly two-thirds of the 318 LEAs had not used their powers, but this number decreased despite the Royal Commission's recommendations and the propagation of its views through books published in its wake.[52]

Table 1   Special schools provided under the 1893 and 1899 Acts

Year	Total no. of schools	Total no. of pupils	Schools for [a]						
			Blind	Deaf	MDs	PDs	Epil.	TB	Open air
1897	95	4739	40	55	—	—	—	—	—
1909	304	17 600	39	48	159	53	5	—	?
1914	367	28 511	42	51	180	64	6	19	13

[a] MDs, mentally defectives; PDs, physically defectives; Epil., epileptic; TB, tuberculosis.

At the 1912 London County Council Conference for teachers, the increasing awareness of the differing needs of the varying levels of feeble-mindedness was shown. A schools' medical officer described Brighton's special system. The dull and backward had been separated from the intermediate grade who were split from the severely mentally defective. The intermediate grade had been placed in 'practical' classes. To avoid stigma, the word special had not been used. A deliberate policy of partial integration was followed: 'The class joins in with others at prayers, opening and closing of school sessions, scripture, and play. They interchange rooms with other classes for reading, writing and drawing etc.' Forbes said that this method freed the normal teacher to concentrate on the children of average intelligence while the backward child in the practical class finds 'he is no longer an outcast'. He becomes keen, his attendance improves, he does not want to leave school at 14, and because of the practical curriculum he is better prepared for employment.[53]

These partially integrated special classes resembled similar classes in the United States which had been described by the Royal Commissioners. In 1905 Ellen Pinsent found the parents of the feeble-minded in Boston objected strongly to plans for their children's placement in special schools. The school board established special classes instead, from which the more able children went into the regular classes in the afternoons. In Chicago she heard of a similar situation. The special classes were all situated in the ordinary schools and the special children mixed with the non-handicapped children at play-times.[54] New York had started 'ungraded' classes in 1900 but, in this city, H.H. Goddard was to campaign for separate special schools.[55]

Awakening to the Needs of the Physically Handicapped

Only a minority of the physically handicapped were managing to attend the ordinary board classes at this time and the majority remained at home, many with no assistance from outside their families. Helping to explain why they had not been brought within the education system is a short dialogue between Chairman Sharpe of the 1898 Departmental Committee and a pioneer teacher of the crippled, Miss Sewell. Sharpe had seen her class some time before and seemed to have expected many to have died. Miss Sewell assured him that most still lived and that many former pupils had become self-supporting, working adults.[56] In a utilitarian age, where state intervention was still anathema to many, investing money in the handicapped who were thought unlikely to survive childhood did not make sense. Ignorance of the nature of physical handicap was further compounded by the common contemporary confusion of the physically with the severely mentally defective.

However, in the 1890s, bodies such as the COS and Invalid Children's Aid Association (ICAA) enlightened society and prompted pioneer provision other than in the rigid, over-disciplined Marylebone and Kensington Industrial Schools which forbad holidays and only allowed rare visits from parents. In 1893, the COS published a report entitled *The Epileptic and Crippled Child*, while the ICAA, founded in 1888, was providing home teaching and welfare assistance to 2200 physically handicapped children in the London area by December 1892.[57]

The COS Report preferred a day option for the crippled child. If residential support was needed, then boarding-out should be used rather than institutional placement. The Report conceded that the practical difficulties, e.g. lifting a child in a wheelchair up staircases or requiring the pupil to remain in a lying-down position, could make their first option, integration, impracticable. For children such as these, special classes were necessary.

In the 1890s, the ICAA assisted in the setting up of the Old Church Road School for cripples in Stepney. Children were transported to the school in a wagonette. This was the envy of Miss Sewell, Warden of the Women's University Settlement in Southwark and organizer of a class for the physically defective in 1894, in a classroom loaned by a London board school for the deaf. She was to tell the Departmental Committee in 1897 that her class's roll would double if transport could be provided. Teaching was by volunteer staff from the Settlement and could only be arranged part-time. She calculated that, of 106 school-age cases in her Blackfriars area, 11 were thought very delicate and only fit to be taught at home, 24 were suited to a special class, 5 were in such a class, but 66 'we consider fit for ordinary school and we do all we can to urge them to attend' with, she later claimed, a high degree of success.[58]

Integration was clearly as much to the forefront as it was for other witnesses. Thomas Aldis, HMI, once again displayed his strong views: 'I met the other day with the case of two little paralysed children, nice intelligent children I am told, whom it was proposed to send to a centre; surely what was wanted was a chair that they might be carried to their proper department.' Similarly, Henry Major told of physically defective children being carried upstairs to their classes in Leicester.[59]

Charles Loch, the energetic secretary of the COS again repeated his organization's preference for ordinary schooling and allowing the children to live at home or, failing that, boarding-out. He was also anxious to work closely with parents. He expressed impatience with people who too readily condemned children's natural homes as bad. He apparently believed that, with more voluntary social work with the family, the need to remove children from their homes would decrease.[60]

In 1897, while this evidence was being gathered, the ladies of the Victoria Settlement started a part-time special class for the physically defective in Everton, Liverpool, with ICAA help. In 1900, this was taken under the wing of the Liverpool School Board and became the Shaw Street special school, the second board school of its kind, the first having opened at Tavistock Place in London in the previous year. In 1900, the London School Board decided to make separate provision for cripples in the wake of the new Act.

The general terms of the 1899 Act, described in the previous section, applied equally to the physically as to the mentally defective. Power was also given to school authorities to provide guides to escort defectives to school and, where necessary, transport.

The financial clauses of the Act also eased the formation of pioneer residential establishments where convalescent and orthopaedic care could be provided as well as some education. In 1901, a school was attached to the West Kirby Convalescent Home in the Wirral. In 1903, sponsored largely by the Bermondsey University Settlement, the Chailey Heritage Hospital and School was founded in Sussex. In 1905, the Swinton House School of Recovery was opened near Manchester and, in 1908, after two years' fund raising, Lord Mayor Treloar's Cripples Hospital and College near Alton, Hampshire.[61]

The rural setting of these was in accord with the views of Eicholz, who in 1899 had called for boarding schools just outside London, where part of the children's treatment would be fresh air and a well-balanced diet. Delicate and undernourished children as well as the more obviously physically handicapped would also benefit in these surroundings.[62] Given the poverty, the unclean city air and the appalling living conditions of so many children's homes, added to the poor physical standards in so many day schools, Eicholz's preference for the rural or seaside setting made much sense. There seems little evidence for the modern assumption, made in an age of smokeless zones, strict building regulations and general affluence, that this was a policy of deliberately cutting off the physically handicapped from society. This is not to say that some of the disabled boarders themselves did not feel that they had been placed 'out of sight and out of mind'.

Only a few school authorities were to use their new powers to provide special classes, although there was steady development in some areas, notably London. A decade after the Act there were 53 certified day and boarding schools in England and Wales, rising to 64 by 1914. In addition, reflecting the Board's concern for classification and specialization, 19 schools had been founded to meet the needs of children with tuberculosis and 13 open air schools.

The formation of the latter copied the example set in Europe and reflected the government's growing concern for the physical well-being of the nation. Among other factors, the large number of those who applied to join the army to fight the Boers and who were subsequently rejected on medical grounds worried the government. Enquiries in Scotland and England discovered large numbers of schoolchildren in poor physical health. As a result, the importance of regular physical training was stressed in many contemporary documents between 1900 and 1940, as was the need for a proper diet. In 1906, LEAs were allowed to provide school dinners.[63] In the following year, LEAs were required to carry out medical checks on all their pupils, giving rise to the school medical services[64] and the appointment of George Newman as the Chief Medical Officer of the Board of Education.

It was against this background that the first British open air school was opened in 1907 by London County Council at Bostall Woods, Woolwich. Other schools followed elsewhere in the country. Pupils with weak hearts, bronchial complaints or suffering from malnutrition were subjected to a somewhat spartan regime with lessons spent out of doors or in three-sided rooms, with meals provided and a compulsory rest period in the middle of the day. For the sickly child from an unhealthy inner-city area who used to attend a poorly ventilated and overcrowded ordinary school, the contrasting regime of the special school did aid his or her physical condition. The open air movement was to influence other special and ordinary schools. Classes out of doors became an increasingly popular approach in many parts of the country.[65]

For epileptics, the Maghull Home had opened in 1889 with the help of a private bequest, with the rich first-class patients subsidizing the poor third-class ones. In the 1890s, some schooling was provided for the majority of its pupils, although it was not formally certified as a school until 1908.

The success of the Maghull Home was praised in the 1893 COS Report. This stressed the importance of the country setting with its fresh air and opportunities for farming and gardening. It was noted that when linked to a regular wholesome diet, the number of patients' fits was reduced significantly. This treatment was preferred to regular doses of bromides of potassium. If severe epileptics did need full-time residential care, the COS preferred the cottage style and once again displayed their dislike for the large institution. They thought certain epileptics liked the asylum and the support offered by a community of fellow sufferers. Epileptics were said to be 'very sensitive, and the sense of inferiority which they experienced when in association with sound patients was harmful'.[66] Fund-raising was encouraged for a new rural colony which was later to contain Chalfont St Peter School, certified by the Board of Education in 1909. Other schools were certified at Much Hadham, Hertfordshire (1903), Lingfield, Surrey (1905), Starnthwaite, Westmorland (1905) and Soss Moss, Manchester (1910).[67]

The COS had accepted the need for segregated residential care with reluctance. The report hoped the epileptic child would where possible receive his education in the ordinary elementary schools.[68]

Children who were Deaf or Blind

In 1895, William Stainer expressed a widely accepted view:

> The attractive theory of mixing deaf and hearing children in classes for instruction has failed in practice wherever it has been attempted, and the necessity of specially-trained teachers who understand the idiosyncrasy of the deaf has been fully acknowledged.[69]

Reflecting this, the Education Department stipulated after the 1893 Act that deaf children must be taught apart from hearing children. Meanwhile, opinion on the wisdom of segregating the blind was hardening but far from assured.

The Act had made education compulsory for both blind and deaf children (see p. 29) and required school authorities to pay the boarding fees of pupils at certified residential institutions. As support for integration had declined, the latter were thus assured of a steadier flow of pupils and money which enabled the sector to expand and to modernize in line with new government building regulations. In 1894, the new Cross School for the Deaf, Preston, opened and rapidly increased its maximum roll from 50 to 66. In 1896, the Northern Counties

School, Newcastle, expanded its roll to 154. Five school boards in North Staffordshire combined to build an institution for both the blind and the deaf. Meanwhile, Birmingham continued to favour the institutional approach for both the deaf and the blind, as did Manchester and Liverpool, although there was a sizeable day-pupil minority at the Liverpool schools for the deaf. Elsewhere, schools for the blind moved into new buildings on edge-of-town sites in Newcastle and Liverpool, and Henshaw's, Manchester, expanded.

However, returns to the Education Department show that, in 1897, more deaf children were being educated in special classes and day schools than in residential institutions. This was for a number of reasons – some pragmatic but some reflecting the continuing strong desire for integration in some areas.

By 1897, special classes for the blind were being provided by 18 school boards and for the deaf by 39 boards. Though an increasing number, this represented a tiny fraction of about 2500 existing boards. Sharpe, the Senior Chief Inspector, complained that many were apathetic and too readily overlooked the needs of their few handicapped.[70] However, some large boards were admitting the children of nearby smaller ones. London provided a service for the Home Counties where, in 1897, 500 places were provided for the deaf in 17 centres. By 1900, 100 of the pupils attending these were boarded-out, a practice encouraged by Sharpe. Meanwhile, the number of London's day centres for the blind was reduced from 20 in 1893 to 8.

Elsewhere in the country, the Burnley Board provided day classes for 89 deaf and 26 blind children. In contrast to the preference for boarding north of the Tyne, South Shields and Sunderland had board school classes for blind children, while Stockton and Middlesbrough provided classes for the deaf. Whereas Exeter preferred boarding, Plymouth School Board provided day classes for 79 deaf children. Also using day provision were Hull, Great Yarmouth, Oldham, Leicester and Cardiff. In Scotland, the Glasgow School Board continued to provide a degree of functional integration for the blind not matched in many of the largely segregated classes described in this paragraph. However, there was also support for the residential approach, witnessed by the 154 deaf children attending the Glasgow Institute for the Deaf and Dumb in 1899, although most of these came from outlying country areas.[71]

In short, opinion remained divided on the best way of providing for the deaf and blind with Education Department officials not taking sides. There was generally movement towards greater segregation but heated debate continued over the desirability of the partial integration made possible by day classes. In Lancashire, shortly before becoming Head of the new Cross School in Preston, the newspaper editor, J.G. Shaw, used often repeated arguments of this period. He complained of the difficulties of wide-age, mixed-ability groups necessitated by a diffused system of special classes appended to ordinary day schools:

> In provincial towns there will be even more difficulty in securing proper classification and graduation than in London, and the best friends of the London Board School classes never think of pretending that those classes give an education to deaf children equal to that obtainable in a good institution.[72]

At nearby Burnley, his views were fiercely attacked by families actively fighting to keep their handicapped children at home. In November 1896, the parents of 21 deaf children presented a successful petition to the Burnley School Board, asking for local day school provision for their children. Arguing on their behalf was F.W. Steele in a pamphlet which paraded many of the familiar arguments against residential schools and sought to answer the line taken by Shaw. In day classes, deaf children would not 'lose their individuality as they do in institutions, where all are like treated'. The isolation and confinement of institution life was said to depress the spirits, deprive them of the happiness of home life, and check their powers of observation. Girls would not be able to learn domestic knowledge if split from their mothers. Deaf children attending institutions were likely to marry other deaf people when grown up. Conversely, for the day school pupil: 'Intercourse, out of school hours, with other children possessed of all their senses, rather than those similarly afflicted, would sharpen their intellects and extend their knowledge.' As the deaf learn so much by sight they should see as much of the normal world as possible. He talked of the ability of the day pupils at the Liverpool Institution to go around town, to see the steamers crossing the Mersey and, consequently, to bring into school 'outside ideas'. Regular attendance, he claimed, was not a problem; classification difficulties were offset by the degree of individual attention each child received in a small special class. He quoted reports he had read on the success of day classes in Hull, Nottingham and elsewhere.[73]

Steele's enthusiasm would have been questioned by W. Nelson, who had taken over Stainer's job in London, before later becoming Head of the Manchester Schools for the Deaf. He was very concerned about the need for better classification:

> It is found that small isolated centres of not more than two teachers cannot do the most efficient work. The teachers' energies are too much spread out over pupils at all degrees of educational attainment.

He was not happy with the existing system where all grades of intelligence were mixed at small local deaf classes. Like Stainer, he wanted the less able who needed to learn signing segregated from the intelligent children who could master lip-reading and benefited from a pure oral approach. Echoing a call made by Dr James Kerr Love, the Glasgow Institution's ear specialist in 1893, Nelson also wanted the 'semi-mutes' to be brought together into classes of their own 'to take advantage of the foundation of language in their possession, and to build upon it by methods more rapid and more nearly approaching those of the ordinary schools'.[74]

In 1900, Miss Greene, the Superintendent of the Instruction of Blind Children for the LSB, also had strong doubts about small wide-age, mixed-ability classes. She told of the shift in policy in the capital after the Act.[75] In 1893, 156 blind children had attended 20 London centres in ordinary board schools and, reflecting the contemporary concern for social integration, only two deaf children were allowed to board-out in any one home. In 1897, the Bloomfield Road class for blind children contained only six pupils. To counter the unsatisfactory nature of these small scattered classes, the Board created eight large centres which provided half-time special instruction. Using powers given by the new Act, they boarded-out pupils from distant homes and paid for guides and travelling expenses for others. Senior pupils went into the ordinary sighted classes in the mornings whereas juniors were integrated in the afternoons. However, a further important step towards complete educational segregation was taken in 1901 when the LSB decided that children in Standards 1–4 should henceforth spend all the school week in their special classes. Only older pupils in Standard 5 and above should continue to enjoy part-time integration.[76]

The 1902 Westminster Conference for workers with the blind was similarly concerned about classification and commented on the poor existing provision for backward and the mentally defective blind. These were refused admission to many institutions and were said to need a special institution, or section of an institution of their own.[77]

Sharpe's annual reports show he agreed that small day schools were expensive and inefficient. One teacher could not 'do justice to children in different stages of progress'. Regular attendance could also be a problem. However, in large towns 'it seems desirable that all scholars who enjoy the happiness of a good home, a home where the efforts of the teachers are seconded by the parents, should attend day classes', but for the child from the poorer home a kindly institution with its arrangements for industrial training should be selected.[78] His colleague, Mrs Holland, HMI, agreed. She claimed poor care in the home undid the good work of the day classes. Further, deaf children in these homes were not encouraged to use language and were allowed to sign. Only institutional life could ensure the pure oral environment necessary if a deaf child was to grow into an adult able to integrate into open society, thereby avoiding the intermarriage of the deaf and the creation of Bell's feared deaf race. Her views were formed from her many inspections of institutions and having seen at least five where 'the children look upon speech as the only means of communication'.

Diverse opinion in Britain reflected contrasting views abroad. In the American mid-west, the day class/partial integration movement continued to grow. In 1897, Chicago parents called for more deaf children to remain in the public schools and praised the continuing success of the 10 such classes in Wisconsin.[79] In the same year, the first three classes in ordinary schools were opened in Chicago for the blind after a 10-year campaign led by Frank Hall prevented the state building an institution.[80] Critics of the day school approach largely repeated the British views of Shaw (see p. 53). In Europe, the bulk of opinion now favoured helping the deaf and blind in institutions.

In the second half of this period disappointment was shown with the performance of the special schools for the deaf. Macleod Yearsley, the London County Council's (LCC) ear specialist, was dismayed that one-quarter of a sample he tested were 'absolute failures' at lip-reading and it was very difficult to understand the speech of over one-half. He shared the hopes of George Newman and the National Association of Teachers of the Deaf that performance could be improved by earlier and more scientific assessment and by better classification.[81] A necessary corollary of this was increasing educational segregation of not only the handicapped from the unimpaired, but of one group from another. The mentally defective deaf should be split from those of normal intelligence in boarding establishments which used sign language, perhaps leading some into permanent care. The oral approach would then be given a fairer chance. Further, the semi-deaf must be distinguished from these, and perhaps the hard-of-hearing from the latter. While segregation was best for the profoundly deaf, those with some hearing should be encouraged to mix with hearing children in the normal day schools although under the tutelage of trained teachers of the deaf. To achieve homogeneous teaching groups, Newman pressed for five-class schools.

These views were sometimes reflected in practice. By 1911–12, Dovehill School for the semi-deaf was operating in Glasgow. A special class for the hard-of-hearing had been started in Bristol and the Manchester Schools for the Deaf had set up Clyne House, a separate department for the backward and a new junior department under Irene Goldsack (later Ewing). In London, Homerton Boarding School had provided for the mentally defective deaf since 1900.[82]

As part of the revolution in London's provision, in which childhood integration took second place to efficient education leading hopefully to adult integration, council boarding schools were started at Anerley for older deaf boys in 1902 and Oak Lodge, Wandsworth for older deaf girls in 1905. At these schools, three years' industrial training was given. By 1914, only seven day schools for the deaf remained in the capital for children under 13. The small, scattered classes had been congregated into a few large special schools. Six of these were on sites adjacent to ordinary elementary schools but, deliberately, they had separate playgrounds, entrances and toilets. Dr Stainer's boarding houses had been closed when he retired in 1896. Pupils living near the boarding schools were allowed to be day pupils however. In 1913, only 35 deaf children were educated in conjunction with the ordinary elementary schools, while 716 were in the special schools.[83]

Meanwhile, the situation of the residential institutions elsewhere in the country did not show dramatic change (see Table 1). Following the 1902 Education Act, they and the new LEAs were now legally able to provide secondary and higher education for the deaf and blind. The financial burden on voluntary schools was eased in 1907 when they were freed from their duty of having to raise a third of their income. In 1908, the Thomasson Memorial School, a boarding and day school for both the deaf and the blind, opened in Bolton. This combined approach, providing a variation on integration, was generally disfavoured on both sides of the Atlantic, but was copied by various East Anglian authorities in 1912. The unique partial-integration situation at Donaldson's, Edinburgh, continued to receive praise in these years.[84] A kindergarten for the blind was opened at Harborne by the Birmingham Institute in 1905. Closures included the small Aberdeen Institution in 1904 which led to a renewed attempt in north-eastern Scotland at the functional integration of the blind. This was described at the 1905 International Conference held at Craigmillar School, Edinburgh. After a balanced paper on the advantages and disadvantages of day and residential schools, including the result of a somewhat biased survey in which 19 out of 21 experts favoured the residential approach, J. Keir spoke for integration from the floor of the Conference. He explained that the Aberdeen blind had for the past year been educated side by side with the sighted under the ordinary teachers, supported by peripatetic specialists. He was convinced this aided the development of their habits of self-reliance 'which are a vast help to them in their after-life'. If a child needed to board for social reasons, would it not be better to improve the living conditions in the cities which made this necessary rather than take the child away?

A related plea for the community approach was also heard from B.P. Jones, Superintendent of the London special classes and schools since

1901. While he had been instrumental in forming the three London boarding schools whose main purpose was to teach useful trades to 13- to 16-year-olds, he recognized the value of day schools for the younger blind. Finding their way to school in the company of guides on the trams and trains was educative and they could live at home. Bad homes could be improved by educating the parents. He visited many poor homes all over London in the course of his work:

> In some cases, after advising the parents they have altered, and have sent their children to school clean, tidy and well cared for. The worst cases we board out with foster parents near the school. I hope that before long dinners will be provided at the centres. There is no reason why young children from five to thirteen years of age should be taken away from home if the day system is carried out efficiently.

Within a couple of years he was able to provide school meals. He also pleaded that those over 16 in boarding institutions should board out in the community as was happening in Nottingham. A day school teacher from Bradford, W.H. Tate, was not convinced and complained of the impossibility of combating ruinous home influences. He preferred homely cottage-style boarding schools with the children looked after by housemothers.[85]

This last view certainly agreed with the thoughts of the majority of delegates but it is clear that concern for integration of the blind still existed and the aim of older children going to boarding schools was to give them the best available preparation for self-sufficient, integrated adulthood. In the light of the above, it is not surprising that, in 1913, over a third of London's blind remained at least partially integrated in the ordinary schools.[86]

At the 1914 Westminster Conference the flame of integration still burnt. The lively Winifred Holt spoke on day provision and 'co-education' in America. She was founder of the New York and later the worldwide Lighthouse Movement, which adopted a community-based, integrationist approach to helping the blind, and had the support of US President Taft. She called on London to opt for a similar approach. She cited the example of a listless 15-year-old who was transformed on leaving boarding school by travelling 10 miles a day by rail, ferry and tram to reach the New York Lighthouse. He went on to high school and Columbia University. This showed the effect of placing the blind with the sighted:

> The blind children have for years been in your public schools, but why not put them side by side with the seeing, and give them a chance to win their way in healthy competition in the schoolroom and playground, as later they must win their way as blind men and women competing with seeing men and women in the struggles and victories of the big world.

Miss R.F. Petty, Assistant Superintendent of the London day centres replied that this had been done for years but with very poor results. Even the intermediate arrangement of only the older children spending half their time in the sighted classes had now fallen into disuse 'because it was found that very few children had that sort of intelligence that will profit by the teaching given in an ordinary school. The children are apt to sit apart and dream because the work is not suitable to them.'[87]

Scottish delegates from Paisley would not accept this and gave examples of blind children faring well in the seeing schools, and winning scholarships to grammar schools. Frew Bryden reminded the conference that 'co-education' had now been successfully practised in Glasgow schools for over 30 years. Winifred Holt then returned to the fray with an argument which foreshadowed the comments of critics of special schooling in the 1970s and 1980s:

> My own schooling interfered with my education: I was bored; I played hookey in every possible way. It was my teacher's fault; and if your experiment here has failed it probably means that the teachers have bored and not interested the pupils.

Miss Petty did not refer to London's integrationist attitude to the partially sighted. The first English class for myopics started in Boundary Lane, Camberwell in 1908. The class joined with sighted children for oral work but, as belief grew in the need to conserve the limited eye-sight by using it as little as possible, the children were separated for language and number lessons. The success of this model led the LCC to place subsequent 'sight-saving' classes in or near to ordinary elementary schools for combined oral work and to ensure the partially sighted were not stigmatized as blind. The first Scottish class was to start at Govan in the school year 1913–14. By that time there were 15 schools and classes for the partially sighted in England including a day school in Leicester.[88]

Meanwhile, the American day movement with its partial and occasional full educational integration grew, although it only catered for about 8 per cent of blind pupils[89] and the day/residential issue was frequently debated.

Moral Defectives and Street Arabs

G.E. Shuttleworth was among the first to describe the 'moral imbecile' – the innocent looking but cunning child for whom punishment was of no use and who was given to sudden naughty impulses. He was 'the despair of his parents, the *bête noir* of the institution' and 'the perplexing puzzle of the jurist'.[90] Sharing the opinion of some writers in the 1980s, Mary Dendy was similarly worried. She told the 1908 Royal Commission that such children were better if they were not herded together in special establishments of their own. Little if anything was done as yet for them, although Medical Officer James Kerr of the LCC, told of a local authority home for the morally defective and plans for more.[91]

Another noteworthy exception was the Little Commonwealth run by the former American streetgang member Homer Lane. He was brought over to England and sponsored by the future Lord Montague. This non-punitive and largely self-governing colony for disturbed boys and girls, which opened in 1912 in Dorset, is sometimes seen as the first progressive boarding community for maladjusted children. It lasted for four years before being closed following unproven sexual allegations of two girl absconders and the Home Office's demand for the resignation of Lane – a course of action the school's managers would not agree to.[92]

Other children who in later years would probably have been placed in schools for the maladjusted went to the mainly residential industrial schools. In 1902 there were also 14 day truant schools. In 1896, the Committee enquiring into the reformatory and industrial schools found it necessary to stress that industrial schools were not meant to be places of punishment and that no child should be removed from home and placed in one unless no other option existed. In keeping with the age, they were suspicious of boarding institutions and worried about mixing 'at risk' non-offenders with confirmed delinquents.

In 1910, the Akbar Affair brought opprobrium on the reformatory and, by association, the industrial schools. Following the sudden suspicious death of a pupil at the Akbar Nautical School at Heswall, Cheshire, the *Daily Mail* made allegations of brutality and lack of discipline against staff which led to a government investigation. This adverse publicity put many off the notion of placing children with behavioural and social needs in industrial schools and it was the late 1920s before they were once again in favour.[93]

The 1915 report of Chief Inspector C.E.B. Russell shows that concern for classification had invaded this sector of education as much as any other. Among 150 industrial schools, there was a special establishment for mental defectives, the deaf and for cripples, respectively, as well as 17 day schools. With the inmates of the 44 reformatory schools added, there were 25 878 pupils.

In keeping with the contemporary doubts on boarding, Russell commended the growing practice of boarding-out children under 10 years old. This started in 1909 and, by 1915, 58 children had been fostered. Wanting a home-like life-style for these children, he praised the ending of silence at meals in industrial schools. This practice was once common and also existed at Mary Dendy's Sandlebridge School.[94] He asked that more liberty be given to children and praised Mossbank

School for giving children pocket money and allowing them to keep pets. He urged more schools to give their pupils home leave, described at this time as an 'innovation'. His desire to limit the cold, regimented practice, which so easily invades understaffed or apathetic residential establishments, reflected the concerns of many late Victorians and has been mirrored in periodic criticism of boarding schools in every decade of this century.

Summary

The 1893 Act made education compulsory for deaf children from the ages of 7 to 16 and for the blind from the ages of 5 to 16. After this, opinion grew that deaf children could best be helped by placing them with children of similar age and ability. To achieve this, it was necessary to gather children into fewer, larger centres. In most areas this could only be achieved by boarding schools, but this was thought to have the advantages of providing a pure 'oral' environment, good physical care for the children from poor homes, and could concentrate on specialist trade training to prepare leavers for adult integration. By the 1890s, support for functional childhood integration hardly existed, but some parents actively pressed for their children's education in day classes.

Similarly, for the blind there was a steady drift away from integration, except in central Scotland. However, in London, children in the higher standards continued to receive some of their education in classes with the sighted, before going as teenagers to receive trade training in residential schools.

In this period the needs of the less seriously handicapped were increasingly recognized and pioneer classes were formed for the partially deaf and partially blind in the ordinary elementary schools. For these, a degree of integration continued to be favoured.

Similarly, the influential Charity Organization Society and Invalid Children's Aid Association strongly favoured a high degree of functional integration for as many of the physically handicapped as possible, although for some severe cases, segregation in day classes or boarding schools was considered necessary. In the 1890s experimental voluntary classes started, which were followed by a few local authority classes and schools after the 1899 Act encouraged them and allowed government money to be spent on them. The first residential schools for severe cases were formed, sometimes attached to hospitals. These were generally situated in the country or by the seaside to escape the city smog. The healthy diet and regular life-style of a boarding school was often considered beneficial. Concern for the health of sick and debilitated children was also seen in the starting of a few open-air schools, whose purpose was the restoration of the child prior to reintegration. By 1910, six residential schools catered for severe epileptics, but the majority were encouraged to attend ordinary schools.

The apparent success and popularity with some parents of special classes for the educable feeble-minded and campaigning by voluntary bodies, allied to the desire of board school teachers struggling to meet their needs in their overcrowded classes, prompted the 1899 Act. This encouraged school authorities to provide classes and schools for them. Largely for financial reasons, the Act was not mandatory, but it perhaps preferred to 'sit on the fence' anyway as opinion was far from unanimous that it was wise to segregate the feeble-minded from children of ordinary intelligence, as evidence to the 1898 Sharpe Committee showed. The latter did support the placing of idiots and imbeciles in residential colonies, however.

This was more strongly desired by the 1908 Royal Commission chaired by Lord Radnor. The latter was dominated by people who feared the degeneration of the race if the feeble-minded, noted in some influential people's view, for their large families and association with crime and vice, were allowed to continue breeding. They questioned the efficacy and logic of the growing number of day special schools. If, as the Committee wanted, many feeble-minded were to be segregated in colonies for life, it was better that they became accustomed to this life-style as children by attending boarding schools. However, the Board of Education was not convinced by their eugenic fears and their more extreme opinions seemed at variance with the opinions of the nation for practical and moral reasons. The 1914 Education Act made the education of all but the lowest grade of feeble-minded children compulsory in classes and schools which were to continue to be run by the LEAs and only the lowest grade, a tiny number, were to be referred to the new Board of Control.

The Radnor Report had advocated special classes in ordinary schools for backward children who, unlike the truly feeble-minded, were thought to have educational difficulties for environmental rather than inherited genetic reasons. The first classes for these children started in this decade in a few towns and were encouraged by the Board of Education. They were situated within the ordinary elementary schools and some functional integration was encouraged.

The problems caused by so-called *moral defectives* were also noticed, but virtually no provision was made other than in the industrial schools.

Notes

1. J. Lawson and H. Silver, *A Social History of Education in England*, Methuen, London, 1973, p.329.
2. L.R. Klemm, *European Schools*, Appleton, New York, 1890.
3. D. Pritchard, *Education and the Handicapped*, Routledge and Kegan Paul, London, 1963, pp.119–20.
4. D. Wardle, *Education and Society in Nineteenth Century Nottingham*, Cambridge University Press, Cambridge, 1971, p.107.
5. COS, *The Feeble-Minded Child and Adult*, Swann Sonnenschein, London, 1893.
6. Ibid., pp.126–7.
7. *Report of the Departmental Committee on Defective and Epileptic Children* (Sharpe Report), HMSO, London, 1898, vol. 2, pp.97–9.
8. Op. cit., note 4, p.107.
9. Op. cit., note 7, vol. 2, pp.101–5.
10. Ibid., vol. 1, pp.12 and 24.
11. Ibid., vol. 1, p.4.
12. Ibid., vol. 2, p.19.
13. Ibid., vol. 1, pp.3–4.
14. Ibid., vol. 2, pp.135 and 144.
15. Ibid., vol. 1, p.12.
16. Ibid., vol. 2, p.131.
17. Ibid., vol. 1, p.7; vol. 2, p.19.
18. Ibid., vol. 1, p.4.
19. Ibid., vol. 1, p.25.
20. Ibid., Appendix B, p.258.
21. Ibid., Appendix B, p.257.
22. Ibid., vol. 2, p.216.
23. Ibid., vol. 2, pp.91–2.
24. Ibid., vol. 2, pp.202–6.
25. 1899 Elementary Education (Defective and Epileptic Children) Act, Section 2(vi).
26. *Board of Education Circular 432* (Revised), Section B(2), November 1904.
27. *Annual Report for 1909 of CMO of the Board of Education*, HMSO, London, 1910, p.152.
28. G.C. Shuttleworth, *Mentally Deficient Children*, 2nd edn, Lewis, London, 1900, p.34.
29. A. Eicholz, 'Report of the Congress on the Education of Feeble-Minded Children, held at Augsburg, April, 1901', in Board of Education *Special Reports on Educational Subjects*, HMSO, London, 1901, vol. 9, p.597.
30. C.P. Lapage, *Feeblemindedness in Children of School-Age*, Manchester University Press, Manchester, 1911, p.8.
31. *Report of the Royal Commission on the Care and Control of the Feeble-Minded* (Radnor Report), HMSO, London, 1908, vol. 1, p.206.
32. Ibid., vol. 1, p.44.
33. Ibid., vol. 1, p.327.

34. Ibid., vol. 1, p.401.
35. Ibid., vol. 8, pp.79–82 and 103.
36. Ibid., vol. 8, p.198.
37. Ibid., vol. 8, p.171.
38. Ibid., vol. 8, pp.232 and 498.
39. Ibid., vol. 3, pp.46–7.
40. Ibid., vol. 8, pp.182–3; vol. 1, pp.205–9.
41. Ibid., vol. 1, p.209.
42. Ibid., vol. 1, p.495.
43. Ibid., vol. 1, p.418.
44. Ibid., vol. 8, p.101.
45. Ibid., vol. 1, pp.617–19.
46. Ibid., vol. 3, p.25.
47. J.S. Hurt, *Outside the Mainstream*, Batsford, London, 1988, p.163.
48. Ibid., p.148.
49. *Annual Report for 1908 of the CMO of the Board of Education*, HMSO, London, 1910, pp.115–17.
50. *Annual Report for 1910 of the CMO*, HMSO, London, 1911, pp.210–13.
51. Statistics taken from *Report of the Committee of Council on Schools for the Deaf and Blind, 1897–8*, HMSO, London, 1898; CMO's Report for 1908, note 49, op.cit. and Annual Report of CMO for 1913. Throughout the book Education Department, Board of Education, Ministry of Education and DES statistics should only be viewed as guidelines, albeit fairly accurate ones. Changes in methods of collection and collation from year to year and varying degrees of thoroughness in school returns mean that absolute accuracy cannot be assured.
52. For example, op. cit., note 30.
53. D. Forbes, 'An experiment in the treatment of backward children', in *LCC Conference of Teachers, Report of Proceedings*, King, London, 1912, p.41.
54. Op. cit., note 31, vol. 8, pp.50 and 116.
55. H.H. Goddard, *School Training of Defective Children*, Harrap, London, 1914.
56. Op. cit., note 7, vol. 2, p.192.
57. COS, *The Epileptic and Crippled Child*, Swann Sonnenschein, London, 1893, p.121.
58. Op. cit., note 7, vol. 2, pp.192–3.
59. Ibid., vol. 2, pp.91–3 and 137.
60. Ibid., vol. 2, pp.155–62.
61. Op. cit., note 49; op. cit., note 3, pp.154–62.
62. Op. cit., note 3, p.143.
63. 1906 Education (Provision of School Meals) Act.
64. 1907 Education (Administrative Provisions) Act.
65. Op. cit., note 49, p.129.
66. W. Rathbone, COS, *Proceedings of Council*, June 1893, p.267.
67. Op. cit., note 3, pp.175–6.
68. Op. cit., note 57, p.100.
69. W. Stainer, 'Recent legislation as carried out by the School Board for London', *Report on Conference of Head Masters of Institutions and of Other Workers*, London, 1895, p.11.

70. *Report of the Committee of Council on Schools for the Blind and Deaf*, HMSO, London, 1897, p.5.
71. Glasgow Society for the Education of the Deaf and Dumb, *Annual Report*, Blackie, Glasgow, 1899.
72. J.G. Shaw, *Compulsory Education for the Deaf and Dumb*, publisher anon., 1893, p.2.
73. F.W. Steele, *Education of Deaf and Dumb Children*, Nuttall, Burnley, 1896, pp.3–18.
74. W. Nelson, 'The deaf', in T. Spalding, *The Work of the London School Board*, King, London, 1900, pp.251–4.
75. Miss M.C. Greene, 'The Deaf', in Spalding, op. cit., note 74, pp.248–51.
76. Op. cit., note 31, vol. 1, p.417.
77. *Report on the Westminster Conference organised by Gardner's Trust*, Farmer, London, 1902, pp.61–4.
78. *Report of the Committee of Council on Schools for the Deaf and Blind, 1897–8*, HMSO, London, 1898, pp.5 and 16.
79. Chicago Association of Parents of Deaf Children, *Public School Classes for Deaf Children*, Chicago, 1897.
80. O.H. Burritt, 'Education of the blind with the seeing', *Outlook for the Blind*, vol. 4, Spring, 1910, p.173.
81. M. Yearsley, 'The education of the deaf', *The Lancet*, February/March, 1911; National Association of Teachers of the Deaf, *Handbook of International Conference*, Edinburgh, 1907.
82. *Teacher of the Deaf*, vol. 11, August 1913; Royal Residential Schools for the Deaf, Old Trafford, *Centenary History*, 1923; A.J. Story, 'How London educates the deaf', *Teacher of the Deaf*, vol. 12, April 1914.
83. *Report for 1913 of CMO of the Board of Education* (Report of Dr Hamer), HMSO, London, 1914.
84. For example, in Bolton, Bury, Rochdale and District Deaf and Dumb Society, *Quarterly News*, vol. 15, 1908, pp.3–5.
85. *Report of the International Conference of the Blind*, Craigmillar, Edinburgh, 1905, pp.20–1 and 83–4.
86. Op. cit., note 83.
87. *Report on the International Conference on the Blind*, Westminster, 1914, pp.470–86.
88. Op. cit., note 83, p.195; *Annual Report for 1914*, Glasgow and West of Scotland Mission to the Out-door Blind.
89. O.H. Burritt, 'Tendencies in work for the blind in America in the twentieth century', in *Report on Westminster Conference*, op. cit., note 87, pp.450–62.
90. Op. cit., note 28, p.126.
91. Op. cit., note 31, vol. 1, p.43; vol. 8, p.78.
92. E.T. Bazeley, *Homer Lane and the Little Commonwealth*, 2nd edn, George Allen and Unwin, London, 1948.
93. J. Carlebach, *Caring for Children in Trouble*, Routledge and Kegan Paul, London, 1966; *54th Report of the Chief Inspector of Reformatory and Industrial Schools*, HMSO, London, 1911, p.68.
94. *59th Report of the Chief Inspector of Reformatory and Industrial Schools of Great Britain*, HMSO, London, 1916, pp.21–5.

CHAPTER 4

Between the Wars: 1918–39

Political and Educational Summary: 1918–39

Major Events and Ordinary Education

1918 War ends: votes for women over 30

1918 Fisher Act provides for nursery education and more 'senior' schools; 14 is leaving age

1918 Burnham Committee started

1919 *Lloyd George's* (Liberal) coalition wins landslide; Liberals fatally split

1921 A.S. Neill opens Summerhill

1922 *Bonar Law* (Conservative) becomes PM

1922 Labour Party publishes *Secondary Education for All*

1922–3 Financial crisis forces cuts in teachers' salaries

1923 *S. Baldwin* (Conservative) becomes PM

Special Education

1918 Education (Scotland) Act raises school leaving age to 18 for blind

1918 NIB's first UK Sunshine Home (nursery school), Chorleywood

1919 A. Eicholz made Chief Medical Inspector at Board of Education

1920 NCTD campaigns for lowering compulsory school-age from 7 to 5 years for deaf

1921 Education Act consolidates previous acts; recognizes five categories (blind, deaf, mentally defective, physically defective and epileptic). These children must be certified and provided for *only* in special schools and certified classes

1921 NIB starts Chorleywood College for higher education of the blind

1923 Second Sunshine Home at Southport

1920s Partial integration of blind continues in Glasgow

1924 First Labour government under *R. MacDonald; Baldwin* resumes premiership in autumn after 'reds under beds' election; Liberals reduced to 40 seat rump

1924 Active NID grows out of quiescent National Bureau for the Deaf; campaigns for government inquiry
1924 Wood Committee appointed
1925 First Child Guidance Clinic in Scotland started at Glasgow University

1926 General Strike
1926 Hadow Report pushes end-on primary and secondary education with transfer at 11; wants easier access to grammar schools, 'modern' schools plus experiment with 'multiple-bias' schools

1926 Jewish Health Organization found CGC in London
1927 Mental Deficiency Act: local authorities to provide training for severe mental defectives

1928 Votes for women over 21
1928 Board of Education pamphlet praises Hadow; survey shows 21 out of 75 LEAs use IQ tests for selection but opinion on their value divided
1929 *MacDonald's 2nd Ministry;* Wall St Crash leads to Great Depression of 1930s

1929 Wood Report attacks stigma caused by certification; attacks all-age small special classes; favours large special schools despite integrationist feelings
1930 Glasgow closes last remaining day industrial schools in Scotland; over 9000 children in 94 Scottish special schools and classes

1931 *National Government* formed under MacDonald, supported by Baldwin
1931 Teachers' and other civil servants' pay cut; freeze on school buildings expenditure
1931 2nd Hadow Report pushes activity/experience (rather than remembering facts) through project work etc. in primary schools
1932 22% unemployed (2.8 million)

1931 NIB opens Court Grange school (Devon) for defective blind

1932 Eicholz's report on the deaf for Board of Education favours the efficiency of the large separate special school
1932 Birmingham start first LEA child guidance clinic

		1933	About 19 000 children in London's 114 day and 10 boarding special schools
		1933	Children and Young Offenders' Act turns reformatory and industrial schools into Approved Schools
1934	Gordonstoun founded	1934	Integrationist leanings of Crowley Report on needs of the partially sighted
1935	*Baldwin* becomes PM; some re-armament in face of growing Nazi threat		
1930s	IQ testing gains in popularity		
1936	Accession and abdication of Edward VIII	1936	NIB/Coll. of Teachers of Blind Report wants big schools; all London day schools for blind now closed
		1936	Act allows education of Scottish deaf aged 3–5 years
1937	*N. Chamberlain* becomes leader of the National Government	1937	Education (Deaf Children) Act reduces compulsory school age to 5 (but not implemented until after the War)
1938	Spens Report on Secondary Education, believing in IQ tests, wants separate grammar, modern or technical schools for the majority but a few experimental multilateral schools	1938	Glover Report on children with defective hearing favours careful classification in special schools
		1938	Donaldson's Hospital and Edinburgh Deaf and Dumb Institution merge, ending partial integration of deaf
		1938	11 CGCs in Scotland (10 are voluntary)
1939	Second World War starts	1939	22 LEA CGCs in England and 10 LEA educational psychologists employed
		1939	Partial integration of Glasgow blind continues (but ends during War); still three classes for deaf in ordinary schools

The Great War destroyed four empires and came close to ruining Britain's. In 1918, the country had lost much of its wealth and was to experience recurring financial crises. World trade problems and foreign competition led to high unemployment in the early 1920s as well as the early 1930s. Grinding poverty in unhealthy cities before the creation of the Welfare State made life precarious for many of the working class. Many of the latter placed their faith in the Labour Party as the hopelessly split Liberals rapidly shrank in significance. Labour formed their first government in 1924 and shared power with the Conservatives in the 1930s when the spreading Nazi shadow and rearmament came to dominate the nation's affairs. In 1926, the first Hadow Report urged the development of end-on primary–secondary education with the transfer age set at 11, reflecting a growing feeling that everyone was entitled to secondary education in some form.

The 1921 Education Act consolidated previous special education legislation and required that children in the five categories of blind, deaf, mentally defective, physically defective and epileptic should be certified as such and then educated in special schools, which were funded differently from the ordinary public elementary schools and inspected by the Medical Branch of the Board of Education. This last provision was abandoned in 1934 and HMI took over inspection again in an attempt to bring special schools more within the educational mainstream.

Adult integration of the severely handicapped was the aim of the 1921 Act although the Board of Education hoped where possible children would be fed back into the ordinary schools as well – and from schools for the physically handicapped, this happened frequently. The influential Chief Medical Officer (CMO) of the Board of Education, George Newman, and his assistant, Dr Alfred Eicholz, recognized that segregation was necessary for some, but in the CMO's annual report for 1923:

> The aim throughout should be to remove the child for as short a time as possible from the ordinary school, and so to organise all Special Schools and classes that the transference of a child to and from special and ordinary schools should be as easy as possible.[1]

To the Board's medical officers 'the guiding principle' was that ideally every child should go to an ordinary school. Such sentiments were reflected strongly in the government-sponsored Crowley Report of 1934. Special schools, it said, were not schools for training a special class of adults. They were schools for 'bringing a special class of children as fully as possible into the stream of normal life'. This had to be 'borne in mind in every detail of their work'.[2] While the 1929 Wood Report[3] continued to worry about the low-grade mentally deficient, it envisaged that many of the far greater number of backward children could receive suitable instruction within the ordinary primary and the newly emerging secondary schools.

Thus children were segregated with reluctance. There continued to be support for the maximum degree of childhood integration felt consistent with efficient education and the physical and social welfare of the child. Newman and other leaders were clearly aware of the stigma sometimes attached to special schooling and some parents' opposition to boarding.

These concerns when added to the acute financial situation, which in 1931 led to a virtually complete embargo on all school building development, explain the situation portrayed in government statistics for the period (see Table 2). For most categories, it was a period of standstill and under-usage of the existing provision. The percentage of children in special schools did increase from about 0.7 per cent in 1920 to nearly 1 per cent in 1938[4], but this was largely explained by growth in the single area of open-air schools. Significantly, the latter were often cheap, temporary wooden structures which LEAs *could* afford. Also significantly, and in keeping with the contemporary concern for integration, they were usually short-stay schools, which boasted restoring children to good health and returning them to ordinary schools.

Later sections of the chapter will refer again to the vacancies existing in schools for the deaf, the blind and the mentally defective. In 1929, there were nearly 3400 spare places in English and Welsh special schools. Reflecting the falling incidence in some categories due to better medical knowledge, but also increasing doubts about the value of some special schooling, notably that provided in separate schools for the mentally defective, this figure rose to over 8000 in 1938. Nearly 3000 of these were in schools for the mentally defective, 1200 in schools for the blind and over 900 in schools for the deaf.

Table 2 Certified English and Welsh special schools and accommodation between the wars

School[a]	Number of schools			No. of available places		
	1919	1929	1939	1919	1929	1939
Blind	58	77	73	3180	4558	4644
Deaf	51	50	45	4610	4726	4517
MD	196	180	154	15 343	17 008	16 385
PD	69	78	72	5921	6922	7127
HS	?	52	53	?	4086	6104
TB	48	45	35	2635	2507	2475
Open-air	37	100	157	2293	8965	17 010
Epil.	6	6	6	496	561	606
Misc.	?	1	3	?	254	900
Total	465	589	609	34 478	49 587	59 768

Sources: *Chief Medical Officer's Annual Reports* for 1918, 1928 and 1938.

[a] MD, mentally defective; PD, physically defective; HS, hospital school; TB, tuberculosis; Epil., epileptic; Misc., miscellaneous.

In short, this was a period of gathering knowledge and experience of the needs of the handicapped, in which major enquiries looked into the needs of most categories and the Board of Education's Medical Officers collated and spread the increasing flow of information; however, a shortage of public money and, at times, self-doubts, prevented any significant expansion of special education, either in segregated schools or within the elementary or emerging secondary schools. The one exception was the open-air school sector.

The Epileptic, Physically Defective and Delicate

The 1918 Education Act made education for the epileptic compulsory, but this was not to be a reality for many years. Table 2 shows that there was some expansion in the six boarding schools for epileptics, but not a great deal. In 1925, half of the severe epileptics outside London were still not attending school and a quarter were in ordinary schools.[5] In 1932, there were 18–24 month waiting lists. To ease the situation and to obtain the best value for government money, the Board of Education urged the strict exclusion of mentally defective cases who were thought to gain the least from the education provided. Newman apparently accepted the view of the teachers, who saw him in October 1932, that the residential approach was the best means of assisting the severe epileptic. Quiet rural surroundings, a regular life, medical care and sympathetic training were said to suit these children.[6] However, in line with the Board's 'guiding principle' that as many children as possible should remain in ordinary schools, over 4000 less severe cases attended the elementary and other normal schools.

Similarly, the vast majority of children with physical defects or chronic illness remained in the ordinary schools. By 1919, a range of day special and 12 boarding schools for cripples, orthopaedic hospitals with schools attached, schools for tuberculosis victims and open-air schools for delicate children with weak hearts, respiratory and other conditions existed. But these only catered for about one-third of those in need and only 28 out of the 318 English LEAs maintained their own schools with London making the most extensive provision. Most were content to use voluntary facilities and many were dilatory in providing any help. The Board's medical officers were delighted that the 1918 Education Act forced all LEAs to ascertain and to provide suitable education for their physically defective pupils from 1 April 1920.[7] North of the Border, Glasgow led the way in providing for the physically defective, although in contrast to London and in keeping with its own integrationist tradition, Scotland favoured special classes attached to ordinary schools.[8]

Given the severe financial constraints under which local government laboured and the desperate condition of some of the existing school buildings, it was not possible to expand the provision for the physically defective as much as Newman had hoped. New schools were opened but old ones were closed or amalgamated to form bigger units where classification was easier, so that the number of certified establishments only rose slightly (see Table 2). The figures for 1923 show that there were 6000 pupils in day schools, although they were only meant to accommodate 5642. However, probably reflecting the reluctance of parents to be parted from their handicapped children, a phenomenon well-known to the Board, there were over 100 vacancies in the residential schools.[9]

However, as the inter-war years proceeded the need for extra places declined to some extent. Increasing numbers of crippled children were ascertained, treated in hospital and then returned to ordinary day schools. This was helped by the establishment of LEA orthopaedic schemes linked to hospital treatment. Such schemes increased from 85 in 1925–6 to 216 in 1930–31. Progress was being made against club-foot, spinal curvature, rickets and other deformities, while deaths of children under 15 years with tuberculosis fell from 6978 in 1921 to 4167 in 1930. In his report for 1930, the CMO recorded with satisfaction that in Leeds 75 per cent of 1506 cripples (mainly rickets victims) had been treated and then reintegrated into ordinary schools. The figures for Staffordshire showed a 90 per cent rate and other successes were given.[10]

The Board's passion, shared by many of the local school medical officers, for open-air schools allied to the the cheapness of the required wooden three-sided sheds and pavilions with corrugated iron roofs, was reflected in the marked expansion of these establishments. These were often short-stay schools. In the 1930s, 4000 London children a year would be sent to open-air boarding schools for a few weeks. More commonly, delicate children would remain for periods of 6–24 months in day open-air schools. However, a minority of children would remain in the delicate school for many years, sometimes until leaving age. The London County Council (LCC) reported that initial parental doubts about these schools' value had been replaced by a recognition of the improvement they could bring in children's health.[11] Given the physical conditions of some of the public elementary schools, the spartan life allied to a regular diet and rest, could be better. Not only might the delicate child have to suffer the smog and poor living conditions of the city slums, he could also be attending the many schools with dark, damp, poorly ventilated classrooms with repairs undone and toilets which did not flush. Such poor conditions were not confined to the big towns. In Hertfordshire in 1925, 52 schools did not have their own water supply, and in some which did, dirty 'privy middens' contaminated it.[12]

Such conditions could also hasten the transfer of less handicapped children into the cripple schools where hygiene, diet, exercise, fresh air and regular medical supervision played a major role. They were seen as havens from the rough-and-tumble of the ordinary school and places where the frequent backwardness of pupils, sometimes caused by long stays in hospital, could be helped in relatively small classes of about 20 pupils. To Newman, and to most school medical officers and educationalists, the all-important goal was integration of the physically defective as adults. This, they believed, was best achieved by the special school route in severe cases, although the curriculum they received should resemble as closely as possible that provided for the child in the public elementary school. However, special emphasis must be laid on preparing the youngster for a self-supporting adult life. Thus, the Annual Reports of the Chief Medical Officer devote repeated attention to trade training and applaud the reports of the LEA medical officers which generally indicated that a large majority of the severe cases leaving hospital schools could be trained to earn a living. For the physically defective in the day schools of London, Birmingham, Liverpool and Manchester, vocational courses were provided for pupils aged from 13 to 16 years. As a result, in 1927, 80 per cent of crippled children in London between 16 and 18 years of age were known to be in work. The Board wanted similar training schemes to be developed in smaller towns and country districts. The CMO applauded the jewellery, copper and leather work taught, even to recumbent pupils at the Heritage, Chailey, and the boot-making, tailoring, book-keeping and shorthand at Alton College, both residential establishments which showed what could be achieved for the rural child if boarding schools were expanded.[13] In 1933 when mass unemployment had returned after an absence of about 10 years, the LCC was to claim, in part corroborated in other sources, that its special school leavers were finding work almost as successfully as the non-handicapped, thus boosting those who favoured segregation for the special child. In some major cities, such as London and Birmingham, voluntary after-care committees aided the handicapped in their search for work. The Invalid Children's Aid Association continued to help, as did its 23 associated provincial branches (e.g. Dundee, Darlington, Plymouth) from 1920.

The Board knew that effective trade training was not provided in the many ordinary schools which were still bound up in forcing children through the Standards. Nevertheless, the majority of crippled children continued to attend the mainstream schools despite this obstacle to their achieving adult integration. In any case, other advantages probably outweighed it.

Information on these integrated pupils is frustratingly sparse. When in 1919, about 4000 children attended London's schools for the

physically defective, Dr Bishop Hamer's survey of the capital's schools
showed that 15 883 physically defective or delicate children remained in
public elementary schools. Reports from the school medical officers of
Camberwell, St Pancras and Willesden tell of the stresses on families
caused by having a handicapped child at home in small houses unsuited
to the special needs of the disabled and of the practical and time-
consuming difficulties of taking their children by tram to out-patient
clinics.

In the same report, Dr J.J. Butterworth, Schools' Medical Officer for
Lancashire, briefly debates which physically defective children should
attend a special school and which an ordinary school. He gives as an
example from his own experience a polio victim, paralysed in his lower
limbs, who goes to school on a tricycle 'on which also he moves from
room to room in acrobatic fashion'. This lad is bright and keeps up with
his class. He is able to attend ordinary school but Butterworth worries
that he is not receiving the physiotherapy which would be provided in a
special school. In contrast, and definitely in need of special school
treatment, is a child crippled with palsy from birth, for whom regular
physiotherapy and training in self-help and independent living skills is
essential.

A rather unusual practice was carried out at Grimké Ward Hospital
School in Salford, where children (mainly rickets victims) were treated
in their immediate neighbourhood and then sent home each weekend.
Regular contact with their families was felt to aid recovery. The Board
seemed surprised that 'Treatment in a slum district is preferred to an
open-air school in the country.'[14]

In the United States during this period, services by way of a mixture of
segregated special schools and classes and semi-integrated classes in
regular schools were growing rapidly, but were only thought to have
catered for one-quarter of the physically handicapped in need of special
treatment. Chicago had been a pioneer in providing public school
classes for cripples; New York had followed. Smaller cities are reported
to have adopted multigrade special classes attached to the regular
schools, which are said to have been popular.[15]

The Deaf and Partially Deaf

In 1922, Dr A.G. Bell's body was lowered into a grave on a mountain top
in Novia Scotia as 13 million American telephones went silent for two
minutes.[16] A few months earlier in December 1921 during a visit to
Britain, the expatriate Scot spoke at a luncheon held in his honour at the
Derby Institute for the Deaf. Here he was lauded and made a Vice-
President of the National College of Teachers of the Deaf.[17] Perhaps

diplomatically, or perhaps because his ardour for childhood integration had lessened, he merely expressed satisfaction that speech training and the oral approach were now almost universal in British schools. A last bastion of the combined manual and oral approach, the small Aberdeen Institute, had recently been absorbed by the oralists of the local authority.[18]

Partial integration of the profoundly deaf was virtually a dead issue. The periodicals did not discuss it and Eicholz's brief historical review in his 1932 report did not mention it. Even the century-old integrationist situation at Donaldson's Hospital School ended when it merged with the nearby Edinburgh Deaf Institution in 1938. In that year the spirit of the times was shown in West Ham when the Mayor, Mayoress and various local dignitaries showed much civic pride at the opening ceremony of a new school, equipped with the latest scientific devices, which replaced two smaller schools. The *British Deaf Times* saw this as 'another link in the chain of educational progress'.[19]

The 1921 Education Act had earlier confirmed the supremacy of the segregated approach by stating that the deaf must be certified and educated only in special schools. In 1922, at a time of government cutbacks, it was reassuring to educators to hear H.A.L. Fisher, the President of the Board of Education, defend the cost of special schools, particulary those for the deaf and blind: 'There is perhaps no form of education', he said, 'which yields so definite a return of happiness and wage-earning independence'.[20] Only the special school, it was generally felt, could produce self-supporting adults and thus save the state the long-term expense of looking after indigent deaf adults. This line was often repeated by senior officials at the Board over the next two decades.

The special schools were of a varied size and administrative status. In 1918 there were 21 boarding and 30 day schools. Large regional voluntary schools such as those at Manchester and Margate had nearly 300 pupils each in 1930 and contained infant, junior, senior elementary and training sections. In contrast, the William Morris Deaf Council School in Walthamstow had a mere 12 pupils and the LEA school in Middlesbrough 13. Some areas, for example Lancashire, had more than adequate provision. London largely maintained its new pre-war system.[21] In Scotland, in 1930, there were five boarding schools for the deaf mute, two for the deaf and blind, four day schools and three special classes attached to ordinary schools.[22]

The shrinking number of special school places in the 1930s reflected the decreasing number of candidates for these schools (see Table 2); by 1930, there were 700 spare places. The number of deaf pupils in London, where ascertainment was perhaps most thorough, fell by 22 per cent between 1923 and 1930.[23] However, the vacancies are also explained by other factors. First, the vacancies were often in the wrong places – one in

Northumberland was of little practical use to a child living in the south. Secondly, there were parental objections to special schooling, as will be discussed later. Thirdly, screening and early diagnosis by school medical officers linked to improved treatment reduced incidence. Fourthly, some LEAs probably restricted the extent of ascertainment to the number of *local* vacancies or budget limits.

Finally, scientific progress was being made in the measurement and amplification of residual hearing which increasingly enabled children in the 1930s to cope with ordinary schooling. In 1925, the recently opened Maud Maxfield School, Sheffield, was experimenting with a group hearing aid. Meanwhile, Macleod Yearsley was successfully trying out hearing aids in London schools.[24] Irene and A.W.G. Ewing bought a pure-tone audiometer for the Deaf Department at Manchester University in 1928 and, in 1931, recruited T.S. Littler, an expert in electro-acoustics. The Manchester team, consisting of scientists and, in Irene Ewing, a leading educationalist and trainer of teachers of the deaf, proceeded in the 1930s to make considerable scientific progress in the measurement of hearing loss and the development of economical hearing aids. By 1934 they knew that as many as 70 per cent of children in the deaf schools had some residual hearing, some of whom could be effectively helped by the new hearing aids.[25]

These advances focused attention even more strongly on the differing needs of the hearing-impaired and convinced leaders of opinion of the importance of separating the partially hearing from the profoundly deaf. Yearsley had asked for this before the Great War. Bristol LEA opened the first class for the partially hearing in 1908, followed soon afterwards by London. These were not copied on a national scale, however. Partially deaf children were often treated as though they were profoundly deaf and placed in schools for the deaf.

This contributed to the situation described by a reporter at the 1920 Conference of the National College of Teachers of the Deaf (NCTD):

> It is universally recognised that the present method of dumping the mentally deficient, the congenital deaf and dumb, the deaf speaking, the semi-deaf, and the hard of hearing altogether is wrong...upon the proper classification of the deaf depends the whole future of deaf education.[26]

The NCTD, supported by the National institute for the Deaf (NID) after its foundation in 1924, wanted a national scheme which ensured efficient classification. Their concern was for adult integration of the deaf, achieved by efficient education in homogeneous groups, even if this meant segregation as a child in residential schools at a distance from their homes. The backward and mentally defective, they held, must be separated from the average child, and a grammar school was needed to meet the needs of the intelligent to supplement the work of the small private grammar school in Northampton and Mary Hare's at Burgess Hill, Sussex.

Their aims continued to be shared by the senior HMI as well as Eicholz and Newman, but these men had a clearer idea of the difficulties that were faced. In 1930, in part a response to pressure from the NCTD and NID, Newman asked the recently retired Eicholz to inquire into the social and educational needs of the deaf. In his resulting 1932 report,[27] Eicholz briefly outlined the continuing debate between proponents of the day and residential approach using the familiar arguments described in earlier chapters.

He also recorded progress in trade training, noting the London model, and pushed the need for more effective schemes elsewhere if the adult deaf were to win and hold employment at a time of increased mechanization and industrial depression, when unemployment was at record levels. This was part of a wider concern for a more efficient organization of schools in which small schools disappeared and larger units were formed, of necessity residential in most areas. He preferred to proceed by persuasion, realizing that it would be difficult to force voluntary schools and council schools to agree upon a plan. He had already made attempts to persuade schools in the south-east and Lancashire to agree areas of specialism. No-one was keen to take just the backward or mentally deficient.

Eicholz was also acutely aware that many parents would not agree to their children being placed in boarding schools a great distance from their homes, which would result from a truly national scheme designed to achieve the most homogeneous groupings. Furthermore, parental objections also made him shy away from the NCTD's demand for compulsory education at the age of 5.

Parental opinion also influenced him on the needs of the partially hearing. In 1930, Eicholz discovered that of 1882 children outside London who were ascertained as being partially deaf, over 70 per cent were left in ordinary schools without special help.[28] He worried about the medical supervision and educational progress of these children, but pointed out that they sometimes remained there through parental opposition to placement in boarding schools with departments for the partially hearing or local day schools designed primarily for the profoundly deaf.

He had earlier recorded with satisfaction the falling number of profoundly deaf children remaining illegally in public elementary schools, but was disappointed that so few cases came to court.[29] However, other than by gentle persuasion, he realized how difficult it was to go against the wishes of parents.

His realism was greeted with some hostility by the NCTD which claimed he made too much of parental opposition and not enough of other parents' approval of special schooling.[30] More often, they claimed, it was the reluctance of LEAs to meet the cost of boarding – seven times the per capita cost of day elementary schooling – which prevented a placement. Nor did they approve of his dismissal of a national scheme and compulsory schooling from age 5 years. But with Eicholz and the NID they pressed for a further enquiry into the needs of the partially hearing.

The government responded by appointing a committee in 1934, with Dr Alison Glover, a Senior Medical Officer at the Board, as Chairman. In 1938 *Children with Defective Hearing* was published. This split affected children into three grades: Grade I pupils could function in ordinary schools, despite hearing loss, without special help; Grade IIA children required hearing aids and perhaps extra tuition in lip-reading but benefited from remaining in ordinary schools; Grade IIB pupils were the partially hearing who could not cope with ordinary schooling; and Grade III children were the profoundly deaf who needed their own special schools.

The Committee clearly hoped that as many children as possible would be placed in Grades I and IIA:

> If a child with defective hearing is keeping up with a class of similar age and ability, then there is no reason why he should be removed from it, however severe his deafness, provided only that he is evincing no signs of undue strain.[31]

Transfer to a special school should only be made on educational and not on medical grounds and only when a child had clearly proved to have failed in an ordinary school. However, the Committee was dubious of attempts made by towns such as London, Oldham and Bristol to provide partial integration by way of special classes in ordinary schools. They recognized the social advantages of mixing with the hearing in the playground, access to better facilities, the preference of many parents for such an arrangement and the possible feelings of normality it would bring to the child. However:

> To make him join the hearing children only for physical training and handicraft would not make him a full member of the school community. His small part in general school activities would make him feel more out of the stream of ordinary interests than if he were educated entirely separately from hearing children.[32]

Although separate special schooling was preferable, ideally with other partially hearing children, special departments shared with Grade III children would probably have to be set up in existing schools, due to the fall in the numbers of partially deaf children. To encourage social integration, they could possibly be boarded-out to enable them to attend a day school.

The Glover Report met with a generally favourable reaction from the NCTD, although it naturally defended the boarding schools against some critical comments in the Report. They also warned that in their present early stage of development, hearing aids could inhibit learning and might lead to children being left in ordinary schools who would progress better in a special school. The Second World War was to intervene before practical action could follow.

In 1937, the NCTD had won another minor victory when it was enacted (though not implemented) that all deaf children should start education at the age of 5 instead of 7. The NCTD had long argued that an earlier start to the education of the deaf would help to raise standards. Further, if 5 was the right age for the blind then why not for the deaf child?

Meanwhile, the adult deaf communities continued to doubt the efficacy of the oral approach. The cover of every edition of the *British Deaf Times* consisted of a diagram of the finger-spelling alphabet and the instruction 'To help the deaf – please learn this'. In May 1933, at an Eastern Counties Association for the Deaf meeting at Cambridge, C.H. Wilkinson suggested the creation of a 5000 strong, entirely self-contained colony for the deaf, claiming this would best provide for their happiness.[33] Clearly, many of the deaf themselves, in this generation as in others, did not accept the wisdom of the prescribed oral education and some doubted the wisdom of adult integration in open hearing society.

The Blind and Partially Sighted

This period saw an increase in the number of certified schools for the blind, but also their under-usage. There were nearly 1000 spare places in 1926, although by 1932 this had shrunk to 450. Progress towards providing a better classification continued with the opening of Sunshine Homes for the 'under fives' at Chorleywood in 1918, followed by Southport and Leamington a few years later. For intelligent girls of secondary age the grammar school at Chorleywood was opened in 1921, while Worcester College continued to provide for bright boys, with 50 per cent of its leavers going on to university. In 1931, Court Grange, at Abbotkerswell in Devon, opened for the backward blind, while the LCC Penn School in Buckinghamshire continued to cater for the multi-handicapped, including the deaf and the blind. In 1932 the largest school was the Royal Institution at Harborne, Birmingham, with 120 pupils in the junior and senior departments and 42 children in the kindergarten. A third of the children there were not taught by braille. The smallest school was at Rhyl with a mere 14 pupils on its roll but room for 24. In Scotland, there were three boarding schools for the blind, including Craigmillar in Edinburgh and one for the deaf and blind. In the 1930s, the number of semi-integrated classes for the blind was reduced from five to two, as the Scots blind population fell. At one of the latter, many of the pupils boarded at a nearby children's home.[34]

Continuing integration in Glasgow reflected the American beliefs of 1919, where many educators of the blind were said to believe that the institution was 'more or less out of place in modern conceptions of child welfare', and was to be accepted 'only in the absence of anything better'.[35] In this climate semi-integrated braille classes in the regular schools and day schools expanded in some areas, although the residential school continued to have many supporters. To a lesser extent, opinion on this side of the Atlantic was also divided. A Local Government Board Enquiry in 1917 noted that some parents resented having their children placed away from home and the segregation of blind children from the sighted was believed to be undesirable. Nevertheless, the majority of the Committee decided that boarding was best for most pupils. It provided better discipline, skilled supervision, more individual attention, regular physical training and medical supervision, as well as better educational facilities.[36]

Differing opinions were to last throughout the inter-war years. Newman and Eicholz, while fully aware of counterarguments, remained committed to boarding, and supporters of day special schools, or full functional integration, generally lost ground. The Board believed that a young child left with his family developed blind mannerisms and did not develop the self-help or mobility skills which he would do in a boarding school helped by expert staff. The parents could not be blamed for negligence but had a natural reluctance 'to press discipline upon an afflicted child'.[37] Further, in a day school it was not practicable to correct bad habits because the child still spent a major portion of his life at home.

Reflecting the dominant view, contemporary historical accounts failed to discuss the integrationist situation of late Victorian Britain.[38] However, until the mid-1930s, London children under the age of 13 continued to attend day schools before transferring to boarding schools which specialized in trade-training, but by the time the National Institute for the Blind and College of Teachers of the Blind published the Ritchie Report in 1936, this practice had ended and all children boarded from an early age. Only in Glasgow did a degree of functional integration survive at the Wolseley and John Street elementary schools. While this was praised by the local HMI in 1939, war-time evacuation and falling numbers of blind put an end to the practice.[39]

For partially sighted children, however, the integrationist position gained rather than lost strength. In 1918, the LCC ophthalmologist, Dr Bishop Hamer, reported the difficulties of persuading parents to allow their children to go to separate myope schools.[40] Less difficulty arose with the special class attached to the ordinary school, making use of the main school facilities. When the Crowley Committee set to work in December 1931, they discovered that of 37 certified special schools and classes for the partially sighted, 11 were in London and catered for 820 of the 2030 certified children in England and Wales, and another 6 classes were in Liverpool. In total, only 22 LEAs were making any special provisions at all. While most schools were small self-contained units, having little to do with the host school in whose grounds they usually stood, the Liverpool classes were integral parts of the ordinary schools under the active control of the Headmasters.[41] This approach was in line with contemporary American practice, where a 1931 survey of 344 sight-saving classes found that over 80 per cent of the sample schools adopted a 'coordinative' rather than a 'segregative' plan.[42] To lessen the stigma felt to be attached to special class placement and to make for more normal social development, pupils mixed with the sighted for lessons not requiring the use of vision. The 1934 Crowley Report contained a whole chapter called 'Segregation Versus Non-segregation', which supported this type of approach, observed by Crowley Committee members in Cleveland, Ohio. In Liverpool, partially sighted pupils at the Birchfield Road School spent a third of their timetable in oral History, Geography and Scripture lessons as well as attending assembly and having breaks at the same time as the sighted.

However, this approach had been tried and abandoned in London. Mr Dobson, a London Head, said that a non-segregated class usually meant a wide-age, mixed-ability class and was not as satisfactory as the good classification achieved in the larger segregated special school. Apart from this, serious administrative difficulties arose, a point repeated by Eicholz. It was further developed by Edward Evans, formerly a teacher in a non-segregated class but then Superintendent of the East Anglian School for the Blind and Deaf. He claimed that a suitable timetable was difficult to arrange and 'ordinary class teachers were generally impatient of the interruptions caused by the introduction of the special class children'.[43] Eicholz had made a similar point. Evans also believed that partially sighted children suffered a feeling of inferiority when closely associating with fully sighted children. At playtime they flocked together and did not mix with the seeing. Evidence from America backed up this last claim. Ralph Merry warned that unless the school was suitably organized and staff actively fostered the regular social intermingling of the sighted and partially sighted, the latter:

> may remain in a group by themselves, and may develop a sense of inferiority and a grudge against the seeing children who fail to accept them as social equals. Seeing children have a definite tendency to regard blind children as 'queer', and seldom make overtures towards them unless encouraged to do so.[44]

However, the Committee felt that any difficulties could be overcome. They were more worried by the practice, existing in nine English schools, of educating partially sighted children in exactly the same way as the blind. They realized that with falling numbers of blind children due to improved medical treatment, it was realistic for the institutions to keep up their numbers by admitting the partially sighted, but to teach them by braille methods was 'indefensible'. The Crowley Committee found that 27 per cent of children in the schools for the blind were partially sighted and that this was increasing.[45] Despite this, and perhaps reflecting the preference for integration, the number of vacancies in the schools for the blind increased from about 350 in 1929 to some 1200 in 1938.

Eicholz was the Chairman of the NIB/CTB Committee of Enquiry until his death in 1933 when J.M. Ritchie, a man with many years' experience of residential institutions, took over. The 1936 Report devoted a chapter to discussing the advisability of educating the blind in schools for the sighted, but the Committee was convinced that this was unwise. They mentioned Barnhill's work and braille classes in Cleveland but were not impressed. If the integrated system was desirable, undoubted administrative difficulties might be overcome. However, the blind, they held, needed a normal curriculum but one which emphasized the particular needs of the young blind:

> The most important features in whose education should be sense and habit training, training in confidence and in independence of movement, eradication of blind mannerisms, and training in the reception of the countless non-visual impressions from the outside world which are a substitute for the visual stimuli of the child endowed with sight.[46]

The normal formal education of the sighted would be likely to preclude much of this. Furthermore, teaching braille reading and writing as isolated subjects, as happened in partially integrated special classes, involved an artificial separation. Their teaching, they held, should be bound up in the teaching of history, geography and other subjects. Ordinary class teachers would have to adapt their methods to suit the needs of the blind, possibly to the detriment of the sighted majority. The Committee's witnesses further believed that educating the blind among the sighted accentuated their sense of being different and enhanced their feelings of inferiority. They also doubted if the trade-training in the ordinary schools, even if it was given, was of the same quality as that given in the special institutions.[47] Vocational courses in handicrafts such as basket-weaving and, for the musical, piano-tuning, had helped many children when leaving special institutions to earn a living.

The Committee further contended that the alleged institutionalization and isolation of residential schools were not intrinsic to these schools. With sympathetic staff and modern forms of organization which encouraged links with the local sighted community and life-skills training in the local town and which developed closer communications with pupils' homes, these criticisms lost their weight. Elsewhere in the Report they noted the more relaxed, happier atmosphere now said to exist in boarding schools, in contrast to the tough discipline of some schools in former times. However, Oscar Myers' reminiscences of spartan dormitories, eating in silence and general regimentation in 1930s boarding schools suggested a continuing rigid life-style.[48]

The Report pressed for the amalgamation of small schools into large units where better classification could be effected.[49] A prime candidate was the north west where 18 schools existed within a 50-mile radius of Manchester. Some schools should be allocated to the mentally defective blind. Single-sex schools were thought to produce better educational results. However, the Committee conceded that the gifted blind child might benefit from schooling other than segregated boarding. In short, they shared the Board of Education's firm belief that segregated special schooling was the best road for most pupils to self-supporting independent living in the adult seeing world.

The Mentally Defective and Backward

In 1917, Marion Bridie, the Birmingham Assistant Superintendent of Special Schools, reflected various widespread views which were to be repeated in the Wood Report of 1929 and largely accepted by the Board of Education. There had been a rapid increase in the numbers of the feeble-minded, she reported:

> The preservation of life by higher medical skill has resulted in the survival of many unfit. Generations of neglect and sin have left their mark in the defective child of to-day, so frequently the offspring of defective parents. Intermarriages in country districts by healthy yeoman stock have left weaklings in the rural neighbourhoods; while the herding together in the unwholesome slums of cities is in a sense both the cause and the result of the present position.[50]

Thus the fears of the 1908 Royal Commission were still alive and echoed in other contemporary publications. But what was there to do about the problem? Permanent care might have been desirable in theory, but its cost in a period of repeated government financial crises as well as ethical considerations limited its use.

In 1919, Mary Dendy's Sandlebridge, with space for 200, only had 108 pupils. While some of the 18 residential special schools were full, others such as Pontville (over 40 vacancies) and Sandwell (over 80 vacancies) were clearly under-used.[51] Sandwell was to resign its Board of Education certificate in 1922. By 1929, however, the boarding schools were being fully used, but more to relieve poverty and other social problems rather than as a method of effecting permanent care. In 1929, the Wood Committee reported that perhaps 10 000 feeble-minded children were catered for in poor law establishments or boarded-out, while only 13 per cent of the low-grade feeble-minded were in Board of Control institutions. About 40 per cent remained at home receiving no education or training and 20 per cent went to ordinary schools.[52] Others were attending the growing number of day occupation centres, of which there were 111 by 1929, catering for 1200 children. Sterilization was also shunned as it tended to be in the USA, although many states had the power to use this measure.

Further doubts regarding permanent care arose as the dubious methodology used to produce 'family histories', which purportedly showed the venality and fecundity of the feeble-minded, came to be more widely realized. Tredgold's study of 150 families has already been mentioned (see p. 44). A reworking of Dugdale's 1877 study of the Jukes family by Estabrook in 1915, claimed half of the Jukes were feeble-minded and many of the latter were criminals. H.H. Goddard, in *The Kallikak Family* (1912), traced the family produced by a liaison between a soldier in the American Revolutionary Army and a supposedly feeble-minded tavern girl and found that only 46 out of 480 descendants were 'normal'. However, the soldier's later marriage to a respectable Quaker girl produced no feeble-minded in that or subsequent generations.[53] In 1908, Alfred Eicholz had not been convinced by claims such as these (see (p. 45), and both he and George Newman, at the Board of Education, were aware that although defective parents often had defective children, many feeble-minded children did not have defective parents. Furthermore, as Eicholz had known for many years, regression to the mean meant that the children of the defective were likely to be less handicapped. Cyril Burt's painstaking research into backwardness in London during the Great War,[54] confirmed by further work in Birmingham in 1920, further showed that the severe feeble-minded could rarely be blamed for crime and venality as formerly assumed;

however, the dull and backward could. These people, increasingly identified with an IQ in the range of 70–85, and constituting about 10 per cent of the population, were far too numerous to segregate in colonies as a preventive measure. Furthermore, Burt was firmly convinced that environmental factors such as bad housing and stressful impoverished life-styles were often the cause of educational backwardness and associated social problems.[55] So, in the inter-war years, the permanent care of the feeble-minded reduced in importance as the far greater problem of turning the dull and backward into useful members of society occupied educators' minds. However, the apparent increase in numbers of the mentally defective did worry both the Wood Committee and the Board.[56]

This was a period of uncertainty for schools for the mentally deficient. While some old buildings were replaced and smaller schools amalgamated, there was no significant growth (see Table 2). Dr Lewis, the investigator attached to the Wood Committee soon after its appointment in 1924, discovered that some special schools were only a half or even a third full, and that 69 per cent of the feeble-minded continued to attend elementary schools.[57] Nevertheless, their work, particularly their practical curriculum, was praised by Wood and a call made for more boarding schools to cater for social cases for whom fostering was felt to be unsuccessful and also for the rural mentally defective. However, it was realized that few parents would allow their higher-grade, well-adjusted children to board.

Contemporary sources including Burt, Bridie and Wood were also clearly impressed by many parents' hatred of the demand of the 1921 Act that the mentally defective should be certified as such by LEA medical officers. Explaining the special school vacancies, Wood records that many teachers and medical officers were loath to carry out their legal duties, only certifying the most clear-cut cases or the children who were most troublesome in class. Parental resistance to having their higher-grade mentally deficient children placed in special schools was heightened by the practice, continuing in some areas, of retaining low-grade defectives in the special schools rather than excluding them and referring them to the Board of Control.[58]

The 1929 Wood Report called for the abolition of the 'notorious' certificate. A new definition of the educationally defective, i.e. a wide group embracing both the old educable mental defectives and the backward, was suggested. Children possessing an IQ of under 50 were assumed to be 'ineducable' and should become the charges of the mental deficiency committees, although it was felt that many of these might learn social habits by staying in the ordinary schools. Higher-grades under 11 should certainly remain in public elementary schools, unless vicious or immoral, and could be taught without any serious inconvenience with children two or three years younger than themselves. These children would 'derive considerable benefit' from many junior department activities. However, when a child over 11 developed a growing consciousness of his own inferiority, he was better placed with children of his own age and ability.[59]

Large special schools were favoured in the cities, from which all low-grade children were excluded. Placement in such a school should be viewed 'not as something distinct and humiliating but as a helpful variation of the ordinary school',[60] and pupils would be stimulated by the chance of returning to the latter. In medium and small communities, however, these larger schools would be impracticable, and the existing one or two class wide-age range, segregated units were condemned. Far better were the practices already existing in many parts of the country, e.g. making special provisions within the ordinary schools by way of special departments with a modified curriculum, backward classes, withdrawal for individual tuition, and the formation of sub-groups within ordinary classes. The Committee saw the advantages of children continuing to mix with other children of average ability for the parts of the curriculum where special instruction was not required. In low population areas, peripatetic support might be given – an 'expedient which has been tried with marked success in one or two places'.[61]

Due largely to the government's acute financial problems, the Committee's recommendations did not result in legislation for many years but were echoed in the writings of the 1930s and in developments in the emerging secondary schools whose establishment had been encouraged by the 1926 Hadow Report.

In Scotland, special classes in ordinary schools for the mentally defective were nothing new. In 1938, a total of 43 ordinary schools contained such classes.[62] In 1932, the Glasgow special education lecturer, David Kennedy-Fraser, stated his preference for special departments for the retarded in large schools for children with IQs between 60 and 85:

> Wherever possible, the special classes for the backward should be kept in the same building as the ordinary classes. This facilitates the inconspicuous transfer of the children both into and out of the special class in a manner which would be impossible if it were in a different school or centre.[63]

Placement in the special class was often desirable to help backward children escape from the failure, discouragement and inappropriate curriculum they experienced in the ordinary classes. However, a few separate Scottish schools had been developed.

Back in England in 1934, Newman had to face up to increased uncertainty caused by the Wood Report's suggestions, though they were not followed up by the government. The Chief Medical Officer found it necessary to remind local medical officers that they still had a duty to ascertain the mentally defective, and, aware of the many vacancies, he talked of the 'mistaken idea that there is no longer any use for M.D. schools'.[64] Readers were reminded that the Wood Report had envisaged a broader role for such schools, perhaps with a new name, when some of the backward as well as the mentally defective might be placed in them. In the meantime, particularly in most areas where alternative arrangements in the ordinary schools did not exist, they should be filled, as nowhere was there over-provision. It seems that the Board was having to 'sell' a product whose value was doubted by many consumers. In 1938, there were 2854 vacancies in English and Welsh day schools for the mentally defective and 93 in the boarding schools.

Newman also commended the new practice started in 1934 of ordinary HMIs taking over the inspection of the educational aspects of their local day special schools from the Board's medical inspectors. This move reflected official recognition, already seen in the Wood Report, that special schools were often isolated, low-status places, staffed by teachers who lacked the professional identity of their mainstream colleagues. In a report of the Chief Medical Officer it was noted that in the past too many teachers and pupils in special schools had been regarded 'rather as outcasts from the school system'.[65] In 1938 Scotland followed suit.

In 1937, a number of people published their views on the education of the backward, including the Board of Education, C. Burt, F.J. Schonell and a Committee of London County Council inspectors. They clearly shared Wood's hatred of certification and saw the need for what Burt called 'intermediate' schools. Special classes in ordinary schools were also favoured, and the LCC inspectors found 51 out of 90 LEAs surveyed had responded to the CMO's repeated call and that of the Wood Committee for them. They were impressed by their success in aiding pupils' self-reliance, self-image, usefulness to the wider school community, better relations with staff, diminution of awkward behaviour and their 'remarkable progress especially in the school direction'. The LCC Committee recommended that 200 'experimental' classes should be formed in London's schools. Foreshadowing the 'unit approach' which was to become popular 40 years later, it suggested two, three or four classes in the chosen host schools.[66]

Alternatively, they suggested that larger post-Hadow secondary schools could be divided into A, B and C streams with the backward receiving an appropriate curriculum in the C stream. This 'treble-track' system was also favoured by Burt,[67] who urged the rapid segregation of the backward into special classes to free them from the confidence-sapping failure of placement in ordinary classes where such children tended to slip into truancy and criminality and where the teacher found it very difficult to meet the demands of wide mixed-ability groupings.

Schonell argued along similar lines. In a comment which suggested that leading educators' views did not mirror those of many ordinary teachers on streaming or special schools, he complained of headteachers who disapproved of any segregation and allowed the backward to 'drag along at the bottom of a class'. Elsewhere he defended the special class against charges current at this time that placement in them meant stigma and isolation. Where this did happen he blamed it on poor organization and teaching.[68]

The Board of Education agreed with Burt's and Schonell's views. To avoid the creation of isolated 'sink' classes, they emphasized the need to keep backward children involved in the mainstream of the school. Such mixing with the more intelligent was held to be a realistic and necessary preparation for adulthood: they should have a chance 'of sharing with them such work and pleasure as all children enjoy just because they are children of the human race'.[69]

This reference to the human rights of the handicapped is not unique during this period. The Wood Committee had wanted the school leaving age for the mental defectives lowered from 16 for similar reasons. Newman had also referred to the rights of the least able to a full education even if this was not of economic use to the nation. In America, where partly integrated special classes grew from 133 in 1922 to 483 in 1932,[70] a Californian administrator told of backward children 'not getting the education to which all the children of all the people are entitled'.[71] To meet these rights, the special class was deemed necessary to free the backward child from the neglect and failure he endured if left in an ordinary class. Contemporary American concerns and views were similar to the British ones described above.

The Maladjusted and Child Guidance

The Mental Deficiency Act of 1913 talked of 'moral imbeciles' with permanent mental defect, vicious or criminal propensities, on whom punishment had little or no deterrent effect. The successor Act of 1927 revised the title to 'moral defective'. In 1917 Burt preferred to talk of the 'unstable',[72] but by 1931 the Board's Medical Officers could allude to the 'group of children who present disorders in behaviour, the so-called "maladjusted child" '.[73] It was noted that their needs were slowly being recognized and help was given to them by the early child guidance clinics. In 1929, their treatment was facilitated when the Board of Education, by placing wide interpretation on Section 80 of the 1921 Education Act, allowed financial assistance for the payment of boarding fees. This required LEAs to attend to the health of the schoolchild. Mental as well as physical health was now deemed to fall within its ambit.[74]

Meanwhile, the phrase 'street arab' lost ground and the industrial schools were used less frequently. In Scotland, enrolments in residential industrial schools fell from 2994 in 1921 to 1479 in 1929,[75] while in London, falling juvenile crime and the expanded use of probation helped reduce placements from a peak of 3600 in 1918, to under 1000 in 1927.[76] School dinners and the school medical service, allied to generally improving social conditions, led to the demise of the day industrial school. In 1930 the last day schools closed in Scotland and soon afterwards those in England followed. The remaining residential schools which had survived years of official doubts about boarding and attacks on their practices became Home Office Approved Schools after 1933.

The disturbed child who truanted or showed behaviour problems or was on the fringes of delinquency might by 1930 receive help from the early child guidance clinics. Voluntary psychological 'laboratories', often attached to universities, had been carrying on small-scale work since before the Great War. Cyril Burt had run a small clinic in Liverpool before becoming England's and London's first LEA psychologist in 1913, a post he was to hold until 1931. In the late 1920s, pioneer clinics developed in Glasgow, Leicester, Bath, Liverpool, Oxford and London. In 1931, the term 'child guidance clinic' was used by the Notre Dame Clinic, which was founded with the help of American funds in Glasgow. It employed a psychiatrist, a psychologist and a social worker – the staffing pattern followed by most later establishments. The first LEA clinic commenced in Birmingham in 1932. In 1937, Glasgow LEA established the first full-time clinic. By 1939 there were 22 LEA clinics in England and 10 LEAs employing psychologists. By 1938 there were 11 Scottish clinics, 10 of them voluntary.[77]

Some maladjusted children were placed in open-air schools or the few experimental classes for difficult children such as that founded in Oxford in 1930. The latter developed into England's second day school for the maladjusted in 1939. The first had been Leicester's Haddenham Road Experimental School, started in 1932.[78] Such schools were directed by psychologists and teachers, and used social workers to investigate the home conditions which were thought to give rise to the children's difficulties. The Board of Education approved of these schools but warned that success depended on early reintegration.[79]

This assertion might have been challenged by the managers of the boarding industrial schools. In 1929, a LCC publication told of the success of the leavers from the London industrial schools who entered the army or trades or were helped to emigrate and were encouraged not to return to their home communities. It would also have been challenged by the few pioneers running independent boarding schools for the maladjusted. Here again, pupils would be encouraged to stay for many years and the goal of adult integration was pursued with apparent success.

The pioneers included F.H. Dodd's small boarding school in Blackheath, London, founded in 1920; George Lyward's Finchden Manor (1930) and Otto Shaw's Red Hill School, Kent (1934). In the latter school, psychoanalysis was used as an important means of therapy. In 1924, A.S. Neill had found that for his new progressive school to survive at Summerhill, Lyme Regis, he had to admit many maladjusted children. In 1927, the school moved to Suffolk. He had visited Homer Lane's Little Commonwealth in 1916, and had taught Lane's son and was apparently influenced by his approach. In the north, in 1935, the psychiatrist Dr Alfred Fitch, having helped to develop a child guidance clinic in Liverpool, founded Dunmow Hall (which evolved into Breckenbrough School) on the Yorkshire/Lancashire border. A few LEAs including Kent and St Helens used Section 80 of the 1921 Education Act to pay for children to attend these schools.[80] In 1940, Glasgow Child Guidance Service used Nerston Home as a residential school for the maladjusted.

By the outbreak of the Second World War awareness of the maladjusted was quite widespread. The seeming success of the pioneer residential establishments, when added to the boarding experience of evacuees during the War, set the stage for the expansion of boarding for the maladjusted, where the adult integration of their pupils tended to be the aim, after the 1944 Act officially recognized their special needs.

Summary

This was a period of acute financial problems for the government which hampered the development of special education and led senior officials at the Board of Education to draw up a list of priorities at the head of which was the education of the deaf and blind, and at the bottom was help for lower-grade mental defectives.[81] For the severe cases of all categories of handicap it was increasingly accepted that education in a carefully classified special school where trade-training or preparation for higher education was given was the best way of helping these children to the desired goal of adult integration. For logistic reasons this necessitated boarding. Conversely, for less severe cases, such as the partially blind and deaf, a degree of childhood integration was actively pursued in major reports and sometimes practised. Scientific advances, for instance the development of hearing aids, helped to facilitate this policy. Similarly for many physically handicapped, the preferred model was treatment and cure in a hospital school, sanatorium, school for the physically defective or open air school, then reintegration into the public elementary schools, or, in the 1930s, after the Hadow Report, the emerging secondary schools. Many epileptic children remained in the ordinary schools, but long waiting lists remained for the special residential establishments and some severe cases received no education.

While low-grade mental defectives should be excluded from schools, and the moderately feeble-minded placed in the schools for the mentally deficient, for the far greater number of backward children, special departments or classes in ordinary schools or in larger day schools closely related to the ordinary schools were advocated. Such arrangements would enable these children to escape from the confidence-sapping failure they endured in the ordinary schools where curricula were unsuitable and class sizes very large. Meanwhile, the existing schools for the mentally deficient attracted stigma and were sometimes under-used, partly because doctors and parents were loath for low-grade children to be excluded from them. This had the knock-on effect of making parents and teachers of the less handicapped feeble-minded reluctant to mix the latter with the low-grade children. Further, the certification process required by the 1921 Act was much hated by parents and often avoided by educators.

The needs of the maladjusted were starting to be recognized and the first LEA child guidance clinics were founded in the hope that such children could be helped in their local areas and kept within the ordinary education system. Failing that, placement in one of the few pioneer independent boarding schools might be possible. Section 80 of the 1921 Education Act allowed LEAs to pay the fees for these children. In Leicester, from 1932, a few children were able to stay at home and attend the country's first day school for the maladjusted. Meanwhile, the day industrial schools closed and the boarding schools were absorbed into the new Home Office Approved Schools in 1933.

Early in the Second World War, the few remaining integrated blind children in Glasgow were moved to a residential school. In a way, this was a fitting symbolic end to this period in which a continuing, wide-spread desire for the integration of children – even the severely handicapped – came increasingly to be subservient to an awareness of the practical difficulties of delivering efficient special education without congregating the handicapped into segregated schools.

Notes

1. *Report for 1923 of CMO of the Board of Education*, HMSO, London, 1924, p.67.
2. *Report of the Committee of Inquiry into Problems relating to Partially Sighted Children* (Crowley Report), HMSO, London, 1934, p.123.
3. *Report of the Mental Deficiency Committee* (Wood Report), HMSO, London, 1929.
4. Board of Education, *Report and Statistics for 1920–1*, HMSO, London, 1922, pp.16–18; Board of Education, *Education in 1938*, HMSO, 1939, p.93.
5. J.S. Hurt, *Outside the Mainstream*, Batsford, London, 1988, pp.165–6.
6. *Report for 1932 of CMO of the Board of Education*, HMSO, London, 1933, ch. VI.
7. *Report for 1918 of CMO of the Board of Education*, HMSO, London, 1919, pp.112–14.
8. *Report of the Committee of Council on Education in Scotland for year 1938*, HMSO, London, 1939.
9. Op. cit., note 1, p.64.
10. *Report for 1930 of CMO of the Board of Education*, HMSO, London, 1931, pp.57–60.
11. LCC, *The Special Services of Education in London*, Hodder and Stoughton, London, 1929, p.98.
12. *Report for 1925 of CMO of the Board of Education*, HMSO, London, 1926, pp.68–9.
13. *Report for 1926 of CMO of the Board of Education*, HMSO, London, 1927, pp.140–4.
14. *Report for 1919 of CMO of the Board of Education*, HMSO, London, 1920, pp.108–20.
15. M.E. Frampton and H.G. Rowell, *Education of the Handicapped*, World Book Co., New York, 1938, vol. 1, pp.137–9.
16. *Teacher of the Deaf*, vol. XX, pp.119 and 125–7.
17. *Teacher of the Deaf*, vol. XIX, p.5.
18. *British Deaf Times*, vol. XVII, 1920, p.80.
19. *British Deaf Times*, vol. XXXV, 1938, p.80.
20. *Teacher of the Deaf*, vol. XX, p.94.
21. Op. cit., note 7, p.108; A. Eicholz, *A Study of the Deaf in England and Wales, 1930 to 1932*, HMSO, London, p.188.
22. *Report of the Committee of Council on Education in Scotland for 1930/1*, HMSO, Edinburgh, 1931, p.31.
23. A. Eicholz, op. cit., note 21, p.17.
24. M.C. McLoughlin, *A History of the Education of the Deaf in England* (published privately), McLoughlin, Liverpool, 1987, p.31.
25. A.W.G. Ewing, 'History of the Department of Education of the Deaf, University of Manchester, 1919–55', *British Journal of Educational Studies*, May 1956.
26. *British Deaf Times*, vol. XVII, 1920, p.74.
27. A. Eicholz, op. cit., note 21.
28. Ibid., p.86.

29. Ibid., p.37.
30. *Teacher of the Deaf*, vol. XXXI, 1933, p.121.
31. Board of Education, *Report of the Committee of Inquiry into Problems Relating to Children with Defective Hearing* (Glover Report), HMSO, London, p.51.
32. Ibid., p.61.
33. *British Deaf Times*, vol. XXX, February 1933.
34. Annual Reports of the CMO and Reports of the Committee of Council on Education in Scotland; CTB/NIB, *Education of the Blind* (Ritchie Report), Arnold, London, 1936.
35. H. Best, *The Blind*, Macmillan, New York, p.308.
36. *Report of the Departmental Committee on the Welfare of the Blind*, HMSO, London, 1917.
37. Op. cit., note 12, pp.45–6.
38. H.J. Wagg, *A Chronological Survey of Work for the Blind*, Pitman, London, 1930; J.M. Ritchie, *Concerning the Blind*, Oliver and Boyd, Edinburgh, 1930. It is mentioned in the Ritchie Report.
39. Glasgow Corporation, *Report on the Work of the Education Committee, 1939–48*, pp.44–5.
40. Op. cit., note 7, pp.144–5.
41. Op. cit., note 2, pp.11–12 and 47.
42. R.V. Merry, *Problems in the Education of Visually Handicapped Children*, Harvard University Press, Cambridge, Mass., 1933, p.85.
43. Op. cit., note 2, pp.64–5. Evans became an MP and spokesman for the handicapped after the war.
44. Op. cit., note 42, p.73.
45. Op. cit., note 2, p.49.
46. Ritchie Report, op. cit., note 34, p.223.
47. Ibid., p.224–5.
48. S.O. Myers, *Where Are They Now?* RNIB, London, 1975, pp.4–6.
49. Ritchie Report, op. cit., note 34, p.12.
50. M.F. Bridie, *An Introduction to Special School Work*, Arnold, London, 1917, pp.4–5.
51. Op. cit., note 7, p.109.
52. Op. cit., note 5, pp.162–3.
53. Ibid., pp.140–1.
54. C. Burt, *The Distribution and Relations of Educational Abilities*, LCC, London, 1917.
55. C. Burt, *The Backward Child*, 3rd edn, University of London Press, London, 1950, pp.118 and 124–5.
56. *Report for 1929 of CMO of the Board of Education*, HMSO, London, pp.96–107.
57. Op. cit., note 3, p.85.
58. Ibid., pp.43 and 116–17.
59. Ibid., pp.100–1.
60. Ibid., pp.116–17 and 133.
61. Ibid., p.134.
62. Op. cit., note 8, p.40.

63. D. Kennedy-Fraser, *Education of the Backward Child*, University of London Press, London, 1932, p.64.
64. *Report for 1933 of CMO of the Board of Education*, HMSO, London, p.143.
65. Ibid., p.145.
66. LCC, *Report of a Committee of Inspectors on Backwardness in Elementary Schools*, London County Council, London, July 1937.
67. Op. cit., note 55.
68. University of London Institute of Education, *The Education of Backward Children*, Institute of Education, London, 1937, p.26.
69. Board of Education, *The Education of Backward Children*, pamphlet 112, HMSO, London, 1937, p.31.
70. Op. cit., note 15, p.187.
71. H.B. Wilson, 'Introduction' to A.D. Inskeep, *Teaching Dull and Retarded Children*, Macmillan, New York, 1926, pp.x–xi.
72. Op. cit., note 54, p.40.
73. Op. cit., note 10, p.64.
74. M. Bridgeland, *Pioneer Work with Maladjusted Children*, Staples, London, 1971, p.149.
75. *Report of Committee of Council on Education in Scotland for Year 1929*, HMSO, Edinburgh, 1930, p.27.
76. Op. cit., note 11, p.122.
77. Op. cit., note 10, pp.66–8; D. Pritchard, *Education and the Handicapped*, Routledge and Kegan Paul, London, 1963, p. 194; op. cit., note 8, p.41.
78. Op. cit., note 74, pp.297–8.
79. Op. cit., note 69, p.57.
80. Op. cit., note 74, pp.135–83.
81. Op. cit., note 5, p.155.

CHAPTER 5

From Butler to Circular 10/65: 1939–65

Political and Educational Summary: 1939–65

Major Events and Ordinary Education		*Special Education*	
1939	Second World War starts: Chamberlain PM	1939–45	War-time disruption, evacuation, etc.; greater use of boarding for children difficult to billet
1940	*Churchill* leads Coalition government	1940	German measles epidemic increases number of deaf babies
1941	Board of Education 'Green Book' on educational reform circulated to canvass ideas		
1943	Norwood Report favours tripartite secondary education (grammar, technical and 'modern')		
1944	Butler Education Act creates primary, secondary and further education model; condemns all-age schools (some linger on until 1960s); leaving age raised to 15 (effected in 1947); Min. of Ed. born; allows multilateral and comprehensive schools.	1944	Education Act requires education according to age, aptitude and ability; special educational treatment can take place in ordinary as well as special schools

		1945	Special education regulations name 11 categories of need; certification and mentally defective label abolished (replaced by ESN category); schools encouraged for part hearing and part sighted; maladjusted recognized
1945	After VE Day, *Attlee's* Labour government returned	1945	Mary Hare Grammar School for Deaf founded
		1946	Min. of Ed.'s Pamphlet no.5 published
		1947	St Margaret's School for cerebral palsied opened
		1947	Over 60 per cent of children ascertained as needing special educational treatment are placed in ordinary schools
		1947	Over 40 000 in English and Welsh special schools
		1947	LCC opens first unit for partially deaf
1947	London plan favours creation of some comprehensives	1947	Moor House School, Oxted, for speech defects opens
Late		Late	
1940s	Nationalization, NHS created, austerity	1940s	Rise in number of blind babies due to retrolental fibroplasia (excessive oxygen given to premature babies)
		1948	RNIB's Condover Hall opens for multi-handicapped blind
		1949	Nat. Assoc. for Educ. of Part. Sighted founded
1950	*Attlee* wins election with reduced majority	1950	London's first tutorial class for maladjusted
1951	GCE exams start	1951	Exhall Grange School for partially sighted opens
1951	*Churchill* (Conservative) returns to power in October	1950–52	Various Advisory Council reports on special education for Scottish Education Department

1953	Anglesey introduces comprehensive secondary schooling but insists on careful streaming	1953	Special Education regulations revised
		1954	Chief Medical Officer in annual report calls for more integration
1954	LCC opens Kidbrooke Comprehensive	1954	Special Education Treatment (Scotland) Regulations
		1954	LCC's first day school for maladjusted opens
1955	*Eden* (Conservative) becomes PM and wins May election	1955	Underwood Report highlights unmet needs of maladjusted; wants comprehensive child guidance service
		1955	Unit for partially deaf opens in day school at Reading
		1955	Over 50 000 children in English and Welsh special schools; nearly 19 000 (two-thirds ESN) on waiting lists
1956	Suez Crisis	1956	Grammar dept for PH boys starts at Lord Mayor Treloar's
		1956	RNIB opens Hethersett College for further education
1957	*Macmillan* becomes PM in January	1957	Units for partially deaf open in Manchester
1950s	Labour leaders defend grammar schools but support growing for comprehensives as doubts grow on validity of IQ testing and 11+ selection	1959	Special education regulations revised
		1959	Mental Health Act urges community care of mentally handicapped; encourages day training centres
1950s–60s	Population boom and teacher shortages	1950s–60s	Rapid growth in day special schools for ESN; some growth in day and boarding schools for maladjusted
1959	Crowther Report wants school leaving age raised		
1959	*Macmillan* wins large majority		
1960	Robbins Committee says IQ depends to significant extent on previous experience	Late 1950s	Decline in schools for the delicate

1960	Beloe Report recommends CSE (starts 1965)	1962	National Soc. for Autistic Children founded
1963	H. Wilson leader of Labour on Gaitskell's death	1962	First blind resident from St Vincent's School, Liverpool, attends local grammar school
1963	Robbins Report pushes expansion of higher education; leads to opening of new universities	1963	D. Pritchard's *Education and the Handicapped* tells of poor provision for special needs in ordinary schools
1963	Newsom Report concerned with untapped talent in under-resourced secondary modern schools; wants ROSLA and better curricula for less able		
1963	*Douglas Home* PM when ill-health forces Macmillan's resignation		
1964	*Wilson* (Labour) becomes PM		
1964	Schools Council founded		
1965	Circular 10/65 asks all unreorganized LEAs to submit plans for 'comprehensivization'	1965	First British school for autistic children (Ealing)
		1965	Over 70 000 children in English and Welsh special schools; over 13 000 (mainly ESN) on waiting lists; nearly 11 000 in Scottish special schools and classes

Before the bomb fell on Hiroshima the nation had voted in Attlee's government. Within a few years, Labour ministers had created the National Health Service and other aspects of the Welfare State, as well as nationalizing major industries. It was also a time of food rationing and the austerity which contributed to the return of the Conservatives under Churchill and Eden in the 1950s. In this period Britain struggled in an ever-more competitive world, yet workers were winning pay awards which the country could ill-afford and management was failing to cope with modern conditions. But, for a time, the nation's credit was good. Consumer spending boomed, the population expanded and expectations of the educational service, in part fuelled by the 1944 Butler

Act, grew. Macmillan told the voters of 1959, 'you've never had it so good', but soon there were balance of payments problems, record unemployment in 1963, the Profumo imbroglio and an ailing leader who was briefly replaced by Lord Home as Premier. The 1964 election saw the return of Labour to power and Harold Wilson promising a state-led technological revolution in a more socialist society.

Until near the end of this period the Labour leadership continued to favour grammar schools. However, in 1965, sounding the symbolic death knell of the classification and scientific selection which dominated post-war thinking for both ordinary and special education, the Secretary of State for Education, Anthony Crosland, issued Circular 10/65.[1] This asked LEAs who had not started to reorganize, to submit plans for the combining of grammar and secondary modern schools into comprehensives. A logical extension of schools for all was the halting of the development of separate special schools which had continued apace in the wake of the 1944 Education Act. However, although the intellectual zenith of the separate special school may have been reached, growth of separate provision was not to cease as dissatisfaction with provision for the backward and maladjusted in ordinary schools continued to override other considerations. However, for the sensory and physical handicapped pressure for integration grew.

The Ministry View

The Second World War brought widespread disruption to special schooling in many parts of the country. To avoid the blitz many schools were evacuated to country mansions or seaside hotels. This experience showed government the practical value of boarding while not erasing a genuine desire to see special help given to more handicapped children purposely left in the ordinary schools. Despite the war, R.A.B. Butler's Education Bill was prepared and passed in 1944. The Act decreed that all children except the severely handicapped deemed 'ineducable' under Section 57, were to receive an education suited to their age, aptitude and ability. Primary education was to be followed by secondary education starting at age 11 in either grammar, technical or secondary modern schools for the vast majority; for some, however, where the local LEA saw fit, education was to be continued in multilateral schools. For a small minority whose placement was to be decided by the LEA rather than by its medical officers, an expanded system of special schooling would be needed.

However, far more children, all of whom had to be identified by the LEAs under Section 34, would need 'special educational treatment'. Under Section 33, LEAs had to see that severe cases received appropriate help in special schools, but where this was impracticable or where the disability was less serious, 'in any school maintained or assisted by the local education authority'.[2] This reversed the 1921 Act's stipulation that special education was to take place in special schools. The stigmatizing 'certificate' which had drawn such an arbitrary line between the official handicapped and the normal was abolished along with the label 'defective'. A continuum of need was thus recognized which logically required close cooperation between special schools and ordinary schools and the inclusion of special schools within the mainstream of education. However, most contemporaries complained that this close relationship could not be achieved and, therefore, special education continued to be viewed in terms of special school provision.

Also under Section 33, the new Ministry of Education drew up an expanded list of 11 categories of handicap which reflected the views of the pre-war reports, in particular the need for a more exact classification to ensure greater efficiency of education and the enhancement of the prospects of special school leavers for adult integration. The blind were to be split from the partially sighted, the deaf from the partially deaf and the delicate from the physically handicapped; the epileptics remained as a separate group. Provision was also to be made for the maladjusted, children with speech defects and diabetics, who, following the discovery of insulin in 1922, could now survive into old age. Largely following the Wood Report, the mental defective label was replaced with the new category of educationally sub-normal (ESN). This broad category was to include both the few children with innate low intelligence (usually taken to mean an intelligence quotient in the range 50/55–70) and the greater number of backward and dull children thought to number about 10 per cent of the school population. In 1946, a Ministry pamphlet indicated that the first group – with low IQs – should attend the new ESN schools, rather than the relatively brighter 'remedial' children.[3]

The few children with IQs of 50 or less were to be deemed ineducable and excluded from local authority schools. This position was made tenable at this time by the widespread faith in the intelligence test as a culture- and environment-free method of ascertaining a child's innate and largely immutable level of ability. It took a further 25 years' experience and research to show that IQs could be affected and could change – rarely in dramatic fashion, but enough to blur the line between so-called educability and non-educability. In this quarter century, the hatred that parents of the mentally handicapped felt for Section 57 of the 1944 Act, also became apparent. Increasingly, researchers, for example Williams and Gruber in the 1960s, were to question the validity of and the need for the concept of educability.[4]

The views of the Ministry were more fully aired in the 1946 pamphlet

Special Educational Treatment. This was a mixture of segregationist and integrationist opinion. For the benefit of the non-handicapped, epileptics were to be allowed to continue in ordinary schools only if they were not a nuisance to others. The ineducable who were said to have 'undesirable social and personal characteristics' and to take up 'an undue share of the teacher's time and energy' were not to be allowed to remain in either ordinary or special schools. In part, this was an attempt to rid the new ESN schools of the stigma attached to the old schools for mentally defectives (see p. 85). Further, openly stating a social control motive, the Ministry stated that the placing of ESNs in their own day schools was a way of relieving the ordinary schools of some difficult children. However, segregation was also required for the good of many of these handicapped children themselves (see p. 104).[5]

Children with less serious physical handicaps or diabetes were to remain where possible in the ordinary schools. Similarly, community care approaches should first be tried for the maladjusted (see p. 109). However, for the more disturbed who were thought not to benefit from · mixing with ordinary children, or those from families under stress, residential schools were encouraged. Boarding, preferably interspersed with half-terms and weekends, seemed a pragmatic way of meeting the demands of the 1944 Act. Between 1945 and 1955, 182 special boarding schools were opened. The Ministry later called this the 'country house period'.[6]

However, by the mid-1950s, attention switched to day schools for the ESN. These were nearer to the integrationist leanings of some influential officials at the Ministry which surfaced in the Chief Medical Officer's Report for 1952 and 1953. In response to persisting tendencies to see special education in terms of what happened in special schools, a whole chapter was devoted to handicapped children in ordinary schools. That a child:

> has a mental or physical handicap does not necessarily involve his withdrawal from a normal environment but, if he has to be withdrawn at all, that withdrawal should not be further or greater than his condition demands. Handicapped children have a deep longing to achieve as much independence as possible within the normal community instead of being surrounded by an atmosphere of disability.[7]

A child should only be removed from his home if there was no practicable alternative.

The Ministry's medical officers were influenced by reports of successful integration of children with different handicaps. They also knew that many parents were strongly opposed to special schooling and to boarding education in particular. Where low rates of incidence existed, partial integration in special classes in ordinary day schools was thought preferable to the small one- or two-class segregated special schools. The medical officers' view was expressed in Circular 276, sent to all LEAs in the summer of 1954, and the 1956 Pamphlet (no. 30).[8] The reports of the Chief Medical Officer in the decade 1955–65 were to tell of the spread of not only special schools (see Table 3) but also the growth of special education in ordinary schools. Statistics showing the latter are hard to come by because the Ministry stopped recording them in response to the integrated handicapped's wish not to be labelled or included in returns. In 1947, before this happened, while 109 272 children were identified as needing special educational treatment, only 40 252 or about 37 per cent of children were in fact in English and Welsh special schools.[9] This percentage reflects, in part, the desire for the integration of the physically handicapped and less severe cases in all categories; however, had more special school places been available it seems probable that they would have been filled immediately.

Table 3 English and Welsh maintained and non-maintained special schools and numbers of pupils for 1947, 1955 and 1965

	No. of schools			*No. of pupils*		
	1947	*1955*	*1965*	*1947*	*1955*	*1965*
Blind	16	22	18	802	1086	1111
Part. sighted	32	27	23	1094	1592	1516
Blind and part. sighted	10	3	2	570	252	231
Deaf	9	14	19	873	1196	1452
Part. deaf	—	4	5	—	418	521
Deaf and part. deaf	34	31	24	2666	3592	2608
Phys. handicap	170	73	82	11 230	4840	4502
Delicate	95	101	75	7544	8898	6708
Phys. handicap and delicate	21	45	52	2097	4789	4486
Delicate and malad.	1	3	2	112	297	209
ESN	135	256	410	12 060	22 639	42 804
Epileptic	6	8	6	563	770	623
Maladjusted	5	33	68	139	1136	2316
Others	3	1	3	502	53	247
Total	537	621	789	40 252	51 558	70 334
Schools with boarding	248	302	336			
Day schools	289	321	454			

Sources: Reports of the Ministry of Education for 1947, Table 72 and 1955, Table 47; DES, *Statistics of Education for 1965*, Table 31. Hospital schools are not included.

Table 3 shows that the Ministry's policies did work to a certain extent. The blind were increasingly split from the partially sighted and, to a lesser extent, the deaf from the partially hearing. Some blind schools were closed and pupils concentrated into larger units enabling better classification. In response to the demands of the 1944 Act and wider ascertainment, there was rapid growth in provision for the ESN although long waiting lists remained. There was also some growth in provision for the maladjusted. Only in the physically handicapped and delicate categories was there a significant fall in the number of pupils. A decline in numbers by nearly 25 per cent is in part explained by better prevention and treatment, but it could also be caused by the more widespread integration of these children in ordinary schools.

In Scotland, now governed by acts passed in 1945 and 1946, the number of physically handicapped in special schools and classes fell dramatically – by almost 70 per cent between 1946 and 1965. Numbers also declined in schools and classes for the deaf, partially deaf, blind and partially blind. A lower incidence of these handicaps was a major factor, but there was continuing support for integration. For those without profound handicaps, this found some expression in the various reports of the Advisory Council on Education in Scotland. In 1955, the Secretary of State issued Circular 300, reviewing these reports. His desire for increasing integration was clear. He noted the international trend towards it and hoped that as medical knowledge and school conditions improved this would be reflected in Scotland.[10] The declining use of special schooling is hidden in official statistics by the increasing number of severely mentally handicapped children attending occupational centres which, unlike in England, were run by the education authorities. The total number of children in special schools and classes were a little under 11 000 in both 1946–7 and 1965.[11]

Educationally Sub-normal Children and the Ineducable

Mary Frances Cleugh spoke for most of her contemporaries when, in 1957, she wrote: 'Were the ordinary education more suitable ... there would be less need of special educational treatment.' Using an argument which attracted much attention 20 or so years later, she continued: 'More lasting good can be achieved for more children by improving the ordinary arrangements than by special measures which are of their nature limited.'[12] Unfortunately, because the necessary improvements were not likely to be implemented in either the short or medium term, given the organization and aims of ordinary schools and the attitudes of many teachers, more special schools were demanded.

The 1945 Regulations had defined the new category of ESN as 'pupils who, by reason of limited ability or other conditions resulting in educational retardation, require some specialised form of education wholly or partly in substitution for the education normally given in ordinary schools'.[13] This description did seem to bring the education of the backward more within the mainstream, but there remained a gulf between government decree and contemporary teacher attitudes. Teachers of the ESN still felt isolated and their work undervalued or dismissed by colleagues teaching children of normal ability. Some still saw special education as a waste of time and resources. To convince these people, there are recurring allusions in contemporary literature to the pragmatic argument of freeing the ordinary child from the burden of having the backward in the same class and taking an unfair proportion of the teacher's time. In addition, doubters were reminded of society's moral duties and it was stressed that society would be saved a lot of trouble if backward children were properly prepared for adult life.

Government and most educators believed that the ESN suffered socially and educationally in overcrowded and understaffed schools, where teaching was geared to academic success – even in the new secondary modern schools. In these, the needs of the C streams were neglected, thus frustrating the hopes of the pre-war commentators (see p. 87). Slow learners were forced to follow the traditional subject timetable – and even in some special classes, a watered-down version of this – often with dire results. Other special classes, under the least experienced teachers, were used as 'dumping grounds' for the awkward and undesirable, with little thought for the children's own needs. Even worse, a 1956 survey found that 31 per cent of 119 LEAs, usually the rural authorities, still made no special provision for the ESN at all.[14]

References to the failure and frustrations of the ESN left in this situation occur repeatedly. In 1946 the Ministry was aware of the restlessness and boredom of the backward forced to follow an abstract curriculum and their feelings of failure when competing with their brighter peers.[15] In 1951, the Scottish Advisory Council talked of a 'ruthless unconcern' for the less able. For the retarded, 'it is a mortifying and hurtful experience for children to be perpetual failures'. Failure in a subject meant a child often developed a sense of 'crippling inability which magnifies the task of recovery' and can spread to other spheres of school-life.[16] The Chief Medical Officer referred to the damaging experience of failure in his annual report for the same year.[17] Later in the decade, M.F. Cleugh referred to the problem and quoted a United States source: 'A child cannot be more cruelly segregated than to be placed in a room where his failures separate him from other children who are experiencing success.'[18] This conclusion was confirmed by the research of another American, G.O. Johnson, who found that the retarded in the regular grade classes were isolated and rejected, experienced repeated failure, and were made to repeat grades.[19] His findings were to reach most English university libraries.

In England, Tansley and Gulliford, writing in 1959, worried about children who 'drag along year by year, unable to keep up with the rest of the class, worried and unhappy about their failure'.[20] In 1964 the new Department of Education and Science (DES) said of the slow learner following the ordinary timetable:

> His failures are exposed many times a day. In such a situation his self-respect is undermined and he quickly loses heart, so that the way is wide open for the development of anti-social conduct.[21]

In the long term it was thought that it might be possible to discard the examination-ridden, competitive ethos pervading most schools, but until that happened there was urgent need for more special classes in ordinary schools and as many special schools as possible.

Most commentators wanted special classes in the ordinary schools to cater for children with IQs over 70 who were retarded for environmental reasons. With an experienced and preferably well-trained teacher, working in a school with a welcoming Head and understanding staff, the special class could work well. In 1956, the London educational psychologist, H.A.T. Child, claimed such a class aided a boy's reading development but more importantly:

> the improvement in cheerfulness, self-confidence and responsiveness is often startling. Whether he is really going to be a reader in adult life or not, the fact that the class enables a child to return to full-time ordinary schooling with the feeling that he is like the other children, and not something inferior, may be the crucial thing.[22]

Reintegration was the definite aim in the best classes. In 1958, Mrs Vaughan, a special class teacher, claimed that over a four-year period, 103 of 154 leavers from her group returned to normal classwork in her junior school.[23] For those in special classes, partial integration through sharing non-academic, extra-curricular activities and mixing with ordinary children out of class were encouraged to lessen any feelings of stigma that might be experienced. This was also the general view in America, where such classes grew substantially. In 1951, Kirk and Johnson believed that the separate special school was 'on its way out. Such schools have usually been stigmatized as "dummy schools".'[24]

In England, however, while many educators shared these concerns, they felt that on balance the separate school was preferable, enabling better classification and the creation of an appropriate ethos, particularly for children with IQs of under 70 who needed protection from the imperfections of the ordinary schools described above. In 1953, James Lumsden, H.M. Staff Inspector, said the Ministry wanted the majority of ESN properly catered for in ordinary schools, but for some children 'so low in ability, so much out of step in educational progress and power to mix freely with others, so utterly convinced of their failure to learn, that they require the specialised atmosphere and life as well as teaching of the special school'.[25]

As this period progressed, it became clear to the Chief Medical Officer and various writers, including Cleugh and David Pritchard,[26] that perhaps a third of the children being placed in the ESN schools were often not very low in ability. As a result, there was often no room for some children with IQs under 70. The spaces had been taken up by children in the low-average range of intelligence who had fallen behind in class or perhaps been a nuisance in the ordinary schools. In the early 1960s, research in South Wales by Phillip Williams and Elisabeth Gruber supported this view.[27] Their work also suggested that brighter 'environmentally' handicapped children usually made much better educational progress than the less-able 'organically' handicapped – often in South Wales at least – leading to the successful reintegration into mainstream schools of the brighter children.

In response to the obvious demand, Circular 11/61 of the Ministry of Education called for the number of places in schools for the ESN to be increased to 54 000. This, it was hoped, would clear the long waiting lists. This call was met by quick action. In 1962–3 alone, 52 new day schools opened. In 1964, the DES still felt that inappropriate conditions remained in many ordinary schools for backward children, and new day schools continued to be opened until the 1970s.[28]

In keeping with the still prevalent view, these were usually built on sites away from the local secondary schools. In 1947, London County Council strongly pushed this policy, and presented its vision of the education of the future. In pamphlets produced for parents and ratepayers, diagrams were printed of a hypothetical 'community area in London'. One was entitled 'As it is', in which the old elementary school and school for the mentally defective shared a site, and the other 'As it will be', in which a newly built special school occupied its own site. In the artists' dreamy impressions which accompany the diagrams, the special school is divided from the primary school and new concrete comprehensive by box-like estates of flat-roofed houses.[29] Ten years later Cleugh also came down in favour of the separate-site special school. She attacked on-site but separate special units, operating different timetables and playtimes.[30] However, this was a view that was not universally held.

Cleugh did not believe that placement in a separate special school heightened the stigma attached to the child. She complained of the 'pious nonsense' which surrounded this subject:

Many of the things that are sometimes said about labelling children can apply with equal effect not only to a special class, but also to C streams, coaching groups, E.S.N. schools, clinic visits, remedial teaching – in short to any and every attempt to provide special help for children who need it. Furthermore, if in fact these children *are* different, it does not help matters to shut our eyes to this and refuse to recognise it.[31]

Her comments suggest that many disagreed with her and the Chief Medical Officer in 1962 and the DES in 1964 complained that some teachers were still not bringing forward slow learners for ascertainment probably because of the attached stigma.[32] Frequent brief references are made to parental objections to the placement of their children in special schools or classes, but they are generally couched in optimistic terms about it being a lessening problem given the greater realization of the value of special schooling. Indeed, there was, and still is, a danger that the objections of a minority hide the acceptance and approval of the majority, and that initial reluctance often changes to approval. *Forward Trends* was thinking of these issues when, in 1958, it published a letter from a parent thanking the Head of a special school for the 'unbelievable difference' placement in that school had brought about in her child.[33]

Predictably, parental objections occurred most often when a child was recommended for placement in the expanding residential schools. The practical reasons for the growth of boarding have been mentioned, but to this should be added the genuine belief of certain influential educationalists, notably the boarding school Head, J. Duncan, that the residential approach offered the backward child from the family under stress, or the neglected or 'at risk' child, on the fringes of delinquency or truanting, the best preparation for a self-supporting and socially useful adult life.[34] A highly practical curriculum, in stark contrast to the new pupil's previous schooling, involving rural science, building projects linked to learning basic educational skills and character building through camping and other outdoor pursuits was favoured by many Heads. This view was shared by some officials at the Ministry, although opposed by some Education Committees.[35]

The costs involved no doubt influenced these LEAs, but John Bowlby's views on the damaging effects of separating young children from their mothers were becoming increasingly well known,[36] and perhaps exaggerated in their telling and wrongly extrapolated to the separated teenager. In 1962, R. Gulliford, in his Presidential Address to the Association for Special Education Conference pondered on the practical implications for residential education of the Bowlby hypothesis.[37] However, the DES still talked highly of boarding in 1964,[38] and not until the late 1970s was it very much forced on the defensive. In this era, it was generally accepted that despite initial reluctance, many parents rapidly became appreciative of the help it gave their child and their family situation.

Of course, the nature of boarding in the better schools was substantially different to the life-long segregation envisaged by some of the 1908 Royal Commissioners and the military style of reformatories. Regular holidays at home and a family-style ethos were fostered, although half-terms were still rare. This was illustrated by Thomas Cole, a pioneer Lancashire Head, in his comments on his work with the ESN in 1953:

> Children should be free to pay visits to friends that they make; they should be allowed to go on shopping expeditions unaccompanied by members of staff; they should be allowed to go for bicycle rides and walks on their own, and unsupervised visits to the cinema or library should be encouraged. It is a simple truth that if these children are not given the opportunity to misbehave they will never learn to behave in a reasonable manner. After all our main object is to fit these children for normal life when they attain school leaving age. This object can never be attained if we insist on dragooning them throughout their school life.[39]

This attitude usually won the appreciation of parents and pupils at Stone Cross, Ulverston and Cole's next school, Eden Grove. Old boys would proudly show their old school to their wives and children. Many were far from ashamed of having attended a special school.

Likewise, the families of the 'ineducable' would have been flattered had their children been allowed to attend special schools. Between 1951 and 1960, 3804 appeals were made by parents against LEAs' exclusion of their mentally handicapped children from the educational system under Section 57 of the 1944 Act. Only 4 per cent of these appeals were successful. However, LEAs were finding it increasingly difficult to draw the line between the educable and those deemed unsuitable for education in school. Separate studies by O'Connor and Stott showed that children's IQs were not immutable as was often assumed.[40] The implications for borderline ESN/'ineducable' were profound. No longer could an IQ of 50 be taken as a safe dividing line.

The National Society for Mentally Handicapped Children (NSMHC) had been campaigning for training centres for the severely subnormal, preferably within the educational system, as existed in Scotland. The 1959 Mental Health Act gave local health authorities the power to provide these and at least one area, Birmingham, was to ask its LEA to run training centres for them. The NSMHC campaign was helped by growing research evidence which showed that eugenic scares about national degeneracy and the criminal propensities of the feeble-minded had been grossly exaggerated. The 1959 Mental Health Act also urged that the severely subnormal should be helped where possible within the community.[41] Ann and A.D.B. Clarke were thus able to entitle their 1958 book *Mental Deficiency – The Changing Outlook*.[42]

Signs of a changing outlook regarding the ESN were also noticeable. A belief in the supremacy of the special school continued and confidence among special school teachers grew. Showing that the work they were doing was effective, their status, perhaps helped by new diploma courses at the Universities of Birmingham, London and Leeds, heightened in the eyes of teachers of ordinary children. Yet in 1960 an article in *Forward Trends* was entitled 'Are special schools necessary?'.[43] In 1962, the Special Schools Association changed its name to the Association for Special Education, deliberately seeking to encourage special educational work in the ordinary schools, and experiments were starting with mixed-ability teaching in junior schools.

Maladjusted Children

The new category of maladjusted children was to be made up of:

> pupils who show evidence of emotional instability or psychological disturbance and require special educational treatment in order to effect their personal, social or educational readjustment.[44]

In 1946, the Ministry urged that they should be helped where possible within the community – pupils could be given a fresh start by transferring them to alternative ordinary day schools, or by placing them in foster homes from where they could attend an ordinary school. Drawing on the success of special war-time hostels for difficult evacuees, they also favoured small boarding homes from which children could attend normal schools. This last approach enabled the maladjusted to mix with the local children and community. It was hoped that the parents of their school mates would 'invite them to their homes and do something to lessen the segregation which residence in even the best hostel inevitably involves'. However, boarding special schools would be needed for those who gained little from mixing with ordinary children.[45] Thus the stage was set for the varied growth of provision over the next 20 years.

In 1945, the only day schools were still at Leicester and Oxford. A few pioneer schools and hostels brought the total number of available places in late 1945 to 150 in England and Wales. London was one of the first LEAs to make extensive provision. In 1950, its first off-site tutorial class opened, which pupils attended for 50 per cent of their time while continuing to go to the ordinary school for the other half. In 1954, the Lilian Baylis day school opened and, in the same year, the LCC placed 563 pupils in various boarding schools.[46] By 1964, there were 49 boarding schools, 36 hostels, 19 day schools (only 3 outside the London area) and 107 special classes nationwide.[47] The Chief Medical Officer pressed for further expansion of these facilities, particularly day schools in the north of England. In Scotland, there were still only 144 boarding and 68 day places in 1962.[48]

In October 1950, the Principal Medical Officer of the Ministry, Dr J.E.A. Underwood, was asked by the Minister of Education to enquire into the medical, educational and social problems of maladjusted children.[49] Five years later, David Eccles, the new Minister, received the report. In the 'Foreword' he praised the emphasis laid on treating the maladjusted child as part of the family and, as far as possible, while he lived at home by using the Child Guidance Clinic (CGC) as the main method of achieving this. In England and Wales the number of CGCs had increased from 79 in 1945 to 300 in late 1954. The Committee hoped the CGCs would be staffed with a ratio of one psychiatrist to two psychologists to three psychiatric social workers.[50] As it was, shortages in all three professions hampered development.

Hopes for a community-based approach were reflected in various aspects of the report. The Berkshire system of hostels was praised – these were some of the 45 hostels which to some extent were thought to reproduce the conditions of normal life. Other LEAs argued that for some children the half-time tutorial classes like those developed in London were sufficient. The report advised that these should be placed off-site, perhaps in social work offices, in contrast to the frustration-inducing ordinary schools with their more rigid expectations and organization. Special classes should allow children to act-out their maladjustments, with teachers waiting until the children were 'ready' to learn. The necessary permissive regime which resulted was better kept off the main school campus. The rapid expansion of day schools was also requested. Boarding schools were only to be used in the last resort. If possible, children in boarding schools should attend the local ordinary school and should return to their homes as soon as possible.[51]

However, realism placed limits on these hopes. Fostering linked to attendance at day school was rarely practicable. It was considered 'the most difficult form of treatment to arrange under conditions conducive to success'.[52] The maladjusted found it hard to accept foster-parents, their natural parents were jealous and antipathetic to the arrangement and suitable foster-parents were hard to find. Further, 'in comparison with other forms of residential treatment, the child also suffers most if it fails'.

The normality of co-education was also considered too difficult to achieve because maladjusted boys by far outnumbered maladjusted girls. Co-education at the primary stage could, however, be followed by single-sex education for pupils over 11 years old.[53]

The Underwood Committee accepted that many maladjusted children could not cope with the demands of the mainstream school. While ordinary schooling was seldom the chief cause of maladjustment, it was often a contributory factor. The duller child, the Committee thought, might be overstretched by over-demanding teachers and an inappropriate curriculum whereas, conversely, the bright maladjusted child might be bored. The school could also be of the wrong social mix for the child transferring from another school.[54] The more severely disturbed were thought to need a period apart from their families in residential schools for 'treatment', a word which occurs frequently in the Report and reflects the influence of the seven doctors on the Committee. However, this did not necessarily mean help of a psychiatric nature. The Committee noted 'a considerable difference of opinion about the need for psychotherapy'. More experience of it was felt to be needed both in group and individual settings before its value could be properly judged.[55]

The psychodynamic approach was only one of four sometimes overlapping styles observed by the Committee. During this period, psychoanalysis continued at Otto Shaw's Red Hill School, where good results were claimed for highly intelligent adolescents. A related approach was to be found at Barbara Dockar-Drysdale's school for junior children, founded in 1948. At the Mulberry Bush, anti-social behaviour was tolerated as children were thought to need to work through emotional problems for themselves. Staff were not to repress this behaviour, rather they were to help the child through phases of love and hate, damage and restitution, until the child was able to sustain normal relationships with adults. Elsewhere, Bill Malcolm, at the instigation of the Freudian-leaning psychiatrist, Dr Marjorie Franklin, opened Arlesford Place in 1948. However, he lost faith. By the early 1960s he had joined the ranks of the many special school heads who doubted the usefulness of psychiatrists in helping most maladjusted children. Maurice Bridgeland later recorded how Malcolm came to see the psychiatric approach as 'damaging to the idea of a normal process of individual development and to social integration'.

However, Malcolm retained faith in the second of the styles noted by the Underwood Committee, namely the use of democratic meetings in which the pupils themselves decided much of what happened in their community. David Wills, a founder member of the Association of Workers with Maladjusted Children in 1951, became Warden of the co-educational Bodenham Manor School in 1950. He became the best known exponent of this approach and something of a cult figure. The permissive nature of Bodenham in some respects echoed Chaigeley School in Cheshire. The latter had evolved from an evacuation hostel and was the first school for maladjusted children to be recognized under the 1944 Act. It favoured pupil meetings, courts, psycho-drama, group therapy and a sometimes disorganized, liberal regime which tended to be viewed with distrust by the Ministry. Chaigeley received a poor assessment from HMI in 1948 and was threatened with closure unless it became an all-boys school.[56] The Chief Medical Officer still had doubts about pupil self-government in 1960. Generally, 'children are not capable of making judgements on standards of behaviour, or decisions concerning other children, unless they have reached a level of stability and maturity of judgement at which they can be relied on to do so responsibly'.[57] Rarely did this happen and then only in schools for older, more intelligent children.

The Ministry felt safer supporting the more common styles identified by the Underwood Committee. First there was the 'benevolent dictatorship' in which the staff imposed a regular pattern on the children's lives, on the assumption that emotionally immature children cannot cope with an excess of freedom. Finally, was the rather similar style where, after initial tolerance, maladjusted children were expected to learn the difference between right and wrong and could be punished for wrong-doing. They could and should be treated like normal children. Staff in these schools, rather than searching the depths of a child's psyche for forgotten early childhood trauma, tended to see the maladjusted as normal children reacting to abnormal circumstances. For many such children Underwood agreed with the London County Council that a contrasting, usually country environment, a regular life-style and normal education were the main mode of effecting improvement.[58]

Measuring the 'success' of maladjusted schools was notoriously difficult depending upon choice of criteria, a host of shifting variables and the impossible task of separating effective treatment from spontaneous remission; yet in the 1960s attempts were being made, notably by Roe in the Inner London Education Authority (ILEA) in 1965.[59] Results seemed sufficiently encouraging for calls to be made for the further experimentation and expansion of provision – hopefully, in the Chief Medical Officer's view, in day schools. The CMO and his colleagues remained hopeful of keeping segregation to a minimum.

The Physically Handicapped, Delicate, Diabetic and Epileptic

In the post-war drive for efficient classification, the 1945 Regulations divided the physically defective into the physically handicapped and the delicate. There was also some movement towards more homogeneous teaching groups within categories. For example, Lord Mayor Treloar College opened secondary grammar and technical departments in 1956.

Also listed were the epileptic, speech defective and diabetic categories. Working in reverse order, the diabetic category was to be short-lived. In the 1953 revised Regulations it was absorbed into the delicate. It only concerned a few children who, with daily insulin injections, were found to be able to cope in delicate or ordinary schools. In London, diabetic children had been evacuated during the war to a boarding school but, in 1954, they were moved to a hostel in Hammersmith from where they went to local day schools. In 1958 there were five hostels of this type.[60]

For children with severe speech defects, Moor House School, Oxted, was opened in 1948 for primary and secondary age pupils. A decade later, the Invalid Children's Aid Association opened the John Horniman School in Worthing for children of primary age.[61]

In 1946, the Ministry stated that epileptics could be educated in ordinary schools if they did not upset other children or the schools' organization.[62] For regular medical supervision, boarding was thought necessary, although this happened less often as the years passed. The number of boarders fell from 770 in 1955 to 623 in 1965 – a small proportion of the estimated 12 000–14 000 epileptic children in England and Wales. A widespread survey by school medical officers in 1950–51 found that of 430 children, 316 of whom had severe attacks, about 75 per cent were attending ordinary schools, 35 were thought 'ineducable', and 44 were in their phraseology 'emotionally disturbed'.[63] As methods of controlling epilepsy continued to improve, it was the disturbed who tended to remain in boarding schools. However, younger pupils could be placed there until, with medical help, the epilepsy was effectively managed by the children themselves. Between 1955 and 1960, as many pupils transferred back to ordinary schools as left the epileptic schools at leaving age.[64] Despite the decline in use of boarding schools, the Chief Medical Officer saw a need for the retention of some of them for medical and psychological assessment, particularly those children whose parents were thought to misunderstand the problem and mishandle their children.

The value of open-air schools had been questioned as early as 1930 when the Industrial Health Research Board had attacked the 'blind belief in the virtue of being out of doors in all weather'. Doubts increased when medical officers surveyed the schools for the Ministry in 1949–50. They were shocked by some decrepit day schools, held in three-sided, unheated wooden pavilions and rest sheds. 'In wet, windy weather', reported the survey team:

> when the canvas curtains were drawn, rain drove in and above the curtains so that the floor and furniture were often wet. We saw children scraping frozen snow off the desks and chairs before they could be used. We also saw children sprinkling sand on the ice-covered floors before the shelters could be occupied.

They continued in similar vein before concluding: 'As doctors we cannot feel that refrigeration or dampness contributes to health and therefore, we strongly condemn the "band-stand" type of classroom.' The residential schools were also attacked as spartan and cheerless, and doubts were expressed about the need for a midday rest, enforced silence at mealtimes and lack of contact between children and their homes. It was also claimed that it was possible for delicate schools to be dumping grounds for an ill-assorted group of physically handicapped, delicate, maladjusted and partially sighted children. Ill-assorted or not, in 1965 there remained many thousands of children in this kind of school.

With an increasing number of modern, well-lit and -ventilated school buildings in cities with cleaner air, was there really any need for open-air schools? The Chief Medical Officer thought so, albeit a declining one. This is reflected in Table 3, where it is shown that the numbers rose between 1945 and 1955, but then fell by over 2000 in the next decade, and the number of schools declined by 25 per cent. However, in well-run schools, there was likely to be less risk of infection, an increase in stimulation and plenty of exercise, which could still benefit the delicate child from an industrial area. The homely atmosphere, small size and high degree of individual attention given to pupils sometimes helped disturbed pupils. The length of stay in a boarding school was often only 3 months – and very rarely over 18 months – before a child was reintegrated in a much improved physical condition.[65]

Increasingly the delicate were intermingled with the physically handicapped. The number of combined schools increased from 21 in 1947 to 52 in 1965. This blurring of the categories was in contrast to developments elsewhere in the field of physical handicap.

In 1946, St Margaret's School, Croydon was opened. This catered exclusively for children suffering from cerebral palsy, a condition which often brought defects in hearing, vision, speech and intellect, in addition to severe physical disability. By 1964, there were 18 such schools, in many cases founded and run by the National Spastics Society. Other schools also specialized in helping these children, such as Hesley Hall, near Doncaster, while still taking non-palsied pupils as well. In Scotland, Westerlea School in Edinburgh also specialized in cerebral palsy.[66]

In 1959, the Shaftesbury Society opened the first school for spina bifida children at Hayes in Kent. In this condition, severe physical handicap is compounded by soiling problems and often by learning difficulties which to some educators and parents at this time indicated the need for separate provision. However, a survey in the Home Counties in 1964 revealed that 47 out of 160 spina bifida children were receiving their education in ordinary schools.[67]

Their integration reflected continuing and growing pressure for the inclusion of the physically handicapped in mainstream schools. The 1947 London school plan had thought separate schools were necessary[68], but within a few years contradictory evidence was reaching the Ministry. A survey by all the principal school medical officers between 1950 and 1952 showed that about 50 per cent of physically handicapped children were being educated in ordinary schools.[69] In 1954, the Chief Medical Officer was of the opinion that the majority of physically handicapped could 'readily be educated in ordinary schools', including some multi-handicapped children. Several cases were mentioned of children coping well in ordinary schools, including a boy in a secondary modern after his parents had resisted his being placed in a special school, as well as others in ordinary grammar schools. The latter were deriving 'great pleasure and satisfaction from being there'.[70] If extra help was allowed (e.g. extra time for the 11 + examination for slow writers) and, after admission to the ordinary school, special transport was laid on, then such children could manage and should be encouraged. The Scottish Education Department expressed similar sentiments in 1955 and resisted a call for a special technical school for the physically handicapped, preferring such children to attend mainstream schools.[71] In 1954 and 1964 the CMO stated the belief that the integrated handicapped were not subject to teasing by children without disabilities.[72]

This, however, was in opposition to the views of the Liverpool Adviser, C. Holroyde, who, in an article published in 1957, was to pose the question 'Normal school or special school?'. In his experience, teasing was a definite problem for some. He also pointed out that many ordinary schools were still housed in unsuitable physical buildings and had large, overcrowded classes. Furthermore, many teachers lacked an understanding of the needs of the handicapped. The result was that special schools tended to be more suitable for severe cases of handicap. He also reflected on the meaning of the word 'normality'. The pursuit of normality for the handicapped was clearly desirable but this was not synonymous with placing a child in an ordinary school.[73] Miss M. Lindsay, HMI, wrote in the same year: 'It is not a normal situation to be the noticeably handicapped child in an ordinary school.'[74] Being handicapped did single a child out from others. Consequently, to Holroyde and many who thought like him: 'If the child lives a life that is normal for *him* then in what way can a special school be regarded as abnormal providing the child lives the fullest life of which he is capable within that environment.'[75] The special school often provided a fuller and happier life for the handicapped child.

Holroyde's conclusion that school placement must be decided upon children's individual needs – some in ordinary and some in special school – was in line with the opinion of the Chief Medical Officer who, in 1964, complained that people should not see ordinary and special schools as being in competition.[76] The latter were clearly needed, but having recently experienced the parents of severely handicapped thalidomide children pressing for the integration of their offspring, it was noted that there were instances of severely handicapped children being successfully integrated. A survey in the Midlands had found severely handicapped children, including 16 confined to wheelchairs, in ordinary schools. Special schools would continue to be needed, although fewer of them.[77]

Together with lower mortality rates among the multi-handicapped due to advance in medicine, the dramatic decrease in the incidence of some disabling conditions meant that fewer special schools were needed. By 1960, tuberculosis, rickets, diphtheria, poliomyelitis and rheumatic fever had largely been overcome. Milk was pasteurized and polio and BCG vaccinations were almost universally given when necessary.[78]

Better treatment and prevention, reduced incidence and a concern for integration were reflected in the declining number of hospital schools (42 in 1958) and a reduction of 77 in the total number of maintained and non-maintained special schools in England and Wales. Meanwhile, pupil numbers in special schools fell by roughly 25 per cent between 1947 and 1965.

Blind and Partially Sighted Children

Reflecting pre-war opinion, the 1945 Regulations divided the blind and partially sighted into separate categories. In the interests of efficient classification and the concentration of special resources and expertise, the boarding approach was favoured unequivocally for the blind and was preferred for the partially sighted, despite the advice of the 1934 Crowley Report. In 1946, the Ministry expressed its disapproval of partially integrated special classes since 'almost inevitably the age range in classes of this kind would be too wide to allow education suited to all the children to be given'.[79] It was no surprise therefore that the number of boarding places for the two categories increased by 479 between 1945 and 1957 and the number of day places decreased by 190.[80] By 1965, only two schools in England and Wales catered for both blind and partially sighted children. Though the overall number of schools fell from 58 to 43, the rolls of those remaining were swelled by an increase in the number of babies suffering from retrolental fibroplasia. This condition was caused by giving excess oxygen to premature babies. By the middle of the 1950s, the danger was recognized and the practice halted; however, many victims were left to complete their education.

In 1948, efficient classification was made easier by the establishment by the Royal National Institute for the Blind (RNIB) of Condover Hall for the visually impaired with additional handicaps, and Hethersett Further Education College in 1956. By 1955, there were 10 Sunshine Homes, allowing the early intervention so strongly advocated at this time. With knowledge of Bowlby's ideas on maternal deprivation spreading and the greater success of the RNIB in providing help to families in their own homes, a decade later there were only six Sunshine Homes, concentrating mainly on blind children with an additional handicap.

For the partially sighted, Exhall Grange School opened in Warwickshire in 1951 with 240 places, which were soon to be used by half of the LEAs in England and Wales. In 1957, the Priestley Smith School, Birmingham opened. This was the first purpose-built school for the partially sighted and included such features as specially designed lighting. In 1960, to meet another perceived need, a grammar school department was started at Exhall Grange to enable pupils to take GCE examinations.

Despite Ministry disapproval, a single-class school with only 15 pupils continued at Barrow and single special classes in Blackburn, York and a few other towns.[81] They also continued in London where, in 1947, the practice of separating the partially sighted into special classes until age 12, and then transferring as many as possible to ordinary schools, was still followed.[82]

In a book published in 1948, William Lightfoot claimed that opinion on the relative merits of segregation and non-segregation for the partially sighted was very much divided. He repeated familiar arguments against integration. The partially sighted tended not to mix with the sighted in the playground and the seeing could be cruel to the handicapped: 'The differences, far from being evened out, become more outstanding and the gulf becomes wider.' He urged that facts be faced. If a child's eyesight was not normal, 'why then hanker after a pseudo-normality and endeavour to hoodwink the child by attaching it to a normal school'. Better for the child to be in a school where children share a common disability, do not feel inferior to sighted children, have sympathetic staff and a more easily organized common timetable. He also condemned the one-class school as an 'abomination'.[83]

To an extent, official opinion in Scotland diverged from that of the English Ministry. The Advisory Council Report of 1950 accepted that to meet the needs of the blind and to achieve efficient classification, boarding was necessary and small day schools should be discontinued. However, the partially sighted belonged to the world of the seeing and should follow a curriculum which closely resembled that of the sighted, mixing where possible with the non-handicapped. However, for some rural children there might be a need for boarding schools. This was doubted by the Secretary of State in 1955, who again called for the partially sighted, particularly the intelligent, to be allowed to remain in the ordinary schools.[84]

After the War, 'sight-saving' was condemned by experts such as Dr Ida Mann after studies concluded that children should be encouraged to use their residual vision.[85] This removed a major barrier to the integration of the partially sighted, a point stressed by the Chief Medical Officer and his colleagues in 1954. Distancing themselves from the Ministry position of 1946, they now favoured the integration of some pupils. They could not understand why many quite severely visually handicapped children, coping well in ordinary schools, were retained on the waiting lists for special schools. They also noted that Birmingham and Salford were reintegrating pupils after a few years' placement in special provision and commended this practice to other LEAs. Furthermore, the non-academic approach of some secondary modern schools also facilitated integration. Given parents' continuing reluctance to see their children placed in a boarding school, they thought the feasibility of integration must be accepted more widely by teachers.[86]

Later in the decade, the CMO returned to this theme, noting successful experiments at Exeter School and Barclay School in Berkshire where children were fitted with contact lenses, which enabled some of them to transfer back to mainstream schools.[87] There were many examples, it was reported, of the partially sighted doing well in ordinary grammar schools, although the less-able tended to require special schools.

In 1961, the Ministry sanctioned an experiment in integrating the blind in Liverpool. From 1962, a few selected pupils from St Vincent's attended neighbouring schools while still living in the boarding school. The LEA agreed to waive the '11 +' and allow entry for suitable children at age 12. Copying existing practice in Japan and America, local prisoners learned braille and typed out necessary textbooks in the dot system. A similar integration scheme started in Derbyshire.[88]

Sister Kathleen, Head of St Vincent's, had not been aware of nineteenth-century English or pre-war Scots integration. Her inspiration had been drawn from a visit to the United States where the merits of segregation and integration continued to be fiercely debated. Pupils in boarding schools for the blind and partially sighted increased. Meanwhile, 'Resource room programs' increased from 53 in 25 cities in 1945 to 200 in 86 cities in 1956, and enrolments of blind children in public school classes increased from 529 in 1948 to 5300 in 1966.[89] The practice of sending boarders out to day school, copied at St Vincent's, also increased.

Integration was also a major talking point at an international conference in Hanover, Germany in 1962, where an appeal was made for the merits of both special schools and integrated programmes to be recognized. They should be seen, it was urged, as complementary rather than rival systems.[90]

The Deaf and Partially Deaf

The wish of the National College of Teachers of the Deaf for a national educational system which created homogeneous teaching groups according to age, ability and degree of impairment was never to be achieved, although the post-war period did see some limited progress towards it (see Table 3). Neither were the Ministry's hopes for large schools with a class for each year group to be realized on a large scale.

The 1945 Regulations split the partially deaf from the deaf, although they did not demand their education in separate schools. Circular 41 had made it clear that it was acceptable for speech, language and lip-reading training to be taught in separate departments of a combined school.[91] However, the foundation before 1950 of Birkdale School in Southport and Ovingdean School, Brighton for the partially hearing, the Mary Hare Grammar School (1945) in Berkshire and a school for the backward deaf in the West Riding, assisted regional classification. In 1955, to ease national needs, Burwood Park School opened in Walton-on-Thames for the technical education of boys aged 12–19 years. Also of help was the deaf-blind unit opened at Condover Hall in 1952.

In Scotland, bigger schools were created by the closure of Kingston School and the transfer of its pupils, and a further dimension to segregation occurred in Glasgow when the deaf were split according to their religion in 1948–9.[92] In 1950, the Advisory Council pressed for the ending of single classes attached to ordinary schools, preferring five-class, cottage-style boarding schools for the deaf, situated on the edge of towns to allow access to shops, factories, museums and other community facilities to enable life-skills work. One of three proposed schools was to be for Catholics. Similarly, for 'IIB' pupils (see p. 78), they wanted three boarding schools, two for Protestants and one for Catholics. When the Scottish Secretary of State considered their advice in 1955, he rejected the call for boarding schools for the part-ially deaf, hoping that wherever possible they should go to ordinary schools.[93]

A German measles epidemic in 1940, and to a lesser extent

meningitis,[94] led to the increased incidence seen in Table 3, but by 1960 the numbers in the special schools were decreasing. This decline was also explained by the growing popularity of partially deaf units attached to the ordinary school. The first of these was opened in London in 1947. By 1955 there were still only 6, but by 1960 there were 35 and by 1963 there were 117 catering for 916 pupils.[95]

Spreading knowledge of Bowlby's work probably contributed to this. Further, while in the past it had often been argued that only placement in the total environment of the boarding school from a very early age could create the pure oral conditions believed necessary for the successful teaching of lip-reading and speech, the low standard achieved by many boarding pupils did not support this position. Special school teachers explained away their relative failure with talk of the disruption caused by the War, the low standard of entrants to the profession and, for the partially deaf, the distractions posed by inefficient hearing aids. But many were not convinced by these reasons. Arguments for the day classes, cited in earlier chapters, were again used.[96]

Moreover, critics heard that over half of the leavers from the early London units did proceed to ordinary schools at secondary level. Also, the development of transistor hearing aids, which were much smaller than the old valve models, lessened children's resistance to wearing them and made their integration with the hearing easier.[97] To avoid the transfer of others to special schools at 11 or 12, London opened its first unit for secondary pupils in 1959. This practice was followed increasingly elsewhere, adding to the rapid growth of units, renamed 'partially hearing' by the Ministry in 1962.[98]

Teachers in the special schools felt increasingly threatened as accounts of the units' apparent success appeared in the specialist press and praise for them occurred in the Chief Medical Officer's reports. In 1958, the Association of Non-Maintained Schools for the Deaf argued against full and partial integration of the partially deaf, stressing the need for effective classification and claiming that almost all the partially deaf in boarding schools had already failed in varying degrees, emotionally and educationally, in normal schools. They needed their confidence rebuilding in special schools. Boarding schools were said to aid the development of social living skills, provide better sporting facilities, ensure regular school attendance and the physical well-being of pupils. They were particularly helpful for the many children from broken homes.[99]

In 1960, the disadvantages of two Manchester units (opened in 1957) were described in *Teacher of the Deaf*. The staff were said to be isolated from the expertise of qualified colleagues and the wide age and ability range posed problems. When the partially deaf mixed with the hearing they were likely to be taught in classrooms with poor acoustics, large teaching groups and unsympathetic staff. It was also claimed that the use of modern 'activity methods' was likely to produce an environment too noisy for effective learning. [100]

In 1962, J.C. Johnson reported 68 Cheshire pupils in ordinary schools with a hearing loss in excess of 30 decibels, some of whom had a severe degree of handicap. Some of the subjects spent all their education among the hearing; others were partially integrated in special classes attached to ordinary schools. The speech of the children in the ordinary schools was felt to be clearer than that of children in special schools and a few of the subjects with higher intelligence, a steady temperament and good parental support were coping well in a fully integrated situation. Many, however, struggled with insufficient help from peripatetic teachers and experienced a lack of understanding from many of their ordinary teachers. Teachers in single-class units sometimes found the wide age and ability range very difficult to master. Pupils rarely wore their hearing aids at home and sometimes teachers were unsympathetic to their use at school. The degree of actual day-to-day integration between the hearing-impaired and the hearing was 'not remarkable, and was often non-existent'. In particular, the timid and withdrawn children were likely to fare better in the supportive environment of the special school. [101] Also, in 1962, HMI Miss E.M. Johnson reached similar conclusions in her study of 33 hearing-impaired children placed in ordinary schools. [102]

During this period, doctors were sometimes accused of unfairly condemning boarding schools, but one of their number, T.A. Clarke, strongly defended their place for some children in 1962: 'Parents', he said, 'know from bitter experience that it is no use pretending their children are normal.' [103] Integration placed a severe strain on many hearing-impaired children and he doubted whether it was desirable. He ridiculed a Dutch writer who had outlined the difficulties experienced in the Netherlands in trying to keep deaf pupils living in foster homes from mixing socially with one another. He repeated the often-spoken view that the deaf liked to be with the deaf.

Some of the adult deaf community had always shared this view and continued to feel great bitterness towards teachers of the oral persuasion who aimed for the adult integration of the deaf among the hearing. They thought this approach only benefited a minority; the majority should have been taught by sign language. In 1949, Leonard Hale, a teacher at Rayner's School for the less-able deaf, one of the few establishments where signing was allowed, attacked oralism as a 'discredited system'. [104] The deafs' strong opinions pointed the way to the return of the 'combined method' in the guise of 'Total Communication' in the 1970s.

Also becoming more common was the use of the phrase 'hearing impaired', preferred by J.C. Johnson in 1962, because it was thought difficult to classify according to the 1938 grades (see p. 78).[105] The tide was turning against both oralism and scientific classification in special schools.

Summary

The 1945 Regulations created no less than 11 categories of handicap, reflecting the dominating concern for precise classification and also the Ministry's official recognition of the maladjusted. 'Certification' was abolished, and special education could take place in ordinary schools. In 1947, of those identified as needing 'special educational treatment', under 37 per cent received it in special schools, although the waiting lists for ESN schools in the next 25 years suggests many more would have been segregated had more places been available.

To help meet the needs of the new ESN category, boarding schools were created in converted country houses, although some LEAs' objections to boarding and the drying up of the supply of cheap buildings led to the building of a large number of day schools after 1955. By then, the Chief Medical Officer's annual reports and government circulars were reminding LEAs that special education should not be equated with provision in special schools and that more needed to be done in the ordinary schools. Sending a child away from home should only happen if there was no practical alternative.

However, given the perceived unsuitability of the curriculum, ethos and organization of many ordinary schools for the ESN, placement for as many as possible in special schools or classes was seen as being necessary to help children to escape from experiencing repeated failure, and its consequent damaging effects on their self-concept and attitudes to education. Most leading educationalists considered this to override any considerations of the stigma attached to segregation. An element of social control in the selection of children for special schools was openly admitted by the Ministry in 1946.

The 1959 Mental Health Act urged provision within the community for the severely subnormal. Eugenic fears had now largely evaporated and there was growing pressure for children to live at home and attend health authority junior training centres rather than stay in subnormality hospitals. Section 57 of the 1944 Education Act was the legal mechanism by which children believed to have an intelligent quotient of less than 50 were excluded from the educational system. Parental hatred of this was increasingly recognized and the justice of their view more widely appreciated as it was confirmed that IQs could change.

Similarly, the helping of the maladjusted was planned to take place within the community wherever possible. Child guidance clinics, part-time 'tutorial classes', and special hostels from where children went to ordinary day schools grew in number. However, for severe cases, boarding schools were found to be useful for long-term treatment and a variety of approaches were tried within them.

As medical practice improved, an increasing number of epileptics were able to rejoin ordinary schools after a period in a boarding school. Similarly, as major diseases such as TB and polio declined and physical conditions in ordinary schools and the children's own homes improved, fewer pupils attended schools for the delicate. Numbers in schools for the physically handicapped also declined, adding to the large number already integrated in ordinary schools. The Annual Reports of the Chief Medical Officer encouraged this trend. However, for the severe cases remaining in special schools, more precise classification occurred as schools opened for cerebral palsy and spina bifida victims.

The Ministry also preferred special boarding schools for the blind, who were meant to be separated from the partially sighted. Partial integration by way of special classes was condemned, although by the end of the period St Vincents School, Liverpool, had rediscovered integration after staff visited American mainstream schemes. Integration was increasingly an international talking point for the visually handicapped and actively encouraged for the partially sighted in Scotland.

For the deaf, greater classification was sought after the War and the oral approach reigned. However, as the period ended, the few pioneer partially deaf units were increasingly copied, reflecting the value of their work, parental dislike of boarding, better hearing aids and a growing desire for school and community integration. Yet there remained many defenders of special schools and the poor classification, low standards and isolation of many partially deaf units were attacked.

Notes

1. DES, *The Organisation of Secondary Education*, Circular 10/65, July 1965.
2. 1944 Education Act, Section 33 (2).
3. Ministry of Education, *Special Educational Treatment*, pamphlet no. 5, HMSO, London, 1946.
4. P. Williams and E. Gruber, *Response to Special Schooling*, Longmans, London, 1967, p.129.
5. Op. cit., note 3.

6. Ministry of Education, *Boarding School Provision for the Educationally Sub-Normal and Maladjusted Children*, Circular 79, January 1940; Ministry of Education, *Education of the Handicapped Pupil, 1945–55*, pamphlet no. 30, HMSO, London, 1956, p.6.
7. *Report for 1952 and 1953 of the CMO of the Ministry of Education*, HMSO, London, 1954, p.68.
8. *Report for 1956 and 1957 of the CMO of the Ministry of Education*, HMSO, London, 1958, p.21; Ministry of Education, pamphlet no. 30, op. cit., note 6, pp.1–3.
9. J. Lumsden, 'Special education for the handicapped', *Teacher of the Deaf*, vol. 46, 4, 1968, p.137; Ministry of Education, *Education in 1947*, HMSO, London, 1948, p.55.
10. The seven reports of the Advisory Council are listed in SED, *Special Educational Treatment*, Circular 300, 1955.
11. SED, *Education in Scotland in 1947*, HMSO, Edinburgh, pp.13–14; SED, *Education in Scotland in 1965*, HMSO, Edinburgh, 1965, p.104.
12. M.F. Cleugh, *The Slow Learner*, Methuen, London, 1957, pp.90–1 (2nd edn. 1968).
13. Quoted in DES, *Slow Learners at School*, pamphlet no. 46, HMSO, London, 1964, p.4.
14. Education Committee of NAHT, 'Provision of special educational facilities', *Forward Trends*, vol. 2, 3, 1958, p.38.
15. Op. cit., note 3, p.21.
16. SED Advisory Committee, *Pupils with Mental or Educational Disabilities*, HMSO, Edinburgh, 1951, p.11.
17. *Report for 1950 and 1951 of the CMO of the Ministry of Education*, HMSO, London, 1952, p.90.
18. Op. cit., note 12, pp.99–102.
19. S.A. Kirk and G.O. Johnson, *Educating the Retarded Child*, Houghton Mifflin, Boston, 1951, p.122.
20. A.E. Tansley and R. Gulliford, *The Education of Slow Learning Children*, Routledge, London, 1960, p.14.
21. Op. cit., note 13, p.23.
22. H.A.T. Child, 'The special class', *Forward Trends*, vol. 1, 1, 1956, p.29.
23. C.M. Vaughan, 'A report on a special class', *Forward Trends*, vol. 2, 2, 1958, p.59.
24. Op. cit., note 19, p.124.
25. J. Lumsden, 'The education of handicapped children', *Teacher of the Deaf*, vol. 51, February 1953, p.5.
26. D. Pritchard, *Education and the Handicapped*, Routledge and Kegan Paul, London, 1963, final chapter.
27. Op. cit., note 4.
28. *Report for 1962 and 1963 of the CMO of the Ministry of Education*, HMSO, London, 1964, p.150; Ministry of Education, *Special Educational Treatment for Educationally Sub-Normal Pupils*, Circular 11/61, July 1961.
29. LCC, *Replanning London Schools*, LCC, London, 1947, p.57.
30. Op. cit., note 12, p.126.
31. Ibid., p.117.
32. *Report for 1960 and 1961 of the CMO of the Ministry of Education*, HMSO, London, 1962, p.140; op. cit., note 13, p.6.
33. *Forward Trends*, vol. 2, 2, 1958, pp.51–2.

34. J. Duncan, *The Education of the Ordinary Child*, Nelson, London, 1942.
35. Op. cit., note 25, p.4.
36. J. Bowlby, *Maternal Care and Mental Health*, World Health Organization, Geneva, 1951.
37. R. Gulliford, 'Growing points in special education', *Presidential Address to ASE Conference*, 1962, p.9.
38. Op. cit., note 13, p.47.
39. T.L. Cole, 'Odd Men Out', unpublished manuscript, 1953.
40. *Report for 1960 and 1961 of the CMO of the Ministry of Education*, HMSO, London, 1962, ch. XIV.
41. *Forward Trends*, vol. 1, 4, 1957, p.107; *Report for 1964 and 1965 of the CMO of the Ministry of Education*, HMSO, London, 1966, pp.73–5; op. cit., note 26, p.218; J.S. Hurt, *Outside the Mainstream*, Batsford, London, 1988, pp.180–1.
42. A.M. Clarke and A.D.B. Clarke, *Mental Deficiency – The Changing Outlook*, Methuen, London, 1958.
43. 'R.S.', 'Are special schools necessary?', *Forward Trends*, vol. 4, 3, 1960, p.99.
44. Ministry of Education, S.I. 1953, no. 1156, *School Health Service and Handicapped Pupils Regulations*, Part III(g).
45. Ministry of Education, *Boarding School Provision for the Educationally Sub-Normal and Maladjusted Children*, Circular 79, January 1940.
46. *Report of the Committee on Maladjusted Children* (Underwood Report), HMSO, London, 1966, pp.33 and 53–5.
47. *Report for 1964 and 1965 of the CMO of the Ministry of Education*, HMSO, London, 1966, p.33.
48. SED, *Education in Scotland in 1962*, HMSO, Edinburgh, 1963, pp.118–19.
49. Op. cit., note 46, p.1.
50. Ibid., pp.iv, 13 and 144–5.
51. Ibid., pp.66–9, 55, 65 and 149.
52. Ibid., pp.70 and 149.
53. Ibid., p.75.
54. Ibid., pp.32–3.
55. Ibid., p.77.
56. M. Bridgeland, *Pioneer Work With Maladjusted Children*, Staples, London, 1971, pp.192–4 and 210–15.
57. *Report for 1958 and 1959 of the CMO of the Ministry of Education*, HMSO, London, 1960, p.120.
58. Op. cit., note 46, p.55; LCC, *Education in London 1945–54*, LCC, London, 1954, p.58.
59. M.C. Roe, *Survey into Progress of Maladjusted Children*, ILEA, London, 1965.
60. LCC, op. cit., note 58, p.58; op. cit., note 57, p.23.
61. Op. cit., note 57, p.26.
62. Op. cit., note 3, p.7.
63. Op. cit., note 17, ch. xii and p.99.
64. Op. cit., note 40, p.115.
65. Op. cit., note 17, pp.101–24.
66. Ibid., pp.81–7.
67. *Report for 1966–1968 of the CMO of the Ministry of Education*, HMSO, London, 1969, p.75; *Report for 1962 and 1963 of the CMO of the Ministry of Education*, HMSO, London, 1964, p.85.
68. Op. cit., note 29, p.50.
69. Op. cit., note 7, p.98.

70. Ibid., p.92.
71. Op. cit., note 10, pp.8–9.
72. Op. cit., note 7, p.90; *Report for 1962 and 1963 of the CMO of the Ministry of Education*, HMSO, London, 1964, p.89.
73. C. Holroyde, 'The physically handicapped child – normal school or special school', *Special Schools Journal*, November 1957, pp.14–18.
74. M. Lindsay, 'Special schools now and in the future', *Special Schools Journal*, January 1957, p.21.
75. Op. cit., note 73, p.16.
76. *Report for 1962 and 1963 of the CMO of the Ministry of Education*, HMSO, London, 1964, p.97.
77. Ibid., p.89.
78. Op. cit., note 57, p.7.
79. Op. cit., note 3, p.13.
80. *Report for 1956 and 1957 of the CMO of the Ministry of Education*, HMSO, London, 1958, p.132.
81. W. Lightfoot, *The Partially Sighted School*, Chatto and Windus, London, 1948, p.21; S.O. Myers, 'A broad survey', *Teacher of the Blind*, vol. 51, 1963, p.138; op. cit., note 57, pp.84 and 88; op. cit., note 26, p.220.
82. Op. cit., note 29, p.48.
83. Op. cit., note 81, pp.20–1.
84. SED Advisory Council, *Pupils Who Are Defective in Vision*, HMSO, Edinburgh, 1950, pp.22 and 32–9; op. cit., note 10, p.8.
85. Sister Kathleen Fothergill, 'The education of the partially sighted', in D.J. Harvey (ed.), *Children Who Are Partially-Sighted*, published privately by the Association for the Education and Welfare of the Visually Handicapped at the George Auden School, Northfield, Birmingham, 1980.
86. Op. cit., note 7, pp.71 and 79–87.
87. Op. cit., note 57, pp.86–7.
88. Sister Kathleen Fothergill, *Turn Over the Page*, RNIB, London, 1979, pp.55–60.
89. G.L. Abel, *The Growth of the Resource Room*, American Foundation for the Blind, New York, 1959; R. Mackie, *Special Education in the United States; Statistics, 1948–66*, Teachers College Press, New York, 1969, p.37.
90. *Teacher of the Blind*, vol. 51, October 1962, p.19.
91. Ministry of Education, Circular 41 (April 1945), in *Teacher of the Deaf*, vol. 47, 277, 1949, p.14.
92. Ibid., p.14; Corporation of Glasgow, *Report of Education Committee on Session, 1948–9*, Corporation of Glasgow, Glasgow, 1949.
93. SED Advisory Council, *Children Who Are Defective in Hearing*, HMSO, Edinburgh, p.43; op. cit., note 10, p.5.
94. *Report for 1939 to 1945 of the CMO of the Ministry of Education*, HMSO, London, 1947, p.86.
95. J.C. Johnson, *Educating hearing-Impaired Children in Ordinary Schools*, Manchester University Press, Manchester, 1962, p.85.
96. See *Teacher of the Deaf*, vols 47, 48 and 51, 1949, 1950 and 1951.
97. C.G. Knowles and M. Owens, 'Partially deaf children and the L.C.C.', *Teacher of the Deaf*, vol. 51, 302, 1953, pp.44–8.
98. Op. cit., note 76, p.55.
99. Association of Non-Maintained Schools, 'Case for boarding schools for the deaf', *Teacher of the Deaf*, vol. 57, 337, 1959, pp.43–8.

100. *Teacher of the Deaf*, vol. 58, 1960, pp.430–32.
101. Op. cit., note 95, pp.14, 60–1, 89 and 105.
102. Op. cit., note 76, pp.58–9.
103. T.A. Clarke, 'Deafness in children', *Teacher of the Deaf*, vol. 61, 356, 1962, p.195.
104. L.H. Hale, 'Oralism and its critics', letter to *Teacher of the Deaf*, vol. 47, 1949, pp.50–3.
105. Op. cit., note 95.

CHAPTER 6

From Crosland to Baker: 1965–88

Political and Educational Summary: 1965–88

Major Events and Ordinary Education

1965 Under 10% in comprehensive schools when Circular 10/65 issued

1966 *Wilson* (Labour) wins election with large majority

1960s Non-streaming, particularly in primary schools, grows in popularity

1967 Plowden Report calls for middle schools and 'educational priority areas'

1966–70 Number of immigrant schoolchildren doubles

1968 Government Commission calls for integration of public schools into state system

1969 Violence flares in Ulster; oil found in North Sea

Special Education

1965 74 PHUs – rapid growth continuing

1967 177 peripatetic teachers of deaf employed by LEAs although 79 LEAs still do not employ any

1968 Summerfield Report calls for more educational psychologists

1968 Lewis Report sees place for some signing in education of deaf

1969 Over 50% of thalidomide children attend ordinary schools

1969–70 10 200 PH children in ordinary schools

1970	Government Commission calls for direct grant schools to go comprehensive or independent		1970	Education (Mentally Handicapped Children) Act transfers severely subnormal from NHS to LEA control from 1971
1970	*Heath* (Conservative) wins election		1970	DES Circulars call for integration of less severe PH
1971	New Tory government increases grants to direct grant schools; free school milk ended		1971	Gulliford's *Special Educational Needs* published; reflects growing doubts over official categorization
1972	Raising of school leaving age to 16 years		1972	Finger-spelling and -signing advocated at NCTD conference
1970s	Press, parents and teachers concerned about discipline in schools while anti-corporal punishment lobby gathers strength		1972	Cautious Vernon Report wants controlled experiments in the integration of the blind into ordinary schools
			1973	Circular 4/73 advises smaller classes for handicapped
			1973	Thatcher announces Warnock Committee which begins work in 1974
1974	*Wilson* (Labour) forms minority government; wins majority of 3 in second election		1974	ASE and Guild of Teachers of Backward Children merge to form NCSE
			1974	School health services move from LEAs to NHS
			1975	LEA special boarding school population peaks at over 18 000; SE forms introduced
1975	Thatcher displaces Heath as Tory leader		1975	McCann Report pushes integration of PH in Scotland
1975	Houghton award eases teachers' pay grievances			
1975	Bullock Report finds no evidence that reading standards have slipped			
1976	Education Act tries to complete comprehensivization; Wilson resigns; *J. Callaghan* (Labour) PM		1976	Section 10 of Education Act requires integration of all handicapped (if practicable and efficient); date to be fixed later
			1976	Snowdon Report favours integration of PH

		1976	Court Report on child health services
1977	Taylor Report wants more power for school governors but opposed by unions and LEAs	1977	463 PHUs in England and Wales
		1977	3-year DES sponsored NFER research into integration in ordinary schools begins under Hegarty
1977–8	Liberal-Labour pact	1977	Society of Teachers of Deaf and NCTD merge to form BATOD
		1978	Warnock Report published; cautious approach to integration welcomed by NCSE, NARE and most bodies; wide concept of special educational needs urged
1979	*Thatcher* (Conservative) wins election	1979	Brennan's Schools Council Report attacks mixed-ability teaching for slow learners and records teachers' doubts on open-plan approach; criticism of existing special school curricula
1979	Education Act: Tories repeal duty of LEAs to submit plans for comprehensivization		
1980	86% of secondary age children in comprehensives	1979	Jay Report pushes community care for mentally handicapped
1980	Education Act makes financial help available for children to attend independent schools under 'assisted places' scheme		
1980s	Dramatically falling rolls mean on-going school closures; independent schools flourish	1981	Education Act says children with SENs should be educated in mainstream where possible; categorization abolished
1982	Falklands War	1983	April: 1981 Act into effect; 'statementing' starts
1983	*Thatcher's* landslide victory over M. Foot	1984	NUT pamphlet calls for properly resourced integration and retention of special schools
		1980s	Curriculum of many secondary schools repeatedly said to be unsuited to children with special needs; many

		1986	reported examples of integration; growing complaints on bureaucracy of statementing procedures
1985–7	Teachers' disruption, including strikes, ends in K. Baker abolishing Burnham Committee and imposing pay award and conditions of service	1986	Greater % in special schools than in 1976
1987	*Thatcher* heavily defeats Kinnock's Labour		
1988	Education Reform Act brings in National Curriculum, age-related testing, open enrolment and local school management	1988	Fears that new Act will halt trend towards integration

By 1965 it was the Labour Government's 'declared objective to end selection and separatism in secondary education'.[1] In the following year, the Scottish Education Department thought it 'a sound principle' that 'special education should be a last resort'.[2] These sentiments were reflected by an increasing number of people who objected as much to the separation of the least able and handicapped as to that of the most intelligent. The comprehensive should strive to be a school for all, meeting the requirements of the child with special needs as well as those of the average or high-flying pupil. However, the achievement of this aim was to be obstructed by educational practices and curricula encouraged by the House of Commons motion passed on 21 January 1965 which gave rise to Circular 10/65. In this, the House welcomed LEAs who were replacing selection with comprehensive schemes which 'will preserve all that is valuable in grammar school education for those children who now receive it and make it available to more children'.

With government thinking along these lines many secondary schools retained systems dominated by the passing of public examinations. This was probably in accord with the wishes of the majority of parents, but the result was a competitive ethos which ill-suited the least able 40 per cent. This situation persisted in the late 1980s and in the wake of Kenneth Baker's 1988 Education Act, might continue into the next century. Against this background functional integration, particularly at secondary level, has been achieved of children with severe special needs in some well-planned instances but has often proved difficult even for determined, well-adjusted children of high intelligence. In mixed ability, less pressurized, primary settings it has been easier, although many schemes have merely aspired to locational and limited part-time integration.

In national terms, although integration was much talked about and a small group of academics tended to dominate the special education press who fervently espoused the cause, DES statistics did not indicate substantial movement towards it beyond what already existed in 1965. The pressure to exclude many disruptive children from the ordinary classes, probably exacerbated by the breakdown in stable family life in a permissive society, led to an explosion in provision for the maladjusted. New schools continued to be opened and many special schools continued to flourish, while others with the active support of the parents of the pupils fought off attempts to close them. A further deterrent was that while special schools were expensive to run, providing properly supported individualized integration could prove more costly.

In the middle of the period the Warnock Committee aroused interest beyond the world of special education. This led to an Act of Parliament of limited effect in 1981 which required integration for all, subject to constraining provisos, and a feeling of disillusionment among many educators by the mid-1980s. This process will briefly be described in the first part of this chapter before the different areas of special education are discussed and the extent of integration examined. As the different categories of handicap were not officially abolished until 1 April 1983, the terms established after the 1944 Education Act are mainly used, but at other times the now well-established shorthand descriptions which were rapidly adopted in the educational world are used instead.

To Warnock and Beyond

The 1978 Warnock Report showed that there had been some development of special education in ordinary schools. Non-designated special classes provided for 494 248 pupils, the vast majority of whom had learning difficulties or emotional and behavioural disorders. This was about 5 per cent of the total school population in England and Wales. These classes existed in 10 845 or 40 per cent of the nation's schools. However, the majority of these pupils attended such classes for under half of the school week. In addition, there were over 21 000 children in designated special classes, 10 000 more than in 1973.[3]

Meanwhile, the nett number of English and Welsh maintained and non-maintained special schools continued to increase until 1981, after which they only began to shrink marginally despite sharp falls in the population:

Year	No. of schools
1974	1354
1978	1449
1981	1462
1984	1441
1987	1393

In 1967, there was about the same percentage of English and Welsh schoolchildren in special schools as on the eve of the Second World War. It was in the 1970s that the percentage in segregated provision rose in real terms, and continued to rise until five years after the Warnock Report, despite the renewed interest in integration. One reason for growth was contained in the title of Stanley Segal's 1968 book *No Child is Ineducable*.[5] The government accepted this view in the 1970 Education (Mentally Handicapped) Act and, in 1971, over 30 000 severely subnormal children were added to the ESN category. The expansion also reflected increased provision for maladjusted children and the growth in the child population until a sharp decline occurred in the early 1980s. These factors are reflected in Table 4 which gives the number of children identified under the 1944 Act or 'statemented' under the 1981 Act and placed in special schools, hospital schools and designated special classes, as well as showing the total population of schoolchildren in England and Wales. One is then expressed as a percentage of the other.

Table 4 Number of children in maintained and non-maintained special schools, classes, etc., compared to the total number of pupils in England and Wales [4]

Year	No. in special schools, etc.	School pop.	%
1957	60 417	7 467 585	0.81
1967	78 256	7 980 940	0.98
1977	135 261	9 663 978	1.40
1987	107 126	7 450 127	1.44

For the time being at least, before the 1988 Education Reform Act took effect, the peak of segregation would seem to have been passed. W. Swann calculated from DES figures that 1.54 per cent of 5- to 15-year-olds were in special schools in 1983, or at least on their rolls.[6] However, some of these children remained on special school rolls while in fact attending ordinary schools for a part of the timetable. This practice might have increased and may obscure the possible advance of integration.

Under the new statistical procedures which followed the 1981 Act, a record was started of children with statements placed in ordinary classes. This figure increased from 5292 in 1985 to over 15 000 in 1987, although this figure is of limited significance given the delays in implementation and the inconsistencies in the use of statements. Thousands of children were not statemented who might have been and many were receiving special support in reading centres and units which count as 'ordinary' classes.

All-in-all Table 4 shows only limited movement on a national scale away from the use of segregated provision, although there are variations between one LEA and another, and between groups of children with different special needs. Research by Swann in 1988 showed that whereas 66 LEAs reduced their use of segregated provision between 1982 and 1987, 30 increased it. On a national scale, he also found that there was a greater inflow of pupils aged 11–14 to special schools in 1985 than in 1982, and that there was also a renewed trend towards segregation for primary children.[7]

Section 10 of the 1976 Education Act had decreed that all children were to be educated in ordinary schools, at a date to be fixed later, but subject to practicability, efficiency and cost. This was never implemented and was superseded by the 1981 Education Act which likewise decreed that children with special needs should be educated with the non-handicapped in ordinary schools but, as in 1976, subject to the same constraints. These constraints would seem to have been powerful deterrents to the advance of integration. LEAs preferring the special school approach could always use them as an excuse for inaction. Further, within 'practicability' lay the potent factor of human inertia. Most professionals probably preferred to leave undisturbed a system which had taken a long time to develop and was generally working quite well, with a high degree of parental satisfaction, despite well-publicized claims to the contrary (see p. 159). In addition, the stresses teachers had to endure in trying to control disruptive children, proved a powerful motive for greater segregation.[8]

In the autumn of 1973, Margaret Thatcher announced the Warnock Enquiry. In 1974, to the background cacophony of Waterloo Station's trains and trundling trolleys, it started to meet at DES headquarters.[9] Before its report was published the American Public Law 94–142 (Education of All Handicapped Children Act) had been passed in 1975, with implementation in 1978. This called for the education of all handicapped children in the 'least restrictive environment', usually taken to mean a mainstream setting, and for each child there was to be an 'IEP' (an individual education programme). Integration laws, although sometimes passed in hope rather than serious expectation, had also recently been passed in Italy and France.[10]

In England in 1974, the DES had issued a cautious pamphlet called *Integrating Handicapped Children*[11] and what looked like a major step towards integration occurred when the Labour Government passed the 1976 Education Act. The Warnock Report was published in 1978, taking its title (*Special Educational Needs*) and many ideas from Professor Gulliford's 1971 book.[12] It stressed that Section 10 of the Act had 'confirmed the direction' of much of the content, although to Dr Mary Wilson the Report was a 'judicious application of the brakes' on the movement to integration.[13] A similar view was taken by the Leeds Adviser, P. Simpson, who saw the Report offering evolution rather than revolution, which was not likely to please 'Section 10 shock troops among local authority officers and members and among the more pushing of the voluntary societies'.[14] However, its cautious style and thorough and wide-ranging recommendations were welcomed by most professionals. Some of these are discussed later in this chapter. However, it regarded the following as areas which needed particular attention: the nursery age group, further education and better training, including a special education content in the courses of all student teachers. Chapter 7 of the Report was devoted to providing more effective special help to the broad range of children who would need some form of special help at some time during their school careers (suggested as possibly 20 per cent of the school population). It discussed individualized integration on a full-time or part-time basis, special class placement with some time spent in regular class and special class placement combined with social contact with the main school.

In 1981, the new Conservative Government, having revoked Section 10, passed the 1981 Education Act. This adopted much of the philosophy of the Warnock Report, preferring to think in terms of children with special educational needs rather than assigning them to the categories of handicap brought into being by the 1944 Act, but abolished from 1 April 1983. For children best served by placement in a special school or class, or preferably provided with the necessary support and educated in ordinary classes, a 'statement of needs' would be maintained. The latter would be drawn up by teachers, psychologists, other professionals and, supposedly, with the active involvement of parents, although in practice the desire for a real parental input often turned out to be more rhetoric than reality.[15] The Statement would be subject to annual review. Appeal procedures were also described.

Further, in a departure from the 1944 and earlier Acts, it was the *duty* of every LEA to educate all children in ordinary schools where this was compatible with parental wishes, the efficient education of other children and the efficient use of resources. The implication was that only the children with the most severe difficulties would need separate special schooling. However, in practice, parents used the new procedures as much for getting their children *into* special schools against LEAs' wishes as for obtaining properly supported integration in mainstream settings.[16]

The Act was a limited measure which only addressed some recommendations of the Warnock Committee. It offered nothing specific to help meet Warnock's priority needs. Disappointingly, for many observers, the government was to make no additional funding available to help implement the Act. During the ensuing years this was often seen as the major reason for the limited advance towards integration. However, allegations of cuts in spending on provision for children with special needs were somewhat punctured by findings in 1987 that 72 per cent of English and Welsh LEAs were spending a higher proportion of their budget on special education and 53 per cent reported an increase in real terms, although they claimed economic difficulties were holding them back from further desired action.[17]

Implementation of the Act was also hampered by the difficult practicalities involved in altering traditional organizational structures and preparing and training staff in the schools receiving the children with special needs. Successful integration was often said to depend on welcoming and sympathetic teachers who had been helped to overcome their feelings of inadequacy when asked to teach the handicapped. The publicity surrounding the Warnock Report and its aftermath did draw the attention of many schoolteachers to children with special needs and perhaps encouraged them to feel more responsibility towards them. In some schools, through local effort, it is probable that many staff did develop greater expertise and understanding for children with special needs. However, preparation of the majority of teachers for greater integration continued to be scant.

Unfortunately, the training of teachers to work with special children had always been low on local and central government agendas and, historically, had contributed much to the low status of special school or special class teachers. In the 1950s and 1960s, Stanley Segal and others had campaigned hard for more widespread training but with only limited results. In the post-Warnock era, some courses did develop at various colleges which trained teachers to work with children with special needs in mainstream settings, but a difficult financial climate prevented many teachers from receiving this help.

It was not therefore surprising that despite a marked movement from separate remedial departments to 'whole school policies' and the supporting of children with special needs in ordinary classes, some evidence in the mid-1980s suggested teachers preferred the old withdrawal system and many still saw the child with special needs as better placed in separate provision.[18]

Further, in some schools where the Head espoused the integration cause, D. Thomas found there were many teachers who, while paying lip-service to the idea, were not strong supporters. He was not the only researcher to find teachers who thought it impractical, discovering that they could not provide the separate curricula needed and that their classes were too large to provide the degree of individual attention required. In practice, union resistance to integration centred on the same point. While supporting it in theory, both the National Union of Teachers (NUT) and the National Association of Schoolmasters/Union of Women Teachers (NAS/UWT) stressed that classes needed to be smaller and that adequate supporting services needed to be provided to allow the extra attention to be given to the child with special needs.[19]

In 1982, the former ILEA officer, W. Brennan, was sceptical about the ability of many ordinary schools to offer education in an integrated setting which matched the standard of care and expertise prevailing in the good special schools he knew, particularly if extra funding was not available. He also stressed the human inertia which militated against integration:

> Teachers in special schools are secure in their role, derive satisfaction from it and enjoy some degree of public acclaim; hence they tend to resist change. Teachers in ordinary schools are stressed by continuous pressures and criticisms and do not welcome additional tasks which may increase both. Parents who have seen their children move from a mainstream where little is done for their special needs to a special school sub-system relatively good at meeting the needs, naturally question any reversal of the move.[20]

However, he went on to describe many examples of successful integration.

Further testimony to the popularity of special schools was to be found in the Fish Report in 1985,[21] knowledge of which was used in the campaign by the Inner London Teachers' Association against planned special school closures. While some parents' groups were campaigning for more integration, the Chair of the ILEA Special Education Committee was caught up in an angry televised row as parents of the Campaign for Choice in Special Education lobbied politicians in April 1987. The group complained that in the wake of the strongly pro-integration Fish Report, parents had to fight the authority to have their children placed in special schools which the parents saw as a form of positive discrimination.[22] Other examples of parents fighting to keep threatened special schools open are quoted later in this chapter.

In America there was a rapid growth in mainstreaming, often using the resource room approach, but the disquiet about integration that existed there was also reaching England. In 1980, Pocklington noted that integration was sometimes forced on children, something which was clearly not in their interests.[23] Two years later, Gresham listed over 40 studies carried out in the 1970s which showed one of three features. First, the non-handicapped interacted less or more negatively with handicapped children; secondly, handicapped children were poorly accepted by non-handicapped peers; and, thirdly, that handicapped children did not automatically model their behaviour on that of the non-handicapped.[24] Also by 1985, the State of Massachusetts, a pioneer since its 1973 Integration Law (Chapter 766), had drawn back from over-enthusiastic mainstreaming practised in the mid-1970s. A lack of resources, among other factors, had led to special children spending less time in regular classes and increasing pressure to segregate the handicapped.[25]

Growing pessimism (or perhaps realism?) in the United States was reflected in the feelings of educationalists this side of the Atlantic. In March 1984, a year after the implementation of the 1981 Act, the editorial of *Special Education – Forward Trends* pondered pessimistically on the nature of the new beast: 'It has an insatiable appetite for paper in all forms, it takes a long time to goad into action and it seems to require a good many extra educational psychologists to keep it up to scratch.'[26] By the mid-1980s, a definite air of gloom had descended on many educational commentators as central government seemed once more to forget about special education. It is reported that officials within the DES had to battle hard in 1987 to prevent the 'statemented' child from being excluded altogether from the newly proposed National Curriculum.[27] Although this segregationist proposal was rejected, the new curriculum's attainment targets, tests and a subject range which seemed to exclude the development of personal and social skills, pointed to a competitive educational system in which there would not be the time or the inclination to meet the needs of special children other than in segregated provision. Many of the hopes engendered by the Warnock Report were fast dissipating. The extra psychologists recommended by Warnock were often not directly involved in helping children or supporting and training staff, but rather in following the long-winded bureaucratic procedures engendered by the Act.

However, many examples were chronicled in the contemporary press of individual integration in various settings and successful organizational examples which worked well. Some of these are mentioned in the pages which follow. Also in 1988, Hegarty was able to report closer links between special and ordinary schools which augured well for the closer future involvement in the mainstream of children with special needs.[28]

The Deaf and Partially Hearing

In 1967, there were under 5500 children in English and Welsh special schools and classes for the deaf and partially hearing, rising to over 10 000 a decade later, but falling back to under 7500 in 1983. In part, these figures reflect the population boom but also the more extensive diagnosis and special placement of the partially hearing. Figures for the partially hearing show a rise of nearly 300 per cent in the first decade.[29]

The world of deaf education continued to be divided regarding both the best teaching method and the best route to adult integration, but the balance of opinion had shifted. By the early 1980s, after a century of dominance, believers in the oral/aural approach (see p. 17) were on the defensive as Total Communication made headway. Increasingly, the latter was found to be useful for the many children with learning difficulties or other additional handicaps who now predominated in the residential schools, and for whom schools such as the Royal Schools for the Deaf at Cheadle, specially catered. However, at the two selective schools, Mary Hare and Burwood Park, strict oral methods continued to be used to good effect. Similarly, Birkdale School for the partially hearing in Southport, many of whose children suffered severe hearing loss, and who enjoyed a high degree of parental support, continued to flourish using a strict oral approach beginning at nursery age. Their headmistress, Morag Clarke, proved a redoubtable champion for the oral cause.[30]

The government-sponsored Lewis Report of 1968 had conceded that finger-spelling and -signing could be useful in the education of some hearing-impaired children and called for more research. Much of this was forthcoming from America from where evidence criticized standards reached by oral methods and claimed success for Total Communication. The adult deaf of the British Deaf Association (BDA) continued to campaign vigorously for its adoption, believing British Sign Language to be a language in its own right. It was gratified to see the Department of Health and Social Security give financial support to the BSL Training Agency which conducted its first course at the University of Durham in 1985. In 1982, it also welcomed the admission by the British Association of Teachers of the Deaf, formed by the amalgamation of the National College of Teachers of the Deaf and

Society of Teachers of the Deaf in 1977, that some hearing-impaired children could not succeed through oral means alone. For many children, the BDA believed that Total Communication would best be taught in the controlled and supportive environment of residential schools, some of which were under threat of closure due to falling numbers but for whose retention the BDA fought.[31]

However, the oral cause was being helped by the growing desire for as many hearing-impaired children as possible to be educated in mainstream schools. It was commonly argued that if the hearing impaired were to be part of ordinary school life they needed to be able to communicate and think in spoken English. Few speaking and hearing people could be expected to learn sign language. Further, if they were to mix in ordinary society as adults, they needed to encounter and work through some of the problems of associating with the hearing world from an early age. Many parents, naturally anxious to be able to keep their deaf children at home, were responsive to these arguments and welcomed the widespread development of units for the hearing impaired attached to ordinary day schools. By 1983 the number of pupils in these units had grown to 4049.[32] An increasing number were in units for secondary-aged pupils. Of course, given the low numbers in some units and the high degree of individual attention available, it was also possible for some signing to be taught where necessary in addition to lip-reading and speech skills.

Further advances in technology also eased the integration of the hearing impaired. In particular, the development of miniaturized hearing-aids worn behind the ear in place of cumbersome 'box' aids strapped to the body and linked to the ears by wires made children less self-conscious about using them. They were also more difficult to break. Radio aids were a further improvement and, in the 1980s, were superseding 'induction loops' as a method of amplification, because they were more flexible and less subject to interference from extraneous sounds.[33]

However, the standard of provision in the units was found to be variable, and the special school continued to have strong support, particularly for those children with severe deafness or an additional handicap. An HMI survey in the mid-1960s praised many units' good work, particularly their ability to help along many quite seriously deaf children in preparation for integration into mainstream classes. However, when it actually came to implementing integration schemes, a mixture of organizational and social difficulties were experienced and some schemes were judged by HMI not to have been successful. Some pupils would have been better placed in special schools and the youth and inexperience of some of the unit teachers was noted. Where the teachers of the main school lacked understanding of the needs of the deaf, the units became small, segregated special schools. The Report urged that units should be reserved for pupils with a fair prospect of learning to speak in a natural way by listening rather than lip-reading.[34] A decade later the Warnock Committee held a similar view.

The latter had found that very few deaf children were fully integrated into ordinary classes, although it was happening to an extent in Haringey in London, Norfolk and Worcester.[35] This situation reflected very real practical difficulties and also the patchy peripatetic service, criticized by the DES in 1969. Support work had operated better in primary schools, but overcrowded classes, noisy environments and lack of time to do effective work directly with the deaf pupils or to counsel their regular teachers, plus the lack of interest in the problems of the deaf shown by some secondary school teachers, limited its effectiveness. However, LEA peripatetic teachers of the deaf increased from 95 to 440 between 1965 and 1983 and many areas placed increasing faith in the service.[36]

Their work was appreciated by Wendy Lynas of the Manchester University Department of Audiology, a well-known advocate of integration. To her, there was a strong moral and philosophical base from which to work. Integration seemed a natural extension of the comprehensive principle and her research suggested that the hearing impaired successfully coped with integration where it did happen and benefited socially. Her 1984 study found four LEAs using contrasting methods of provision. One sent 82 per cent of its hearing impaired to special schools, whereas the remaining 18 per cent were individually integrated into ordinary schools. Another LEA placed 28 per cent in special schools and 72 per cent in units. A third divided its hearing impaired almost equally between special schools, units and individual integration. Out of 137 severely and profoundly deaf pupils, 58 per cent were on the rolls of ordinary schools.

Her interviews with deaf students suggested to her that many more strident critics of integration, for example the Australian school principal, McGrath, were wrong to claim that the deaf in ordinary schools were relegated to a low status. If some were disliked or teased it was rarely because of their deafness, but rather because they exhibited characteristics which would lead to dislike of any hearing children. She claimed that virtually all the deaf children 'who had views on the matter' wanted to be in an ordinary school, despite sometimes admittedly difficult experiences and stress. Education in ordinary schools was seen as the best preparation for mainstream adult life.[37]

Lynas' work was criticized by Susan Gregory of Nottingham University. In 1976, Gregory had warned that while integration was a worthy aim, it should not be assumed to be the best way for either deaf children or their families. Such an attitude often placed unfair stresses on the deaf and on their families who were already having difficulties in coping with the child's handicap.[38] A decade later she challenged the way in which Lynas had questioned her subjects and had underestimated 'the immense communication problems that are apparent from many of the quotes by teachers and pupils'.[39] From Gregory's own interpretation of Lynas' evidence she felt that the case for integration was far from proven.

The divergence of views in Britain in the late 1980s in which most still saw a continuing place for some special schools, reflected contrasting opinion around the world. Germany, the country with the most prolonged experience of integration in the nineteenth century, was perhaps the most resistant to the modern integration movement. Meanwhile, in 1987 in the USA, a century after Bell's campaigns, under 12 per cent of the hearing impaired were in the country's residential schools. The latter, as in Britain, educated the deaf with additional difficulties, acted as a safety net for those failing in the mainstream and as a vocational trainer of the older teenager. The majority of children were mainstreamed, but of the latter only 21 per cent were actually on regular class rolls.[40]

The Blind and Partially Sighted

The numbers of partially sighted children in England and Wales increased by about 17 per cent between 1967 and 1977 before falling back to 2027 in 1983, the last year the DES produced statistics in the traditional form. This is a little below the 1967 level. For the blind, however, there was a steady gradual decline to 929 children in 1983, reflecting the much reduced incidence of retrolental fibroplasia and better medical care.[41] Falling numbers of blind children brought about the demise of some famous old schools, including the Royal Normal College in 1972, and in the 1980s the Royal Victoria, Newcastle. However, some establishments flourished and a few expanded their activities. Exhall Grange continued to provide a national service, while Worcester College was enlarged and strengthened in 1986 on its amalgamation with the Chorleywood Grammar School for girls. Likewise, schools catering for the 50 per cent of blind children with additional learning or physical difficulties continued to be needed. Among these was the RNIB's Condover Hall. For the blind, special classes attached to ordinary schools continued to be rare or non-existent, whereas there were nine such classes in England

and Wales for the partially sighted in 1971.[42]

Not shown in DES statistics are an unknown number of children, some severely handicapped, coping with life in ordinary schools and escaping official categorization. Nor, given changes in the presentation of statistics in 1984, is it possible to say how many children were in special classes for the visually handicapped. However, in 1982, half of the educationally blind were thought to be in special schools for the visually handicapped and the other half in ordinary schools or special schools primarily designed for other difficulties. This calculation does not seem significantly different from two local surveys conducted in the Cheshire area and in Wales in 1969–70. In 1983, only 11 blind and 150 partially sighted children in England and Wales, and a further small number in Scotland, were attending special classes in maintained schools.[43]

It does seem that integrating the visually handicapped into ordinary schools made only limited progress during this period and probably so to the present day. This reflects the caution of most contemporary British commentators and conflicting evidence from America on its advisability.

The Fine Report of 1968 was little concerned with integration other than to record that it was quite common for the visually handicapped to start their schooling in ordinary primary schools with the sighted before transferring to schools for the visually impaired.[44] The following year a Working Party set up by the Scottish Education Department and chaired by A.G. Rodger was also cautious. Carrying on the post-war tradition, the Working Party wanted to see the two larger schools with boarding facilities for the partially sighted in Edinburgh and Glasgow developed and an end to the eight small special classes set in special schools. They were not against mixing the intelligent partially sighted with the physically handicapped in a grammar school, and suggested linking a school for the partially sighted to a local secondary school to give access to wider social and educational opportunities for the academically gifted.

The Working Party favoured special nursery education.[45] The same message was given by Eira Clarke, the former Head of the East Grinstead Sunshine Home, one of the six units existing at this time. In a 1967 article she emphasized the useful service these continued to provide both in relieving family stress and starting effective social education, mobility and other independence training. She regretted the influence of Bowlby, whose ideas discouraged some over-protective and over-busy parents, with little time to aid their blind child's development, from using the Sunshine Homes. She noted the 'liveliness and interest, fun and laughter' of the children.[46] This concern for a very early start to the education and training of the visually handicapped was shared by the 1978 Warnock Report[47] and the 1972 Vernon Report.

The latter was a major, government-sponsored enquiry into provision for the blind, set up in 1968. The Committee concluded that nationally there were adequate educational facilities, but in an attempt to make the larger, more viable schools nearer the homes of the pupils, they reversed the belief of the post-war planners that the blind and the partially-sighted should be educated in separate schools.[48] They also saw that this would ease placement decisions for low-vision pupils at an uncertain and sometimes shifting borderline between blindness and partial sight. This recommendation was reflected in the merging in 1979 of the College of Teachers of the Blind and the National Association for the Education of the Partially Sighted to form the Association for the Education and Welfare of the Visually Handicapped (AEWVH).

The Vernon Committee also strongly favoured turning existing single-sex schools into co-educational establishments.[49]

The Vernon Report devoted a whole section to the subject of integration. They reported that 59 per cent of the blind in the USA were attending sighted schools. They discussed a visit by Elizabeth Anderson to Scandinavia. While impressed by her enthusiasm for what she observed there, they were only prepared to encourage limited and controlled moves towards integration in this country. They commented on the success of the well-supported integration occurring in Sheffield where Tapton Mount had placed a small number of its residents in a hostel at the school from where they attended a local comprehensive. In the latter, a resource centre was set up staffed by two teachers from Tapton Mount, who produced braille materials and gave support to the pupils and mainstream staff. The children chosen were intelligent, persevering and emotionally mature students. They were judged to be mixing freely with the sighted children and gaining substantially in mobility and independence.[50]

This success echoed that of some of the carefully selected children sent out from St Vincent's, Liverpool, to a neighbouring school. Between 1961 and 1977, 10 children were thus integrated. But the experience had convinced Sister Kathleen of the need for caution. For some children who lacked stamina and motivation the placements had not gone particularly well. Other intelligent children were sent to a special grammar school rather than try to integrate them. Sister Kathleen was convinced that both methods had their advantages and disadvantages.

Like many Heads of special schools, she had seen the happy change in children entering her special school who had found the pressure of surviving in ordinary school too great or the organization of the ordinary school ill-suited to their needs, with the handicapped debarred from sport, handicraft and other enjoyable subjects. She had experienced parents pushing for a special school place for their partially sighted child after unhappy experiences in ordinary day schools. She was aware that other parents were reluctant to have their child board, but stressed that this opposition often evaporated and parents became very supportive of the residential approach when they saw their child's progress and contentment. In her opinion, in 1977, integration remained 'a value judgement highly charged with emotion'. She also repeated an old idea: 'There is indeed something to be said for being "ordinary" in a special school, rather than "special" in an ordinary school.'[51]

The same sentiment was felt by Elizabeth Chapman and Juliet Stone in 1988.[52] They were able to look back on research by Jamiesson and colleagues which suggested that the visually handicapped in ordinary schools experienced little teasing by the sighted,[53] the Warnock Report which had endorsed the advice of the Vernon Report, and the DES-sponsored study by the National Foundation for Educational Research into the education of children with special needs in ordinary schools. The latter described a resource area in an unnamed city primary school in 1978. The pupils were carefully selected, but the degree of functional integration for the partially sighted was rapidly increased and even the blind pupils were found, after time, to be able to spend more of their time in regular classes. Care had been taken to prepare the staff, the sighted pupils and their parents before this experiment began, contributing to the reported success. Team teaching and vertical grouping of pupils were believed to be important features.[54]

Similar developments elsewhere were supported by a growing band of LEA peripatetic teachers whose numbers increased from 1 to 60 between 1972 and 1985.[55] Some of the support for children in ordinary schools came from the special schools. Tapton Mount was a pioneer, joined in recent years by Worcester College. This agrees with AEWVH policy of encouraging integration while keeping some special schools. Also to be noted is the planned opening of a vocational college for older students funded by the Royal National Institute for the Blind on the same site as Loughborough Technical college.[56]

In conflict with claims that special schools exclude children from, in the term used by Sally Tomlinson, 'the national credentialling system', Chapman and Stone noted that in the 1980s many special schools for the blind achieved excellent examination results. They further held that parents' appreciation of this was likely to be one of the factors which made them press for special education.[57]

In 1986 in the United States, the great majority of visually handicapped were mainstreamed, but only a third were enrolled in regular classes. Another third were based in resource rooms and nearly a fifth in special classes. About 18 per cent were taught in separate day and residential schools. These national averages hide considerable differences in the 50 states. The American literature often favours integration but other studies showed poor interaction between the visually handicapped and the sighted and their poor social status.[58]

The cautious views of Vernon, Warnock, Fothergill and Chapman seem wise.

The Epileptic, Delicate and Physically Handicapped

The number of epileptic children in special provision increased between 1967 and 1977 before falling back to the 1967 level by 1983. In the 1980s, the schools at Maghull, Kendal and Soss Moss, near Manchester, closed despite parental objections, leaving three remaining centres at Much Hadham and Lingfield in the Home Counties and Warford, Cheshire. Pupils, almost without exception, had other difficulties in addition to their medical handicap. In 1983, 73 children whose primary handicap was epilepsy were being educated in designated special classes instead of boarding schools. For an increasing majority of epileptic children, however, control of fits by medication and integration into regular classes in ordinary schools continued to be the usual course of action. However, referrals for the David Lewis Centre in Cheshire increased in 1988. Places were sought for both very young primary-age children as well as teenagers who could not cope or were posing problems in the third or fourth years of secondary education.[59]

The dramatic decline, commenced in the late 1950s, in the number of delicate children in, or awaiting placement in special schools, and those in hospital schools continued. The numbers for England and Wales fell from nearly 10 000 in 1967 (of whom 955 were in hospital schools or receiving home tuition) to 4603 in 1983 (of whom 212 children were in hospital or at home). Better medical practice (e.g. salbutamol inhalers for the treatment of asthma and the decline of tuberculosis) added to vastly improved physical conditions in many city schools, lessened the usefulness of the delicate schools. They also remained popular with some children and parents. The Fish Committee of 1985 found a very high percentage of both parents and their children appreciative of London's delicate schools. In the same year, Staffordshire closed down Hanchurch Open Air School whereupon the parents and some staff raised £70 000, brought the school and reopened it. In 1989 it still existed as a small unit and was upgrading its boarding facilities expecting to increase its numbers on roll.[60]

When, in 1987, Berkshire proposed to close Hephaistos Boarding

School for the intelligent physically handicapped, Mary Warnock expressed sadness and doubts. She believed that in the present financial and social climate, boarding schools were in 'terrible trouble'. She regretted many people's ignorance of 'the enormous benefits of boarding for some children'.[61]

How typical was the closure of Hephaistos of the times? Did it represent yet another step along the high road to almost complete integration for the physically handicapped? The alterations to the DES collection and publication of statistics makes the task of answering these questions more difficult, but it does not seem that a dramatic increase took place in integration, at least not until the mid-1980s. There were still over 2000 more children in schools for the physically handicapped in 1983 than in 1967. Government circulars in 1970 (85/70 and 13/70), the 1971 Scottish Circular 782 and the 1975 McCann Report continued to call for more integration of the less severely handicapped, as did the Warnock Report,[62] but did they alter the situation that already existed? This is a difficult question to answer.

In most periods, many of the physically handicapped had coped in ordinary classes and had not entered regular government statistics. This continued in this period. In 1972, the Chief Medical Officer reported a wide-ranging survey covering most parts of the country which showed that 10 200 physically handicapped children were in ordinary schools while, in 1970, 8545 were in special schools.[63] Two years later he noted that in a north Midlands city with a well-developed special school system there were 333 physically handicapped in the ordinary schools.[64] In 1978, when the total number in schools for the physically handicapped was about twice as many as in 1970, Anderson and Clarke still found that of their sample of 119 children, a third were in ordinary schools, including 20 per cent of the children with moderate or severe handicaps.[65] In 1969, over half the thalidomide children were also attending ordinary primary schools and taking a full part in school life.[66]

Yet in the 1970s and 1980s new integration schemes undoubtedly started. For example, physically handicapped children, some in wheelchairs, entered Bell Wood Primary School, Maidstone, in 1971. By 1980, nine had moved on to ordinary secondary schools, although many went to secondary special schools.[67] In 1973, 12 children entered a new unit attached to a secondary school in Warley in the West Midlands.[68] Both schemes were judged successful.

However, such partial integration in the 1970s was limited. A survey in 1975 found only 12 out of the 105 recently reorganized LEAs maintained special units in ordinary schools at primary level and 4 at secondary level. Only 14 LEAs provided for the physically handicapped in ordinary classes at secondary level and 11 LEAs placed special schools on the same campus as an ordinary school. However, other LEAs were planning moves in this direction. Cope and Anderson described the benefits of integration for the primary aged pupils but conceded that at secondary level nearly half of their sample of 55 children would need to go to a special secondary school. A decade later, this tendency still existed, but various successful secondary schemes have been reported including examples in Manchester and at the Senacre School, Maidstone.[69]

The need for special education at secondary age reflected the findings of the Chief Medical Officer's Report in 1972, where two-thirds of the physically handicapped in ordinary schools had been of primary age. The greater ease of integration at primary level is mentioned in other contemporary sources.[70] Hegarty and Pocklington's description in 1982 of integrated provision also referred mainly to the primary level. They noted the slow progress of integration but gave three models of good practice for others to follow. In detailed accounts in which difficulties as well as successes were outlined, an individual integration scheme, a special department in an ordinary school and a special school sharing a site with an ordinary school were described. The authors, along with the 1978 Warnock Report, were convinced of the viability of integration of many more physically handicapped, particularly for stable, persevering children of normal ability. Their view took into account allusions in contemporary literature to the lack of proper support, particularly physiotherapy services for the physically handicapped in ordinary schools.[71] These deficiencies were sometimes recognized and put right (e.g. in the schools of South Clwyd after 1978).[72] However, Anderson, Clarke and Spain still found too many schools without ramps and generally poorly adapted to the needs of the disabled.[73]

In the McCann and Warnock Reports, a continuing role was seen for some special schools, including boarding schools where children with social, learning or behavioural difficulties, often in addition to their physical handicap, could receive expert, individual attention.[74] Likely pupils would be some spina bifida children who, due to more active medical intervention to save the lives of babies whatever the degree of handicap in the 1970s, survived in greater numbers.[75] Many cerebral palsied children also had serious learning difficulties. It was for these children that the Spastics Society opened a new purpose-built boarding school at Meldreth Manor, Cambridgeshire, in 1966.

Many pupils from special schools and from ordinary schools found specialist further education (FE) facilities useful. Some establishments, for example St Loyes, Exeter, and long-established schools such as Lord Mayor Treloar's, Alton, had provided FE courses for many years. However, new facilities were developed at Coventry LEA's Hereward

College, sharing a site with an ordinary college (1971), at the Spastics Society's Beaumont College in Lancaster (1977) for the less-able cerebral palsied, and Dene College in Kent (1978). The aim was always to increase students' abilities to cope with an independent adult life integrated as much as possible into mainstream society.

Many other British schools followed the lead of the Spastics Society at Ingfield Manor in 1971, by showing an interest in conductive education.[76] However, the methods of Peto – further developed by Maria Hari in Budapest with such good results for the cerebral palsied – were diluted, and the staff applying them did not receive the rigorous four-year conductor's course. In 1986, a television programme, *Standing Up for Joe*, focused attention on the success of Budapest and contributed to the establishment of the Foundation for Conductive Education at Birmingham University. The thorough training of British conductors was then set in motion; however, it will take a number of years to determine the success of this scheme.[77] One point is clear, however. While conductive education might well lead to the integration of many severely handicapped children at junior age, it has to take place in a specialized environment under the constant guidance of expert staff. Therefore, it would seem likely that the number of primary age children in segregated provision will be maintained, if not increased. In Hungary, most students are residential.

Despite the propagandist tones of bodies such as the Centre for Studies in Integrated Education,[78] the cautious words of the Chief Medical Officer in 1974 sum up the period and reflect the views of most contemporaries:

> There is no longer any justification for attaching a label or category to a child and automatically sending him to a special school. Alternatively, it would be dangerous to decree that all physically handicapped children could attend even suitably adapted ordinary schools. Some children can accept it and some are psychologically, socially, medically or educationally unable to do so.[79]

Maladjusted and Disruptive Children

Statistics are lacking, but movement towards the 'whole school' policies identified by the Warnock and Fish Reports[80] did not apparently halt growth in the number of maladjusted or disruptive children placed in special schools, classes or non-designated special units, even in the late 1980s. Altering traditional curricula and weaning staff away from handing the troublesome over to special teachers in separate departments was often a process which even fervent believers in the approach found difficult. John Sayer talked in 1983 of 'the constant pressure to revert to a closed circle of special educators'.[81]

Segregation increased and almost certainly reflected the difficulties teachers found in maintaining order in the classroom against a backdrop of an increasingly violent and lawless society in which family life was under attack. The appointment in Scotland in the mid-1970s of the Pack Committee,[82] and of the Elton Committee in England in 1988, reflected concern for discipline in schools. Meanwhile, the needs of the majority took precedence over those of the disruptive pupils, but a rough sort of justice often occurred. Selection for special provision could be haphazard and the value of the expanding special schools, classes or units was doubted. Various writers[83] viewed special schools for children with emotional and behavioural disorders (EBD) as expensive and often less effective than normal schooling where the curriculum and ethos were suitable. Echoing the view of Mary Dendy (*c.* 1908), it was thought unwise to mix the maladjusted with other disturbed children as they tended to exacerbate each other's problems. It was further held that placement in a special unit or school was stigmatizing and possibly damaging to a child's life-chances. Reintegration was low and there was little research to show the worth of segregated provision.

But, equally, little research existed to show the *lack* of worth of most schools and, given the many variables, efficacy studies were always likely to be flawed. Policy makers were therefore left with personal accounts of professionals, case histories, and surveys of opinion. Influential authors who, while worrying about segregation, saw considerable value in special provision for the maladjusted, included Robert Laslett (1977) and Wilson and Evans (1980), after their wide-ranging study of 'best practice' schools.[84] When added to the admitted social control functions, the views of these and other commentators made a strong case for continuing special provision – quite often, as I have argued elsewhere, in boarding schools.[85]

Against this background, the number of children identified as being maladjusted in England and Wales rose from 8833 in 1967 to 20 995 in 1977, and to 22 241 in 1983 despite a decline in the overall number of schoolchildren. The change in the presentation of DES statistics prevents a figure for the late 1980s. The number of schools for these pupils increased in the maintained, non-maintained and independent sectors from 92 in 1965 to 191 in 1974.[86] By 1983, there were 136 maintained and non-maintained residential schools and, in August 1985, 69 independent schools were approved by the DES.[87] In addition to pupils in official special education, there was an explosion in the provision of units for the disaffected, including many maladjusted children, which were called by a variety of official names but dubbed 'sin-bins'. Between 1973 and 1977, 199 were established, bringing the total to 239, catering for 3962 pupils. By 1983, the Inner London Education Authority alone had 226 units for 3800 pupils and further rapid growth happened elsewhere with calls continuing for more. In Scotland, provision was less widespread but included boarding schools and units.[88]

Controversy existed not only over whether children should be placed in schools for the maladjusted, but also over what approaches best helped them once they were there. The Underwood Committee had placed much of its hope in psychiatrists and child guidance clinics. However, in 1974, Dr Kingsley Whitmore, Senior Medical Officer at the DES, doubted the value of time-consuming neo-Freudian intervention which had dominated child-guidance thinking for 50 years with little firm evidence of its value. In the late 1970s, the Schools Council Research team was similarly sceptical.[89]

The Underwood Committee had also listened sympathetically to the liberal notions of educators such as David Wills on the nature of good child care. Therapeutic communities still existed which emphasized Rapaport's basic tenets of democratization, communalism, reality-confrontation and permissiveness.[90] However, the word 'liberalism' was sometimes preferred to this latter term, and the need for some structure and for adults to set limits to acting-out behaviour was perhaps more widely recognized. Some communities continued to prosper, mainly on social service department placements, by catering for exceptionally disturbed children. Their clientele and their approach in part explained why their fees were usually more than double those for more conventional special boarding communities. Some children benefited in these settings, and such schools helped by sensible guidance on child care from the DES in 1965 and the DHSS in 1970,[91] and by training courses at Newcastle and Bristol Universities, helped to move some boarding schools away from an over-structured authoritarianism.

In his 1971 account of the somewhat chaotic and ill-disciplined transformation of an apparently flawed and repressive approved school into the therapeutic Cotswold Community, during which 50 children were excluded, David Wills commented: 'Only very rarely is the cure for delinquency and emotional disorder to be found in what normally goes on in the classroom.'[92] This probably reflects a popular view in the 1950s and 1960s, stretching beyond the bounds of Approved Schools for young offenders and into schools for the maladjusted. However, in 1978, the Warnock Committee wrote that, 'Educational failure is now recognised as a significant factor in maladjustment and the contribution of successful learning to adjustment is more widely recognised.'

Warnock thought it was not sufficient for schools merely to concentrate on fostering good personal relationships as had tended to happen in some schools. Education had to be of a quality and width to enable the maladjusted child to profit from further education and training on 'relatively equal terms with their contemporaries'.[93] Denying them a normal education was likely to restrict their chances in adult life.

This comment was in line with HMIs' poor report on the educational standards in community homes with education (CHEs)[94] published in the same year and with the clear message of the wide-ranging Schools Council three-year inquiry under Wilson and Evans into the theory and practice of educational work with disturbed children. Having sounded out the opinions of front-line staff in hundreds of schools and made many visits, they concluded that it was important for schools to seek to enhance the disturbed child's self-image by fostering his successful achievement in as many activities as possible. Foremost was the need, within a warm caring atmosphere, to secure success in reading and writing, or, perhaps failing that, in craft work or sport. Developing social skills and improving relationships were important, but these could sometimes be developed hand-in-hand with educational progress. Many effective schools stressed normality in the classroom and one headteacher talked of 'normality therapy'.[95]

Their enquiries revealed the limited extent to which aspects of treatment associated with the leading lights of the 1960s (e.g. unconditional affection, shared responsibility, opportunity for regression and psychotherapy) were used. However, behaviour modification was even less used and favoured, despite some evidence of its effectiveness in altering the behaviour of the maladjusted. Roger Burland's Chelfham Mill School suggested the usefulness of the behaviourist approach over many years.[96] Here, checklists of carefully defined behavioural goals would be completed by the carers looking after the children and regular rewards given for good behaviour. However, most schools steered a middle course, favouring a liberal but structured community and sharing the belief of the former Approved School Head, Haydn Davies Jones, when he wrote that 'much of residential work relies heavily on the intuitive, the creative and the artistic'. This also applied to day schools.[97]

In the second half of the 1980s, some boarding schools were closed as LEAs moved further towards community-based approaches. Some poor-quality independent schools identified by the Warnock Committee were to a limited extent weeded out in the inspection procedures which followed the 1981 Education Act. This specified that if independent residential special schools were to be used by LEAs, they must be inspected and approved by HMI and placed on a special DES list. If

LEAs wished to place a particular child in an 'unlisted' school (e.g. many schools following the Rudolf Steiner philosophy in the early 1980s), they must first obtain permission from the DES. However, more damaging to the viability of some schools was the ability of LEAs to pick their placements carefully, because the supply of schools exceeded the demand of needy children or strictly controlled 'out-county' budgets. Nevertheless, a few new independent boarding schools, some reflecting the high standards existing in many still flourishing older establishments, opened and provided a useful service, particularly when they stayed open in the normal holiday periods. Meanwhile, indifferent maintained schools largely escaped HMI attention and were a source of concern to LEA officers.

The 1985 Fish Report, while recognizing a continuing need for some residential schools in ILEA, wondered whether social service departments ought to run them.[98] Certainly, boarding schools were in part filling a gap left by the widespread closure of very expensive CHEs and children's homes run by social service departments. Not for the first time, community care in the guise of fostering as well as integration of EBD children was found to have limits. Many Heads of boarding schools experienced the failure of social service departments to find suitable foster homes for older children with special needs, or watched as the fragile hopes of often-disappointed children were again shattered as foster parents rejected them with little warning, leaving the boarding school to pick up the pieces once more.[99]

The Fish Report also suggested that while a minority of parents and children were dissatisfied with their placement and progress in schools for the maladjusted, over half were happy. This majority view was in accord with evidence contained in Wilson and Evans's survey which showed frequent positive pupil reaction to their special school placement.[100] Elsewhere, it was noted how children placed part-time in special classes and units attended these regularly while continuing to truant from the host school which they associated with boredom, unhappy relationships with staff and pupils and general failure. Segregation helped to restore their self-esteem.[101] However, others claimed that attending special schools and classes was stigmatizing. Once again, a study in 1987 found, not surprisingly, that reintegrated EBD children did not wish to return to a special school.[102]

The Schools Council inquiry also established that nearly two-thirds of the children in boarding schools for the disturbed had IQs of under 100, and that 92 per cent were underachievers on arrival and 68 per cent needed remedial teaching.[103] Given this situation, it was unrealistic to expect these children to leave school with a clutch of national examination passes, although some pupils might have been restricted by the narrow curriculum offered in the small special school.

Difficulties in integrating EBD children have been echoed internationally. In 1986, in Massachusetts, sometimes held up as an exemplar of integration, only 8 per cent were in regular classes, although the majority were mainstreamed in resource areas. Meanwhile, in California, 5 per cent were in regular classes, 68 per cent in special classes and 21 per cent in private special schools.[104]

ESN and Remedial Children

In 1971, W. Brennan, then President of the National Association for Remedial Education, wrote:

> The backward child who does not enter a special school is left in the most hazardous situation in the whole of the education system. His educational future is at the mercy of completely fortuitous circumstances which may differ not only from area to area but also from school to school, or even from term to term within the same school.[105]

Classes in remedial departments were still too often taken by the least able or most inexperienced teachers. They were the last to receive resources, the first target for cuts and often held in the worst available accommodation. They were noted for their isolation from the main body of the school and often existed due to the enthusiasm of a particular Head or individual teacher on whose departure the class would be disbanded. It was a period of rapid staff turnover and disruption caused by the creation of comprehensive schools, sometimes magnified, HMI noted, by the change over from streaming to non-streaming and, on occasion, by the change back to streaming.[106] Other leading writers, such as Gulliford, Segal, Peter Bell and Alec Williams, thought the same way to varying degrees.[107] Their views were backed by the findings of Rutter's survey of children on the Isle of Wight and the National Child Development Study, as well as by the wide-ranging HMI survey of secondary schools in 1967–8 of over 90 000 children in 20 LEAs. Brennan's doubts persisted in 1982 and were reflected in the 1985 Fish Report.[108]

However, a survey by HMI in 1980–82 painted a generally more favourable impression. There was praise for several schools' lively and stimulating remedial classes and well-planned mixed-ability work. Good relations were observed between teachers and children and 'there was little indication that pupils equated poor academic attainment with inferior personal worth'.[109] However, some special classes and remedial groups were still thought isolated. They were situated in remote parts of the school, sometimes in separate buildings, although this arrangement was thought to be becoming less frequent. Other children experienced a 'nomadic existence', moving about complicated buildings to a succession of cheerless rooms. Too many children received an impoverished curriculum with too much concentration on basic skills and repetition of arid exercises which emphasized their failures.

This then was the unsatisfactory setting for many of Warnock's 20 per cent in this period, despite improvements in organization and curricula, perhaps aided by movement to 'support' and the 'whole school approach' in the mid-1980s. It is small wonder that separate provision in special schools for as many as possible was the dominant desire in the late 1960s. Neither is it surprising that thousands of children still appeared to fare better in moderate learning difficulty (MLD) schools in 1988 after an often chequered and unhappy time in the mainstream.

In 1967, of 57 580 children identified as being ESN, over 10 000 awaited placement in special schools or designated classes. This number rose to 81 011 for the ESN (Moderate) in 1977 before falling back to 69 174 in 1983 and a waiting list of under 2500, possibly due to the declining population and further integration. The number of pupils in maintained and non-maintained English and Welsh ESN (Moderate) boarding schools fell by 44 per cent from 8899 in 1973 to 4945 in 1983. National statistics are not available but, in the late 1980s, this decline has probably spread to day schools in some areas, as more authorities have pursued a policy of occasional functional and more often social or locational integration for MLD children. In ILEA, the number of children in MLD schools expressed as a percentage of the school population declined noticeably from 1.21 to 0.83 per cent between 1971 and 1984.[110] Cleveland was an example of an authority which kept children's names on the special schools' rolls while an increasing number of pupils received their education in ordinary schools supported by the special school staff.

The movement to a greater degree of integration in some areas found an early advocate in the Coventry educational psychologist J. R. Staples who, in 1967, wrote of his dislike of persuading reluctant parents that their children needed to be placed in special schools. He claimed that a strong element of chance was present in placement decisions and it tended to be the disruptive who were segregated, although the blame for their behaviour should have been attributed to the unsatisfactory curricula and organization in their ordinary schools.[111] In 1971, A. Adams' article was an example of the growing belief that were streaming replaced by team teaching and curricula which did not emphasize competition, there would be fewer disenchanted children needing to be placed in ESN schools.[112] In 1974, Malcolm Stone, HMI, in a talk significantly entitled 'Children with Learning Difficulties', gave a cautious welcome to the notion of integration.[113] He believed this was now a realistic if difficult proposition in true comprehensive schools which sought to meet individual needs, and which were well supported by related professional services. Pushing integration from another angle, the Park School, Blackpool, was admitting children at an early age but managing to reintegrate a significant percentage of them into secondary schools.[114]

In 1974, the Warnock Committee set to work. They wrote their Report in the light of Section 10 of the 1976 Education Act (see p. 134), but members had also observed good practice in some ordinary schools, e.g. the progress units at the Cooper School in Bicester.[115] They were therefore able to recommend with some enthusiasm the improvement of services by way of resource centres, special classes and teachers supporting children in regular classes, adequately helped by specialists such as psychologists. They made early allusion to the necessity for a 'whole school policy' which broke down the old 'them and us' attitude between the remedial department and the rest of the school, in which remedial teachers were assigned an inferior status. The sympathy and support of the ordinary class teacher had to be won if integration was to be beneficial. Assuming this could happen, the number of special schools was likely to decline and to be reserved for children with complex learning and additional difficulties. Some schools could become resource centres, providing expert advice and suitable materials for teachers to use in neighbouring ordinary schools.

Movement in the direction of integration was perhaps sometimes hastened and at other times slowed down by the publicity given in the Schools Council's examination of the standard of curriculum offered in England's ESN schools. Good teaching and good curricula were observed, but rarely together. Brennan's 1979 report drew attention to a generally unsatisfactory situation which did much to puncture claims that special schools were providing 'special' education. Teaching tended to be poorly thought out and badly recorded, mathematics inadequately taught, preparation for leaving sometimes inappropriate, and science as well as the aesthetic subjects ignored. However, in comments which augured badly for the 'whole school approach', his team concluded that team and mixed-ability teaching did not work in practice for slow learners. Further, with implications for many of the new primary schools built in the 1960s and 1970s, open plan designs were thought by many teachers to be less effective than teaching slow learners in specialist rooms.[116]

In the next few years, the disadvantages of special school placement were stressed in a number of books including those by Galloway and Goodwyn, and Sally Tomlinson.[117] Selection for ESN school was said to be arbitrary or made because the ordinary school wanted rid of an awkward child, and was therefore a safety valve for the main system and even a method of social control. Some efficacy studies, although flawed in design and showing conflicting evidence in both America and England, tended to show that the ESN reached higher levels of 'academic' attainment if left in the ordinary schools.[118] Tomlinson argued that the special school system had evolved and was preserved because of the vested interests of the professionals employed within it as much as for the benefit of the children.[119] Resources spent on special schools would be more efficiently spent on improving provision for the special child in ordinary schools. This somewhat crude summary is an accurate reflection of popular interpretations of these authors' work, although it probably distorts the more complex reasoning of their books and their appreciation of counterarguments. To the popular views must also be added the association of racism with special school placement. This belief was common in some inner cities where, reflecting the American experience, a disproportionate number of black children attended ESN schools.[120]

Consequently, supporters of integration argued that the options described by Hegarty and colleagues in *Integration in Action* (1982) were the better course of action. Integration was seen as a dynamic process whereby a child with special needs increasingly participated in ordinary society. There were many degrees of *school* integration. If full functional integration was not possible in practice, then at least partial integration in varying degrees could be provided through special needs departments situated in comprehensive schools, or special centres sharing sites with an ordinary parent school or special classes for children with severe learning difficulties set in infants' schools. In their first example of a Basic Studies Department for 80 pupils in a comprehensive, most children averaged a quarter of their time in ordinary classes. Significantly, difficulties lessened after the transfer of a few severely disruptive children to special boarding schools.[121] The second example also achieved only limited functional integration, because the special centres for MLD and SLD (severe learning difficulty) children were not in the same buildings as the parent school and were operating as 'mini-special schools', with only distant relations with the main school and an 'us and them' attitude was sometimes encountered among staff, although the situation was improving. In the third example, MLD children in a comprehensive were more fully assimilated into the life of the main school, joining mixed-ability groups for games and craft lessons and mixing more with ordinary classes as they became older. However, when the authority wanted to place SLD children in the Slow Learner Department, the Head insisted that they were accommodated in a separate building although on the main school site. This was duly built and the new pupils did share dining facilities and moved around the main site at break-times. The final example of special classes for SLD children in an infants' school did allow a few children to join the reception class for limited periods, but the pupils transferred to special schools at junior age. Parents were reported to be happy with these four options.

More adventurous, but building on local integrationist attitudes of great longevity, was the call of a Regional Study Group in Strathclyde in 1982 for the complete abolition of the few remaining MLD special classes in secondary schools. For some years the trend in the Glasgow area had been away from separate remedial provision and towards mixed-ability organization with more 'banding' as the pupils grew older. For the primary schools, they called for the 'whole school policy' where all staff felt responsible and contributed to meeting the needs of children with learning difficulties. Grampian region, following pioneering 'support' work, also followed a policy of comprehensivization for all children.[122]

Elsewhere in the country, many special schools were forging links with neighbouring ordinary schools in line with the hopes of the Warnock Committee. In Walsall, the heads of local primary schools responded to an invitation to visit the Castle School, as a first step to developing the school as a resource and support centre. From small social beginnings, special school staff started to go into the primaries advising staff and helping prepare materials for children with learning difficulties. Another example was Kirkleatham School in Redcar, where by 1988 about half of the children on its roll attended a growing number of local primary and secondary schools supported by half of its staff, leaving the children with the most complex problems in the special school. Again, from the modest beginnings of integrating the relatively bright and stable MLD children, the scheme had grown to encompass more handicapped children and was county-wide policy.[123]

In 1988, Hegarty was to report that links between special and day schools were becoming commonplace and that three-quarters of the schools he had surveyed had developed them. Schools were being used increasingly as resource centres for advice and materials and the special schools' staff expertise was valued. Furthermore, some individual pupils, and more frequently groups of children, were attending local mainstream schools for a number of periods a week. However, the value of some symbolic mainstreaming, occasionally transmogrified into a new timetabled subject called 'Integration', was doubted in other quarters.[124]

The middle road of locational with a little social integration was apparently liked by parents and was the preferred option of many teachers in Wales in 1984. Gordon Lowden surveyed the opinions of over 200 teachers in 72 primary schools. While four out of five teachers thought integration desirable, nearly two-thirds thought it impractical, and most favoured the system which already existed in some parts of Wales of attaching units to primary schools. Lowden concluded that the results 'did not suggest a generally tolerant attitude toward slow learners as a group'[125] and that there was little determination to see full integration brought about. There was substantial integration for assembly, functions and for physical exercise, but under half the sample mixed with the main school children at playtime and, although the Heads believed that in most cases the children were integrated with the ordinary children at lunchtime, it was common for the dinner ladies to sit the unit children in a separate group. The rare examples of the integration of children in regular lessons depended on the willingness of individual teachers. With 35 children in a class, could the ordinary teacher offer as much to the child as the teacher in the small unit class, Lowden wondered, particularly as support services from psychologists and advisers were poor and those from speech therapists and social services almost nil for even the unit children.[126] In 1985, Croll and Moses also encountered many junior school teachers who found it very difficult with a class of 30 to provide the individual attention required by the child with special needs.[127]

In the same year, the Fish Committee reported that while a substantial minority of parents was dissatisfied with their children's placement in MLD schools, the majority were quite content – as were the pupils.[128] In the following year, the magazine *Special Children*, perhaps reflecting a popular misconception, expressed surprise when parents successfully fought Hampshire's proposal to close a school for children with moderate learning difficulties.[129] Likewise, in 1988, Somerset had to drop plans to close the county's MLD schools in face of opposition from parents, governors and teachers. Teachers in the mainstream schools protested that plans for supporting the children in the mainstream were inadequate. It was concluded that there was a 'clear lack of support for the review and philosophy'. Similarly, in 1988, a Midlands LEA had to withdraw a plan to close its MLD schools and replace them with 45 units in mainstream schools when surveys revealed the high level of support among parents for their continued existence.[130]

The old arguments had again surfaced in the writings of certain foreign commentators. In 1980, Herbert Goldstein referred to 'inept or absent transition programs' when decertified mentally retarded children were returned to regular 'programs' in California and when survival was equated with 'success'. He complained of a stampede to mainstreaming which ignored history and took an uncritical look at the efficacy studies (see p. 157). The isolation, unpopularity and lack of educational success of the retarded in the mainstream should not be forgotten. In Sweden, Stangvik found once again that pupils selected friends of similar intelligence and social rejection was linked to low intelligence and a lack of social skills.[131] Perhaps reflecting these claims, the integration of the mentally retarded and of many of the 'learning disabled' was far from complete in America. In California, in 1986, 94 per cent of the mentally retarded and 30 per cent of the learning disabled attended separate special classes. Massachusetts and many other states favoured resource rooms to varying degrees. Maryland placed nearly half of its mentally retarded in separate special schools. However, Michigan did keep nearly two-thirds and Alabama nearly all of its learning disabled in regular classes.[132]

The least able mentally retarded in America are equivalent to British children with severe learning difficulties. After the 1970 Act, 382 junior training centres and over 300 special care units were transferred in 1971 to the control of LEAs.[133] This was a logical step towards community care and integration beyond the 1959 Mental Health Act. A similar act came into effect in Scotland in 1975. Increasingly over this period, severely handicapped children did not enter subnormality hospitals, but stayed instead at home and attended special care classes in ESN (Severe) schools. The number of children under 16 years of age in Scottish hospitals fell from 1269 to 480 between 1973 and 1981.[134] In 1972, the Campaign for the Mentally Handicapped hoped for more,[135] but achieving a greater degree of integration even for relatively more able pupils such as some children with Down's Syndrome, proved elusive. However, pupils in South Derbyshire, Haringey (London) and Norfolk attended ordinary schools, although mainly for part-time social integration in the latter case. In Sheffield, a pattern emerged that while it was possible for some children with Down's Syndrome to cope with mixed-ability primary school when parents pressed for this, placement in a school for children with severe learning difficulties at secondary age was found to be necessary.[136] Probably reflecting the majority view, Brennan (1982) and Mary Warnock thought it would be necessary to continue to make separate provision for some extremely handicapped children.[137]

In this period, some ESN (Severe) or SLD schools were to use behaviour modification techniques to good effect with mentally handicapped pupils. Similarly, while the Portage System was designed for parents to use with their children at home and was increasingly employed by them, the system's carefully graded and comprehensive behavioural objectives were also found useful by teachers. Monitoring by the DES gave official if qualified approval to this approach.[138]

For older mentally handicapped youngsters, family group or village colonies run by CARE, Home Farm Trust, the Steiner Camphill Village and the expanding L'Arche Communities continued to have long waiting lists. These cottage-style, permanent care establishments encouraged their voluntary residents to join in life in their local neighbourhoods in a limited way and allowed much personal freedom within their mixed communities. This seemed a sensible approach which was liked by the residents and, of course, contrasted starkly with forms of permanent care mentioned in Chapter 3. However, somewhat surprisingly in America, research indicated that family group environments could be more restrictive and less 'normalizing' than some well-organized large institutions.[139]

Also popular were the 18-month life-skills and industrial training courses offered at NSMHC centres at Dilston, Pengwern and Lufton Halls. Some ordinary further education colleges, including the Herefordshire College of Art and Design, started to offer courses for the mentally handicapped which allowed a degree of integration with non-handicapped students.[140]

Autistic Children

In 1971, the DES, for the first time, asked LEAs to make returns of the number of autistic children and what provision they were making or planning to make for them. By 1983, over 1000 such children were shown in the DES statistics, although according to other estimates this was under a quarter of the number of cases. Confusion over the extent of the condition reflects the difficulty in distinguishing autism from other forms of severe handicap and also the fact that there are degrees of autistic behaviour. Although the existence of the syndrome had been known since Leo Kanner's pioneering work in the early 1940s, it remained shrouded in mystery.

Special educational provision resulted from pressure from the National Society for Autistic Children, founded in 1962 by parents. In 1965, the first school was opened by the Society in Ealing with Sybil Elgar as Head. In the same year, the Lindens School in Epsom opened, moving to purpose-built premises in Worcester Park in 1977 and administered by Surrey County Council. In 1974, Sybil Elgar moved with some of her teenage pupils to Somerset Court residential further education community at Brent Knoll in Somerset.[141] In the decade, other special schools opened including Peterhouse School, Southport. Other autistic children have been placed in schools for children with severe learning difficulties.

In most cases, educational and social progress has been limited and more research is needed to try to understand why the normal sensory experiences are apparently not processed by the child's brain, leaving the sufferer alone in a strange world and often exhibiting bizarre or disturbed behaviour which makes meaningful integration with ordinary people extremely difficult.

Summary

During this period a Labour government and then leading special education writers under a Tory government, increasingly encouraged 'schools for all' and yet, until the 1980s, numbers at least on the rolls of special schools and classes grew and the progress of integration was limited. However, the growth in numbers was explained by the inclusion of the mentally handicapped in special schools and the explosion in numbers of the maladjusted. For the latter, unofficially dubbed 'EBD' after 1983, there was clear evidence of increasing segregation whether in official special schools or units on and off the sites of ordinary schools. For many of these children, their placement seems to have been made for 'social control' motives, as complaints of ill-discipline in ordinary schools increased. However, many EBD children appeared to prefer their segregated placement even if evidence of the educational value of their segregation was lacking. The 1978 Warnock Report recognized that segregation of some EBD pupils was necessary.

However, for most children it had encouraged integration, and the resulting 1981 Education Act required the education of all children in ordinary schools but subject to parental wishes, the efficient use of resources and the efficient provision of education for the child with special needs and the non-handicapped. In practice, these constraints ensured the continued existence of the vast majority of special schools and helped the cause of those who still believed in the usefulness of such schools for some children. In practice, many 'mainstreaming' developments managed no more than locational integration, but links between special schools and ordinary schools did become closer. Moreover, the 1981 Act seemed to focus attention more on children with special needs remaining in ordinary schools.

These included a rapidly growing number of children in units for the partially hearing and also some children in units for the partially sighted. However, full functional integration was not common for the profoundly deaf and, for the visually handicapped, rare although perhaps increasing. Changes in the presentation of DES statistics make more definite comment difficult. Meanwhile, support continued for special schools and the high academic standards of some schools for the deaf and for the blind were noted. A few special schools were closed, reflecting the fall in the school population after the Warnock Report.

Better medical care and a continuing growing concern for integration was reflected in the sharp fall in the numbers in schools for delicate and physically handicapped children.

There was pronounced movement away from placing ESN children in boarding schools and selection procedures for the day schools were attacked. At the same time, there was more evidence of these children being neglected in the ordinary schools. While most areas continued to maintain MLD schools and, on occasion, parents fought to keep threatened schools open, in the 1980s a number of LEAs have moved towards some functional but more commonly locational and social integration for these children by way of units attached to ordinary schools. Special schools also opened for some autistic children.

Notes

1. DES, *The Organisation of Secondary Education*, Circular 10/65, July 1965, p.1.
2. Scottish Education Department, *Education*, Cmnd. 3216, HMSO, Edinburgh, 1967, p.3.
3. Committee of Enquiry into the Education of Handicapped Children and Young People, *Special Educational Needs* (Warnock Report), Cmnd. 7212, HMSO, London, 1978, 3.8, p.38; 7.59, p.119; 7.2, p.99.
4. Calculated from DES *Statistics of Education* for appropriate year.
5. S. Segal, *No Child is Ineducable*, Pergamon, Oxford, 1968.
6. W. Swann, 'Integration? Look twice at statistics', *British Journal of Special Education*, vol. 15, 3, 1988, p.102.
7. Ibid.
8. S. Surkes, 'Violence increase predicted by union', *Times Educational Supplement*, 15 July 1988.
9. M. Tyson, 'On being a Warnock member', *SEFT*, vol. 5, 3, 1978, p.35.
10. CERI, *The Education of the Handicapped Adolescent: Integration in the School*, OECD, Paris, 1981, p.16; H. Cullen,' Special educational needs provision in France', *Supp. for Learning*, vol. 1, 2, 1986, p.28.
11. DES, *Integrating Handicapped Children*, HMSO, London, 1974.
12. R. Gulliford, *Special Educational Needs*, Routledge and Kegan Paul, London, 1971.
13. Op. cit., note 3, 19.3, p.325; M. Wilson, 'Schools – An evolutionary view', *SEFT*, vol. 5, 3, 1978, p.14.
14. P. Simpson, 'An adviser looks at Warnock', *SEFT*, vol. 5, 3, 1978, p.32.
15. *Special Children*, vol. 2, 26, Editorial, January 1989, p.2.
16. Ibid.
17. K. Wedell, J. Welton, J. Evans and B. Goacher, 'Policy and provision under the 1981 Act', *British Journal of Special Education*, vol. 14, 2, 1987, p.52.
18. S. Hegarty, 'Supporting the ordinary school', *British Journal of Special Education*, vol. 15, 2, 1988, p.50; C. Gipps, H. Gross and H. Goldstein, *Warnock's Eighteen Per Cent: Children With Special Needs in Primary Schools*,

Falmer, London, 1987, p.128; P. Croll and D. Moses, *One In Five*, Routledge and Kegan Paul, London, 1985, pp.110–17.

19. D. Thomas, 'The dynamics of teacher opposition to integration', *Remedial Education*, vol. 20, 2, 1985, pp.55 and 57; NUT, *Meeting Special Educational Needs in Ordinary Schools*, NUT, London, 1984; *Special Children*, April 1988, p.3.

20. W. Brennan, *Special Education in Mainstream Schools – The Search for Quality*, NCSE, Stratford-upon-Avon, 1982, p.11.

21. Committee Reviewing Provision to Meet Special Educational Needs, *Equal Opportunities for All* (Fish Report), ILEA, London, 1985, 1.15–1.19; 13.27–13.35; 14.40.

22. *Special Children*, Editorial and 'Parents in backlash against Fish', April 1987, pp.2 and 4; *ILEA News*, Special Needs Supplement, September 1987, p.10.

23. K. Pocklington, 'Integration – A lesson from America', *SEFT*, vol.7, 3, 1980, p.23.

24. F. Gresham, 'Misguided mainstreaming', *Exceptional Children*, February 1982, pp.422–9; J. Gottlieb (ed.), *Educating Mentally Retarded Persons in the Mainstream*, University Park Press, Baltimore, 1980.

25. M. Vaughan and A. Shearer, *Mainstreaming in Massachusetts*, CSIE/CMH, London, 1986, p.14.

26. *SEFT*, Editorial, vol. 11, 1, 1984, p.5.

27. *British Journal of Special Education*, Editorial, vol. 14, 3, September 1987, p.93.

28. S. Hegarty, op. cit., note 18, p.51.

29. Statistics in this chapter unless otherwise stated are taken from DES, *Statistics of Education: Schools*, for 1967, 1977, 1983, 1985, 1986 and 1987.

30. See *British Deaf News*, various items, 1977–1987.

31. Lewis Committee, *The Possible Place of Finger-Spelling and Signing*, HMSO, London, 1968; M. Reed, *Educating Hearing Impaired Children*, Open University Press, Milton Keynes, 1984, p.91.

32. W. Lynas, *Integrating the Handicapped Into Ordinary Schools*, Croom Helm, London, 1985, p.13.

33. Ibid., p.23.

34. DES, *Units for Partially-Hearing Children*, Ed. Survey 1, HMSO, London, 1967.

35. Op. cit., note 3, pp.213–15.

36. Op. cit., note 32, p.15.

37. Ibid., pp.17 and 256–7; G. McGrath, 'Integration', *Australian Teacher of the Deaf*, vol. 20, 1979, p.4.

38. S. Gregory, *The Deaf Child and his Family*, George Allen and Unwin, London, 1976.

39. S. Gregory, review of W. Lynas, op. cit. note 32, *British Deaf News*, February 1987, p.9.

40. US Department of Education, *9th Annual Report to Congress on the Implementation of the Education of the Handicapped Act*, 1987, p.E–56.

41. V. Smith and J. Keen (eds), *Visual Handicap in Children*, Heinemann, London, 1979, ch. 11; E.K. Chapman and J.M. Stone, *The Visually Handicapped Child in Your Classroom*, Cassell, London, 1988, p.36.

42. Ibid., pp. 5 and 196; DES, *The Education of the Visually Handicapped* (Vernon Report), HMSO, London, 1972, p. 37.

43. E.K. Chapman and J.M. Stone, op. cit., note 41, p. 5; *Report for 1969 and 1970 of the CMO of the Ministry of Education*, HMSO, London, 1972, p.71.

44. S.R. Fine, *Blind and Partially Sighted Children*, DES Ed. Survey 4, HMSO, London, 1968, p. 25.
45. SED Working Party chaired by A.G. Rodger, *Ascertainment of Children With Visual Handicap*, HMSO, Edinburgh, 1968.
46. E. Clarke, 'The needs of young blind children and their parents', from *Twenty Four Selected Articles, Teacher of the Blind*, 1970, p.8.
47. Op. cit., note 3, pp. 211–12.
48. Op. cit., note 42.
49. Ibid.
50. Ibid., pp. 38–9.
51. Sister Kathleen Fothergill, *Turn Over the Page*, RNIB, London, 1978, pp.63–4.
52. E.K. Chapman and J.M. Stone, op. cit., note 41, p.4.
53. M. Jamieson, M. Parlett and K. Pocklington, *Towards Integration: A Study of Blind and Partially Sighted Children in Ordinary Schools*, NFER, Windsor, 1977.
54. S. Hegarty, K. Pocklington and D. Lucas, *Integration in Action*, NFER-Nelson, Windsor, 1982, p.206.
55. E.K. Chapman and J.M. Stone, op. cit., note 41, p.195.
56. *Insight*, vol. 1, 1, 1979, pp.4–5; *Times Educational Supplement*, 25 September 1987.
57. E.K. Chapman and J.M. Stone, op. cit., note 41, p.195.
58. Op. cit., note 40, p.E-64; M. Hoben and V. Lindstrom, 'Evidence of isolation in the mainstream', *Journal of Visual Impairment and Blindness*, vol. 74, 8, 1980, pp. 289–92.
59. Op. cit., note 3, pp.217–18; Mrs S.M. Warley, Head of David Lewis Centre, personal communication, 10 October 1988.
60. Op. cit., note 21, 2.13.35, p.144; *Special Children* vol.2, May 1988, p.4.
61. *Special Children*, vol. 1, 1, June 1986, p.6.
62. *Report for 1971 and 1972 of the CMO of the Ministry of Education*, HMSO, London, 1974, p.24; SED, *The Secondary Education of Physically Handicapped Children in Scotland* (McCann Report), HMSO, Edinburgh, 1975, pp.1 and 9–10; op. cit., note 3, p.216.
63. Op. cit., note 43, ch. V, p.51.
64. CMO, op. cit., note 62, p.26.
65. E.M. Anderson, L. Clarke with B. Spain, *Disability in Adolescence*, Methuen, London, 1982, p.15.
66. *Report for 1966 to 1968 of the CMO of the Ministry of Education*, HMSO, London, 1969, p.71.
67. M. Spencer, 'Wheelchairs in a primary school', *SEFT*, vol. 7, 1, 1980, p.18.
68. B. Sturges, 'An integrated unit at St Michaels', *SEFT*, vol. 2, 2, 1980, pp.12–14.
69. C. Cope and E. Anderson, *Special Units in Ordinary Schools*, University of London Institute of Education, London, 1977, p.88; *Special Children*, September 1986, pp.10–11; *Times Educational Supplement*, 'Integration scheme wins admirers', 25 September 1987.
70. CMO, op. cit., note 62, p.51.
71. Op. cit., note 54, pp.89–132.
72. J. Davies, 'Physiotherapy in ordinary schools', *SEFT*, vol. 7, 1, 1980, p.29.
73. Op. cit., note 65, p.260.
74. McCann Report, op. cit., note 62, p.12; op. cit., note 3, p.216.

75. E.M. Anderson and B. Spain, *The Child With Spina Bifida*, Methuen, London, 1977.
76. E. Cotton, *Conductive Education and Cerebral Palsy*, Spastics Society, London, 1975.
77. *Special Children*, June 1986, p.4; December, 1986, p.4.
78. CSIE was founded by the Spastics Society in July 1982.
79. CMO, op. cit., note 62, p.25.
80. Op. cit., note 3, 7.21, p.107; op. cit., note 21, 1.1.16, p.3; D. Galloway, *Schools Pupils and Special Educational Needs*, Croom Helm, London, 1985.
81. J. Sayer, 'Assessment for all, statements for none', *SEFT*, vol. 10, 1, 1983, p.16.
82. Report of a Committee of Enquiry, *Truancy and Indiscipline in Scotland* (Pack Report), HMSO, Edinburgh, 1977.
83. For example, D. Galloway and C. Goodwin, *Educating Slow-Learning and Maladjusted Children*, Longman, London, 1979; K.J. Topping, *Educational Systems for Disruptive Adolescents*, Croom Helm, London, 1983.
84. R. Laslett, *Educating Maladjusted Children*, Granada, London, 1977; M. Wilson and M. Evans, *Education of Disturbed Pupils*, Schools Council Working Paper no. 65, Methuen, London, 1980.
85. T. Cole, *Residential Special Education*, Open University Press, Milton Keynes, 1986.
86. R. Laslett, op. cit., note 84, p.52.
87. DES, 'Approved independent schools', *Special Education Letter* (85) 3, August 1985.
88. DES, *Behavioural Units*, December 1978, pp.6–7; op. cit., note 21, pp.22–4.
89. CMO, op. cit., note 62, ch. 2; M. Wilson and M. Evans, op. cit., note 84, p.34.
90. R.D. Hinshelwood and M. Manning (eds), *Therapeutic Communities: Reflections and Progress*, Routledge and Kegan Paul, London, 1979.
91. DES, *Boarding Schools for Maladjusted Children*, Building Bulletin no. 27, HMSO, London, 1965; DHSS Advisory Council on Child Care, *Care and Treatment in a Planned Environment*, HMSO, London, 1970.
92. D. Wills, *Spare the Child*, Penguin, Harmondsworth, 1971, p.102.
93. Op. cit., note 3, p.222.
94. DES, *Community Homes with Education*, HMSO, London, 1978.
95. M. Wilson and M. Evans, op. cit., note 84, pp.65–8, 84–5 and 132.
96. J. Inman, 'Bad boys make good at Chelfham Mill', *Special Children*, February 1988, pp.12–14.
97. F.G. Lennhoff *et al.*, *Learning to Live*, Shotton Hall, Shrewsbury, 1968, p.E35.
98. Op. cit., note 21, 1.5.48, p.40.
99. Personal communications from M. Ince, Headteacher, Eden Grove, and colleagues in Association of Independent Residential Special Schools.
100. M. Wilson and M. Evans, op. cit., note 84, ch. 6.
101. DES, *Behavioural Units*, London, 1978, p.37; A. Skinner, H. Platts and B. Hall, *Disaffection from School; Issues and Interagency Responses*, National Youth Bureau, Leicester, 1983, p.24.
102. H. Askew and D. Thomas, 'But I wouldn't want to go back', *British Journal of Special Education*, vol. 14, 1, 1987, pp.6–9.
103. M. Wilson and M. Evans, op. cit, note 84, p.64.
104. Op. cit., note 40, p.E–54.
105. W.K. Brennan, 'A policy for remedial education', *Remedial Education*, vol. 6, 1, 1971, p.8.

106. DES, *Slow Learners in the School*, Ed. Survey 15, HMSO, London, 1971, p.1.
107. Op. cit., note 12, pp.11 and 129; op. cit., note 4, pp.54 and 354; P. Bell, *Basic Teaching for Slow Learners*, Muller, London, 1970, p.viii; A.A. Williams, *Basic Subjects for the Slow Learner*, Methuen, London, 1970, p.7.
108. Op. cit., note 66, p.98.; op. cit., note 20, p.12; op. cit., note 21, 2.7.53, p.65.
109. DES, *Slow Learning and Less Successful Pupils in Secondary Schools*, HMSO, London, 1984, p.18.
110. Op. cit., note 85, p.9; op. cit, note 21, 2.9.48, p.93.
111. J.R. Staples, 'Some thoughts on the education of educationally subnormal pupils', *Remedial Education*, vol. 2, 2, pp.11–14.
112. A. Adams, 'Some implications of the organisation of secondary schools', *Remedial Education*, vol. 6, 3, 1971.
113. M. Stone, 'Children with learning difficulties: Integration or segregation', in A. Laing (ed.), *Trends in the Education of Children With Special Learning Needs*, Conference report, Swansea, 1974.
114. D. Thompson and C. Jones, 'Towards integration', *SEFT*, vol. 1, 1, 1974, p.31.
115. Op. cit., note 3, 7.30–7.32, pp.110–11.
116. W. Brennan, *Curricular Needs of Slow Learners*, Evans, London, 1979, pp.10, 18, 20, 100 and 111.
117. D. Galloway and C. Goodwin, op. cit., note 83; S. Tomlinson, *Educational Subnormality*, Routledge and Kegan Paul, London, 1981.
118. C. Cave and P. Maddison, *A Survey of Recent Research in Special Education*, NFER, Windsor, 1978, pp.90–124 and 127–9.
119. S. Tomlinson, *A Sociology of Special Education*, Routledge and Kegan Paul, London, 1982.
120. L. Barton and S. Tomlinson (eds), *Special Education and Social Interests*, Croom Helm, London, 1984, p.72; *Special Children*, April 1987, p.4; S. Tomlinson, *Educational Subnormality*, Routledge and Kegan Paul, London, 1981, ch. 1.
121. Op. cit., note 54, pp.24 and 1–87.
122. SED, *The Education of Mildly Handicapped Pupils of Secondary Age*, HMSO, Edinburgh, 1981; Strathclyde Regional Council Study Group, *Pupils With Learning Difficulties*. Strathclyde Regional Council, Glasgow, 1982.
123. J. Bond and C. Sharrock, 'Castle School lends support', *SEFT*, vol. 11, 4, 1, pp.31–2; B. Cornell 'Evaluating integration', *Special Children*, vol. 11, 1987, p.12; B. Cornell, personal communication, 10 October 1988.
124. S. Hegarty, op. cit., note 18, p.51; A. Florek, 'Integration – or bandwagon hypocrisy?', *British Journal of Special Education*, vol. 13, 2, 1986, p.52.
125. G. Lowden, 'Integrating slow learners in Wales', *SEFT*, vol. 11, 4, 1984, pp.25–6.
126. G. Lowden,' The units approach to integration', *British Journal of Special Education*, vol. 12, 1, 1985, pp. 10–12.
127. P. Croll and D. Moses, op. cit., note 18, p. 152.
128. Op. cit., note 21, 2.13.35, p.144.
129. *Special Children*, September, 1986, p.5.
130. Somerset County Council, *Report of the Special Needs Review Panel to the Special Services Sub-Committee*, Part 1, February 1988, p. xv; R. Dawson and J. Kierney, 'A survey of parents' views', *British Journal of Special Education*, vol. 15, 3, September 1988, p. 123.
131. H. Goldstein, Foreword to J. Gottlieb (ed.), op. cit., note 24; G. Stangvik, *Self Concept and School Segregation*, University of Gothenburg, Gothenburg, 1979.

132. Op. cit., note 40, pp. E–48 and E–52.
133. Op. cit., note 43, pp.32–6.
134. *SEFT*, vol. 11, 4, 1984.
135. A. Kendall and P. Moss, *Integration or Segregation?*, Campaign for the Mentally Handicapped, London, 1972.
136. T. Booth and B. Potts (eds), *Integrating Special Education*, Blackwell, Oxford, 1983, p.19; *Special Children*, July 1986, p.18; September 1988, p.16; P. Budgell, 'Drifting towards segregation', *British Journal of Special Education*, vol. 13, 3, 1986, p.94.
137. Op. cit., note 20, p.29; Booth and Potts, op. cit., note 136, p.20.
138. *Special Children*, 'Portage gains qualified approval', September 1986, p.16.
139. *Special Children*, September, 1987, pp.20–1; E. Baranyay, *A Lifetime of Learning*, NSMHC, London, 1976; H.C. Newbrough and J.R. Heywood, *Living Environments for Developmentally Retarded Persons*, University Park Press, Baltimore, 1981, pp.8–10.
140. A. Henshaw, *After 16*, NSMHC, London, 1979.
141. B. Furneaux and B. Roberts, *Autistic Children*, Routledge and Kegan Paul, London, 1977, pp.5–7.

CHAPTER 7

Past and Future Imperfect

The words and actions of professionals concerned with special education like those of academics and politicians espousing a cause, have no doubt been influenced by vested interests and personal beliefs. The continued existence of so many separate special schools is perhaps in part explained by the latter. However, after trawling deeply through the annals, I am left agreeing with John Hurt[1] that early special education pioneers – and indeed more recent practitioners and policy makers, including leading medical officers – generally seemed imbued with a deep concern for the interests of special children. It is true that there have been wider economic motives for helping them, e.g. Victorian enquiries argued that aid given to the blind, deaf and feeble-minded as children would save society the expense and trouble of looking after them as beggars in the workhouses as adults. But this was only part of the story. There was also a genuine wish to help such children achieve the dignity of a self-supporting, integrated adulthood. Acquiring economic independence through a job was probably the most potent touchstone of 'normality' to the handicapped person.

It is true that, for a time, supporters of the eugenic movement favoured the permanent care of some morally defective or incapable feeble-minded in segregated colonies to preserve the purity of the British race and to lessen the vice and crime attributed to them, but only limited practical progress was made towards achieving this social control and there were many people who saw the wide application of this policy as immoral as well as impractical. It is also true that in most ages some children with learning or social and behavioural difficulties have been placed in segregated provision because they were a disturbing influence in ordinary schools.

Thus, the social control hypothesis has some substance, but it should only be seen as one factor in the complicated development of special education and, I believe, subservient to humanitarian motives and, inevitably, government's financial restraints, whatever the age. There is not space for a detailed critique of Sally Tomlinson's[2] account (1982) of the history of special education, but suffice it to say that her major points seem to rest upon a selective view of the late nineteenth and twentieth centuries. I fear that students too commonly fail to remember her comment, which unfortunately is little developed, that 'motives of compassion and humanitarianism play a part'. They clearly played a very major part. Furthermore, social control arguments have little relevance to the deaf, the blind, the physically handicapped, the delicate, the epileptic and other categories who clearly posed no threat to teachers in ordinary schools or society at large. At least, until the mid-1950s, these groups outnumbered those with learning and behavioural difficulties in special provision. It is also worth recalling that Alexander Graham Bell had seen *integration* of the deaf as a method of social control. To him and to others, this seemed the best way of preventing the creation of the feared, deaf sub-culture and race.

Where social control did operate it was usually balanced and sometimes surpassed by a concern for providing help for the special child. On the road to reaching this conclusion I have, on occasion, perhaps accepted that what people said in the source material, is what they actually did. It is easy to mistake *intentions* for actual happenings. However, the views described in the chapters above are usually repeated in further sources which, for reasons of length and readability, I could not include. These sources give stronger support to the humanitarian perspective. A comment by Alfred Eicholz near the turn of the century smacked of sincerity and seems typical of the commitment beyond narrowly meeting demands of contemporary legislation displayed by many senior government officials: 'We no longer confine action to those who fall within the four corners of these Acts [1893 and 1899]. Our duty is to the whole class of abnormal pupils of all ages.'[3] This was not a statement designed for public consumption and it indicates a dedication, borne out by his life's work, which is not explained by social control or economic explanations, and I do not believe he was 'empire-building'.

Until after the Warnock Report, separation into special schools or classes was generally seen as inevitable for some children, given the apparent inability of the ordinary school to provide the class size, curriculum, organization, expertise or ethos suited to their needs. It was genuinely felt that only by segregation could these children's self-respect and confidence be restored and their educational and social skills developed to equip them to cope with life in integrated adult society. Apparently, there remain far too many of these unsuitable mainstream schools where the old problems still exist. In September 1988, Professor David Hargreaves, lately Chief Inspector for the Inner London Education Authority, was to remind a national conference of HMIs' finding that a quarter of the secondary schools visited between 1982 and 1986 were generally unsatisfactory and that a third of 15 000 observed lessons were below par. The figures for ILEA, Hargreaves said, were only slightly better.[4] This unsatisfactory situation in the mainstream, added to the evidence mentioned in the previous chapter, does not augur well for increased integration of a high quality. If many mainstream schools cannot 'get it right' for the non-handicapped, is it likely that they will fare better with meeting the more complex needs of the special child?

It is disturbing that, in the post-Warnock years, the worth of the special school often seemed to be undervalued by the specialist press. This contrasted so sharply with press attitudes existing before 1970. Indicating this shift was the new journal *Special Children*, which in 1986 reported that an LEA found it surprising that parents should fight to keep an MLD school open and that in 1987, unexpectedly, many parents objected to the integration proposals of the Fish Report. Furthermore, in 1988, an article outlining the Russian system of differentiated special schools, which could so easily have been written by Newman or Eicholz 50 years before, appeared under the box heading 'Controversy'.[5] However, by early 1989, there were signs that the press was focusing once more on supporters of special schools. Where was the outcome research showing the superiority of integration, asked *Special Children*? The same Editorial also noted that some LEAs 'had made zero progress' towards integration. Perhaps, it could have asked if these authorities saw it necessarily as *progress*. The same article noted that the number of parents pressing for integration was balanced by parents demanding, against local authorities' wishes, that their children be placed in specialist, often more segregated settings. The pro-special school 'Parents for Choice in Special Education' was reported to be as strong and vociferous as the integrationist 'Parents in Partnership'.[6] In the *Times Educational Supplement*, also in January 1989, Hilary Wilce described the positive virtues of a boarding institution for the autistic, stressing the invaluable support this gave to parents and to the children, and noting the waiting lists for it.[7] In the last chapter, examples (also reported in the specialist press) were given of LEAs dropping integration plans for the MLD in face of parental and other opposition and mention was made of the increasing segregation practised in a number of LEAs.

In the light of history, this rediscovery of the value of special schools comes as no surprise. But why did special schools fall from media and political favour in the 1970s? To return to Eicholz's 1911 memorandum, the doctor proceeded: 'While many of these [children] require special school training there are many for whom adaptations of arrangements which obtain in the ordinary public elementary schools will suffice'.[8] This book has shown how attempts to achieve this have met with varying degrees of success for different groups of handicapped in different places and at different times, but how, in general, it has proved difficult though far from impossible. Attempts in some areas to achieve a wide degree of integration in the late nineteenth century gave way to a preference for the creation of special centres which purported to provide the necessary expertise. Sometimes high standards were achieved, encouraging the expansion of special schooling described in the chapters above.

But, unfortunately, the high levels of excellence were often not realized, even with the high degree of 'scientific classification' so favoured in the first half of this century. It is often unfair to blame special schools for narrow curricula and low standards of academic attainment given the complex social, physical and intellectual difficulties of their children, and also the similar standards prevailing in many mainstream alternatives. However, important educationalists were increasingly influenced by some post-war 'efficacy studies', which, though flawed in design and sometimes trying to measure the immeasurable, suggested that some handicapped children made as good and sometimes better progress if left in ordinary schools.

In addition, the problem of stigma and special education continued to cause dilemmas. Some parents have always perceived a stigma attached to special school placement, particularly in MD or ESN schools. Government labelling in whatever form intensified this problem. Before 1944, certification was hated, while some parents and children in the late 1980s go to great lengths to avoid statementing. Whether the shame of attending a special class or school is more damaging than experiencing daily failure in front of one's peers in an ordinary school is far from established, with research into self-concept related to educational placement giving very mixed results.[9] Further, as Cleugh noted in 1957 (see p. 106) and Lynas in 1985,[10] giving the child with special needs extra help in an ordinary class can be equally fraught. Whatever the truth of this issue, in the 1970s it was increasingly assumed by writers and politicians that segregated education equalled greater stigma, and that integration would much reduce this problem.

That many parents, as Wilce's 1989 article reminds us, have approved of special boarding – usually placed at the extreme 'negative' end of the integration/segregation continuum – also tended to be overlooked. Critics of residental schools made much of parental and pupil opposition, seen in every age and mentioned in the chapters above. Boarding schools' usual country setting, although chosen for health or cost reasons or a genuine belief that a rural education was beneficial, was said to be a means of hiding the handicapped from public view. Fairer accusations were that many were isolated, unreal communities, where standards of child care were poor, and which did not prepare their pupils for ordinary adult life.

There was also a recurring feeling that integration was cheaper than special schooling, and indeed it can be for the less seriously handicapped and for severe cases if they are not given the necessary support. When combined with a powerful desire in the 1960s and 1970s to replace selective education with comprehensive schools for all children, and a growing awareness of mainstreaming schemes abroad, these factors led to a renewed focus on integration.

Helping to make wider integration feasible was the general improvement in housing, health and social service provisions after the creation of the Welfare State. Only rarely could it be argued in the 1960s and 1970s that a child needed rescuing from the appalling physical conditions and the abject poverty which prevailed in Victorian times and the first half of this century. Critics of the Thatcher government might say that the longstanding welfare and social work function of special education, seen repeatedly in the chapters above, will again become a powerful factor, given the sharp and increasing divisions in British society between the affluent majority and an out-of-work underculture. Lack of affordable public housing and alterations to social security payments in 1988 could cause more children with special needs to be taken away from their families for the good of their physical, if not their mental health, as well as for a suitable education. Certainly, television pictures of the homeless of London sleeping under cardboard boxes, or the Salvation Army distributing supermarket bread which had passed its 'sell-by' date to grateful children on a Glasgow estate,[11] are redolent of the Victorian age and the need for 'rescue' and charity. Perhaps these images are too sensationalist and in fact unrepresentative of a government, already investing extra funds in schools and the health service in a way that would not have been anticipated in the early years of the Thatcher era, that will respond to alleviate these problems. Of course, a different party might shortly win a general election.

Pushing aside these wider considerations which might lead to new obstacles on the road to integration, it has not proved easy in educational terms to transform a theoretical desire for mainstreaming into widespread effective practice. In October 1988, a British Psychological Society conference heard of new evidence suggesting the poor progress of MLD children in mixed-ability primary schools, although generally integration has proved more difficult for secondary-aged pupils.[12] While there have been many well-planned and -executed schemes and also schemes which after a shaky start have improved considerably, examinations continued to dominate too many schools and the less able continued to be somewhat overlooked. Further, teachers in ordinary schools have been wary and have complained about the difficulties of meeting individual needs in a large group and about coping with wide-age, mixed-ability classes in partially integrated units, which have too often remained isolated from the host school. Peripatetic teaching and therapy services have been criticized and perhaps too heavy a responsibility placed on them. Meanwhile, in 1988, Somerset found again that the alternative of concentrating children with disabilities into special schools for physiotherapy was more cost-effective.[13] In fact, these are largely the issues which worried the late Victorians and which led to a preference for the separate special school.

Whether Kenneth Baker's 1988 Education Reform Act helps or hinders the quality of the national education service will not be apparent for some years. But while possibly aiding the majority of non-handicapped pupils by making the teaching profession more accountable and by giving it a clearer framework in which to work, might this be at the expense of children with special needs? In 1988 and early 1989, most commentators in the *British Journal of Special Education*, *Special Children* and the *Times Educational Supplement* clearly thought so. Parent power, which had been increased by earlier Conservative Education Acts, local school management and the ability of parents to choose their child's school, might well lead to even more competitive secondary schools, dominated by the passing of attainment tests at ages 7, 11, 14 and 16 and national examinations. This could be popular with the majority of voters and perhaps better for the nation, but will it leave room for the child with special needs? In rural areas, where one secondary school serves a community, there is a 'captive audience', but in the cities parent power might effect a rough-and-ready return to a selective system based on ability and affluence and perhaps, in some towns, on racial lines. There could be pressure for places at those schools with the best academic records, still under local school management, and probably with the most resources; while schools which continue to follow 'whole school' policies and concentrate on the needs of the less able could develop into underfunded 'sink schools'. It is possible that pressure to segregate those who require extra attention or are a nuisance will increase and that extra resources, when available, could be channelled – as an easily-identified symbol of a rich government's humanity – into special units or schools. However, these fears may prove groundless or government will provide the necessary correctives. Integration, with its many fervent supporters and building on the experience gathered over the last 15 years or so, could yet advance. Only time will tell. It is worth recalling that many of the gloomier predictions about Conservative reforms of the 1980s have been inaccurate.

In noticing similarities between issues worrying our forebears and contemporary concerns, understanding is increased and perhaps a few caveats are picked up for the future, but it would be naive to suggest that history repeats itself. Even if a wheel comes full circle, it has rolled on into another age and a different set of variables. If there is a clear lesson of history, it is that timeless questions such as whether one should take the special child to the experts, or the expert to the special child, or whether it is better to be normal in an abnormal special school or abnormal in an ordinary school, cannot be answered as dogmatically as many have wished. Summing up my personal view of the integration/segregation debate in the light of the evidence I have examined – and I have to admit, my own personal experience – I am left adopting the cautious position of the Warnock Report and the many professionals who praised it. The maximum degree of school and societal integration should be provided for the maximum number of children. However, in an imperfect world where special education has always been short of money and a low government priority, it must be subject to the three constraints of practicability, efficiency and cost. To these, as the 1981 Act optimistically decreed, ought to be added parental choice, where, as is usually the case, the parents are putting their child's interests ahead of their own.

The successful examples of integration, whether *c.* 1875 or those occurring in the last 20 years, should be copied and expanded, but the rapid ending of all special schools, as proposed by the Children's Legal Centre for example,[14] would be positively damaging to many children. More distant as well as more recent experience indicates that a continuum of provision is needed which includes on-site special classes and some separate special schools. It should be more openly stated that many children have appreciated and benefited from their special school placement and that many parents, whatever the historical period, have supported and approved of their children's placement there. To claim that integration is essentially a moral issue, and that to place a child in a separate special school usually denies him rights and damages his life-chances, is unconvincing, often inaccurate and certainly insulting to the parents who support special schooling and to the many expert staff who have worked in the schools. Such a claim can further impose damaging stresses on the parents of the handicapped who feel obliged to struggle to keep their children in ordinary day school however ill-suited this might be to their needs and at whatever cost to the health and happiness of the rest of the family. Accepting special school places can be crudely equated with rejection of their children – a sign that they do not love them. The anguish and unwarranted guilt feelings of such parents are cruelly exacerbated by those who see integration as a moral issue to be pursued at all costs.

No doubt many special schools have had and continue to have severe faults, some of which have been mentioned in the pages above, but some have been places of innovation which have brought new hope to the handicapped and their families. The present interest in bringing conductive education to Britain, with its realistic prospect of making many crippled children walk, can only take place in a specialist and, to some extent, segregated environment; in Hungary it has proved to be a road to reintegration.

Meanwhile, in the mainstream, the practical difficulty of teacher resistance to integration should not be underestimated. The fear of being accused of heresy by the new establishment may keep feelings hidden, but Lowden's research (see p.159) allied to the National Union of Teachers' and some writers' doubts, do not suggest widespread enthusiasm among the silent majority, whose priorities probably lie elsewhere. Similarly, the possible unpopularity of mixed-ability teaching and non-streaming among the parents of the non-handicapped majority are under-explored areas which have been indicated in one or two reports: a MORI poll in 1987 found that nearly two-thirds of a sample of over 300 people wanted a return to a selective system of education.[15] Of course, this poll did not explore how these parents would feel if their children failed a successor to the '11+' examination and were placed in secondary modern schools. Nevertheless, given greater parent-power in education allied to the 1988 Education Reform Act, the implications for the 'whole-school approach' could be profound. The assumptions of the opinion-formers of one generation are so often condemned by those of the next.

Whether these fears are real or illusory, the guiding principle for integration must remain that described by Lumsden in 1968: 'If a handicapped child is to be successfully educated in an ordinary school, he must be specifically *placed* there, not left there.'[16] If the size of the teaching group is too large, if the curriculum is inappropriate or the necessary ancillary or peripatetic or technical support is lacking, the good on-site special class or separate special school might still be the best place for some children, despite unsolved problems of stigma and selection procedures.

Whatever transpires, it is encouraging, in the few years preceding the 1988 Education Reform Act, to have seen increasing attention being paid to the needs of the '18 per cent' within the ordinary schools. Hopefully, this will continue in the decade in which the Act is gradually implemented.

It is worth noting that this figure does not represent the constantly widening grasp of the segregationist claws, as has been alleged.[17] It is rather a vague guideline which is in accord with the thoughts of some of our Victorian forebears. In the early 1880s, Dr Crichton-Browne was among those who found that 20 per cent of London schoolchildren were backward.[18] The Wood Report believed at least 10 per cent were to some extent educationally defective. If the large number of physically handicapped – over 30 000 in special provision, and a greater number in ordinary schools *c.* 1929 – plus other handicapped groups in special provision are added, the 20 per cent figure is approached. Similarly, in 1946, the Ministry of Education thought that between 10 and 15 per cent might need special educational treatment, urging that the bulk of this help be provided in ordinary schools.

It is also worth reflecting on the 2 per cent often thought to be in special schools. This is, in fact, a mirage created by incorrect examination of government statistics. This percentage is only approached if children *waiting* for placement in special provision and those in partially integrated special classes in ordinary schools – about 30 000 children in both 1977 and 1987 – are included. The peak in numbers of children in special schools or hospital schools, reached in 1983, was actually below 1.6 per cent (see p. 133). However, the shortfall is more than made up by those children attending non-designated special classes. If the near 500 000 children found by Warnock to be receiving this extra, mainly part-time help, are included, it would be more accurate to talk in the region of 6–7 per cent.

No matter what percentage of children have special needs, it is to be hoped that the advent of the National Curriculum will not disrupt special classes. If the near 500 000 children found by Warnock to be research of Hegarty and others when added to the experience of teachers in different eras has shown that integration can take place more widely than it does in 1989, and that with honest reappraisal sometimes flawed schemes, begun in the belief that 'one has to start somewhere', can be improved. Under the right conditions the experience of the integrated child with special needs can match the high hopes of Barnhill, Alexander Graham Bell and the other nineteenth-century pioneers.

Of course, an even better way forward would be the rapid advance of medical science and the efficient application of existing preventive and

178 _Apart or A Part?_

curative medicine. In 1978, it was claimed that if existing knowledge was applied, 40 per cent of the cases of cerebral palsy, the most common of the physical disabilities, could be prevented.[19] Perhaps with cochlear implants, the numbers of the hearing impaired could be reduced, or by limited and ethical genetic engineering, the intelligence of the mentally handicapped could be enhanced. This would obviously reduce the need for special schools. It might be easier to look forward to a brighter future for these children than for those whose difficulties spring largely from environmental causes. At the risk of my sounding like a Victorian philanthropist, it seems that an increasing number of children of all classes have to endure unstable childhoods, often due to parental irresponsibility or skewed caring, and sometimes unforgivable neglect. Sometimes, the difficulties of poverty are added. This situation would seem likely to produce thousands of backward, disturbed or disturbing children with whom mainstream schools will continue to find it very difficult to cope. For these children, sadly, the integration/segregation debate is likely to remain relevant well into the twenty-first century.

Notes

1. J.S. Hurt, _Outside the Mainstream_, Batsford, London, 1988, p.189.
2. S. Tomlinson, _A Sociology of Special Education_, Routledge and Kegan Paul, London, 1982, ch. 2.
3. Op. cit., note 1, p.150.
4. _Times Educational Supplement_, 9 September 1988, p.5.
5. See Chapter 6, pp.145–6 and 167; V. Lubovski, 'Against integration', _Special Children_, September 1988, pp.6–7.
6. _Special Children_, 'Editorial' vol.26, January 1989, p.2
7. H. Wilce, 'Sunday night's special', _Times Educational Supplement_, 27 January 1989, p.A25.
8. Op. cit., note 1, p.150.
9. J.B. Thomas, _The Self in Education_, NFER, Slough, 1980.
10. W. Lynas, _Integrating the Handicapped into Ordinary Schools_, Croom Helm, London, 1985, p.248.
11. BBC, _Panorama_, 'Children in need', 23 January 1989.
12. K. Beach, 'Classroom unsuitable for slow learners', _The Independent_, 17 September 1988.
13. Somerset County Council, _Report of the Special Needs Review Panel to the Special Services Sub-Committee_, Part 1, February 1988, p.xix.
14. _Special Children_, 'Editorial', September 1986, p.2.
15. H. Wilce, 'Comprehensives get the worst of both worlds', _Times Educational Supplement_, 9 September 1983; _Times Educational Supplement_, 'Parents want selection back', 28 August 1987.

16. J. Lumsden, 'Special education for the handicapped', *Teacher of the Blind*, vol. 56, 4, 1968, p.2.
17. Op. cit., note 2, p.2.
18. Op. cit., note 1, p.123.
19. J. Loring and M. Holland, *The Prevention of Cerebral Palsy*, Spastics Society, London, 1978, p.17.

Index